HOUSE OF WEEPING

ANCIENT NEAR EAST MONOGRAPHS

General Editors
Alan Lenzi
Jeffrey Stackert
Juan Manuel Tebes

Editorial Board
Reinhard Achenbach
Jeffrey L. Cooley
C. L. Crouch
Roxana Flammini
Christopher B. Hays
René Krüger
Graciela Gestoso Singer
Bruce Wells

Number 24

SBL PRESS

HOUSE OF WEEPING

The Motif of Tears in Akkadian and Hebrew Prayers

by
David A. Bosworth

SBL PRESS

SBL PRESS

Atlanta

Library of Congress Control Number: 2019930771

Printed on acid-free paper.

for my father

Table of Contents

Preface ix
List of Abbreviations xiii
1. Prayer and Weeping 1
Attachment Theory 3
Social Sharing of Emotion 11
The Inner Voice, or the Dialogic Mind 15
Weeping 20
Method 35
2. Weeping in Akkadian Prayers 39
*Šuilla*s 41
*Eršaḫunga*s 51
*Dingiršadabba*s 67
*Namburbi*s 76
*Ikribu*s 77
*Tamītu*s 77
Letter Prayers 78
Royal Prayers 79
Hymns 80
Language of Weeping 85
Divine Anger and Human Tears 86
3. Weeping in Hebrew Psalms 89
Individual Laments 92
Communal Laments 115
Thanksgiving Psalms 122
Other Prayers 127
Language of Weeping 132
Divine Anger and Human Tears 133
4. Comparative Perspectives 135
Works Cited 143
Indices 155

Preface

> Man begins as a social being; he does not acquire society. This fact, which seems from one point of view a recognized commonplace, has many far-reaching consequences which are not always considered. Moreover, the fact itself has not always been taken as self-evident.
>
> —Anna Louise Strong, *The Psychology of Prayer*

Anna Louise Strong, largely unknown now, was a household name from the 1920s to 1960s, famed for her reporting from the Soviet Union and China and her advocacy for communism. She begins her best-selling autobiography with an episode from her childhood that may shed light on her later work on prayer and commitment to socialism.[1] When she was eleven years old and playing in a garden, she had a sudden realization of herself as separate from the world and everything and everyone in it. Speaking of her childhood self in the third person, she wrote: "She couldn't get out and nothing could get in through the shell of that hard, round, soul.... For the first time she knew herself as an individual creature, cut off from the world of which she had been a part. She painfully wanted to get back."[2] As she looked back on this moment, she reflected on her life as a quest to find a way out of human loneliness, a condition that she saw as a consequence of our social nature and the brokenness of our social worlds:

> Our individuality is partial and restless; the stream of consciousness that we call "I" is made of shifting elements that flow from our group and back to our group again. Always we seek to be ourselves and the herd together, not One against the herd. And we cannot, for the herd itself is split by struggles, which change in form with the ages: slave against owner, serf against baron, worker against capitalist and the myriad complex conflicts that derive from these.[3]

---

1 Anna Louise Strong, *I Change Worlds: The Remaking of an American* (New York: Henry Holt, 1935).

2 Strong, *I Change Worlds*, 10.

3 Strong, *I Change Worlds*, 11.

Strong's understanding of our social nature coheres with recent discoveries about the inner voice or stream of consciousness and its social origin and orientation.[4] Even when we may seem to be most withdrawn into our individual selves, we remain deeply connected to others because our inmost selves are social and dialogic. Our emotional lives may also seem private, even intimate, but they also reflect our social nature. We are constantly regulating our emotions, thoughts, and behaviors with other people, and we are never as independent or autonomous as we like to believe. Strong's childhood realization of her individuality came as a devastating blow that left her achingly lonely and set her on a life-long journey to lose herself in a larger cause. Loneliness is as bad for one's health as smoking, and, unlike smoking, loneliness rates are increasing in many countries.[5] The United Kingdom recently appointed a minister of loneliness to address the problem. Our social nature becomes problematic when our social institutions inhibit rather than facilitate connectedness to others. Our need to connect informs our entire lives and whole selves, and it lies at the heart of the present study.

We are constantly regulating our thoughts, feelings, and behaviors with other people, even when we do not realize it. In the privacy of our own thoughts, we speak from one aspect of the self to another in a dialogue that has been internalized from the wider world of people around us. Our sense of well-being hinges on the quality of our relationships with other people, and trusted partners help us endure our miseries and celebrate our successes. Like Strong, I am interested in pursuing the study of prayer in light of our social nature. I came to the study of prayer texts through a research project on weeping. Weeping, I learned, is an expression of our need to connect with others, yet many Westerners imagine it is an individual cathartic behavior. As Strong remarks, the observation that humans are by nature social animals is a commonplace, but its far-reaching consequences are not often considered. I hope in the present project to illustrate how profoundly social we are, and how prayer and weeping reveal our social nature. If we were not social, we would neither pray nor weep. The first chapter draws heavily on modern psychological research. The modern discipline of psychology has an individualist bias, yet psychologists who delve deeply into the individual have discovered a community. This first chapter unfolds aspects of human emotion regulation that are important for understanding prayer and weeping. The second chapter applies these insights to an analysis of the motif of weeping in a corpus of

---

[4] See pages 15–22.

[5] Julianne Holt-Lunstad, Timothy Smith, and J. Bradley Layton, "Social Relationships and Mortality Risk: A Meta-Analytic Review," *PLOS Medicine* 7 (2010), https://doi.org/10.1371/journal.pmed.1000316; Julianne Holt-Lunstad, Timothy Smith, and Mark Baker, "Loneliness and Social Isolation as Risk Factors for Mortality: A Meta-Analytic Review," *Perspectives on Psychological Science* 10 (2015): 227–37.

Akkadian prayers. I analyze those that involve weeping in some detail and discuss the distribution and function of weeping in the larger corpus of hundreds of prayers. In the third chapter, I provide the same kind of analysis of weeping within the corpus of the Hebrew Psalter. The fourth and final chapter compares the two corpora to one another and to the scientific findings discussed in the first chapter.

As the research presented here shows, we are never truly alone but are constantly regulating our thoughts, emotions, and behaviors with our fellow creatures. The present book is the fruit of such social regulation and support. The notes provide only an indication of the many scholars whose work has shaped and informed my own. Although writing a book may seem like a solitary activity, it is a deeply communal task. Every work I have read in pursuit of this project is the fruit of a socially embedded and relationally engaged mind that has connected to my own social world and work and helped shape it into what it is, which is much better than it could have been without such help. For example, at an early stage of the project, I planned to analyze a much smaller corpus of Akkadian material reflected in Benjamin Foster's anthology *Before the Muses*. As I worked through Alan Lenzi's helpful *Reading Akkadian Prayers and Hymns*, it became clear that I needed to expand the corpus significantly in order to provide meaningful analysis of the several genres of prayer, which are unevenly represented in *Before the Muses*. This decision, largely informed by Lenzi and the other scholars who contributed to his volume, made it possible to uncover the significant correlation between divine wrath and human tears that is common to Akkadian and Hebrew prayers. My initial corpus would have been too small to uncover this and other insights. The work of other scholars, therefore, shaped my thinking and expanded my horizons, enabling me to do more meaningful analysis. Lenzi is high on the list of scholars whose work has shaped my own, and his work on *Reading Akkadian Prayers and Hymns* has facilitated my entry into this area of research and improved my work. He has also been a source of personal encouragement as someone who saw the initial proposal for this project and built up the reputation of the present series with his own valuable contribution. I hope the present work continues that tradition. The peer reviewers for the Ancient Near Eastern Monographs series offered several helpful suggestions, large and small, that have significantly improved the work. Translations from Akkadian, Hebrew, and Greek are my own.

My work integrating science and humanities research received two foundational supports in recent years. First, the School of Theology and Religious Studies at the Catholic University of America received a Sciences for Seminaries grant from the Dialogue on Science, Ethics, and Religion (DoSER) of the American Association for the Advancement of Science (AAAS), funded by the Templeton Foundation. The grant enabled me and several colleagues to incorporate scientific material into seminary courses, which allowed me to further develop my scientific education and better integrate science into my own thinking, research, and teaching. The grant also allowed me to forge a relationship with Nancy Adleman, a neuroscientist at Catholic University whom I might not otherwise have come to know. She has been enormously helpful in addressing questions that arise for me in my reading. Another outgrowth of the grant is an ongoing commitment at Catholic University to develop relationships among science and humanities faculty and research involving faith and science. Second, from the AAAS, I learned about Sinai and Synapses and became one of the 2015–17 Fellows. The Sinai and Synapses fellowship involves a range of people from diverse professions and expertise who share an interest in science and faith. Arielle Hanien stands out as a Sinai and Synapses fellow who has a strong sense of our social nature and how we coregulate with one another. Geoff Mitelman, who founded and organizes the fellowship at the National Jewish Center for Leadership and Learning, has wide-ranging interests and generously fosters community and encourages the work of the fellows. Several research assistants have assisted with this project. Eric Wagner, CR helped build the corpus of Akkadian texts, especially with tracking down the scattered texts. At an earlier stage, Andrew Litke likewise tracked down many Akkadian prayers and some of the scholarship on these texts. The Catholic University of America's internal grant-in-aid program funded the work of copyediting, page layout, and indexing by Angela Roskop Erisman. I am deeply grateful to both the university and Angela for this help. Important support for this project was close to home. Nothing in my life works without my wife, Britt Silkey, and our son Alex. Becoming a parent has led me to understand and appreciate my own parents more. In the course of this work, my father, Barry Bosworth, received a diagnosis that has made the subject of this project more salient. It is dedicated to him.

List of Abbreviations

AbB	*Altbabylonische Briefe in Umschrift und Übersetzung*. Edited by Fritz R. Kraus. Leiden: Brill, 1964–.
AHw	*Akkadisches Handwörterbuch*. Wolfram von Soden. 3 vols. Wiesbaden, 1965–1981.
AJA	*American Journal of Archaeology*
ANEM	Ancient Near East Monographs
AOAT	Alter Orient und Altes Testament
AOS	American Oriental Series
AOTC	Abingdon Old Testament Commentaries
AOTS	Augsburg Old Testament Studies
AfO	*Archiv für Orientforschung*
BA	*Biblical Archeologist*
BBB	Bonner biblische Beiträge
BCOTWP	Baker Commentary on the Old Testament Wisdom and Psalms
Bib	*Biblica*
BibInt	*Biblical Interpretation*
Bijdr	*Bijdragen: Tijdschrift voor filosofie en theologie*
BMes	Bibliotheca Mesopotamica
BSOAS	*Bulletin of the School of Oriental and African Studies*
BWANT	Beiträge zur Wissenschaft vom Alten und Neuen Testament
CAD	*The Assyrian Dictionary of the Oriental Institute of the University of Chicago*. Chicago: The Oriental Institute of the University of Chicago, 1956–2006.
CBQ	*Catholic Biblical Quarterly*
CBQMS	Catholic Biblical Quarterly Monograph Series
CHSB	Critical Studies in the Hebrew Bible
CM	Cuneiform Monographs
ConBOT	Coniectanea Biblica: Old Testament Series
Dš	*Dingiršaddaba*
Er	A specific *eršaḫunga* text
Ešḫ	A specific manuscript of an *eršaḫunga*

ETR	*Etudes théologiques et religieuses*
FOTL	Forms of the Old Testament Literature
GAG	*Grundriss der akkadischen Grammatik*. Wolfram von Soden. 2nd ed. Rome: Pontifical Biblical Institute, 1969.
HAT	Handbuch zum Alten Testament
HBT	*Horizons in Biblical Theology*
HR	*History of Religions*
HSM	Harvard Semitic Monographs
HSS	Harvard Semitic Studies
IBHS	*An Introduction to Biblical Hebrew Syntax*. Bruce K. Waltke and Michael O'Connor. Winona Lake, IN: Eisenbrauns, 1990.
Il.	*Iliad*
Int	*Interpretation*
ISBE	*International Standard Bible Encyclopedia*. Edited by Geoffrey W. Bromiley. 4 vols. Grand Rapids, MI: Eerdmans, 1979–1988.
IVR^2	*Cuneiform Inscriptions of Western Asia, Vol. IV A Selection from the Miscellaneous Inscriptions from Assyria*. 2nd ed. By Henry C. Rawlinson. London, 1893.
JAOS	*Journal of the American Oriental Society*
JBL	*Journal of Biblical Literature*
JSOT	*Journal for the Study of the Old Testament*
JSOTSup	Journal for the Study of the Old Testament Supplement Series
KTU	*Die keilalphabetischen Texte aus Ugarit*. Edited by Manfred Dietrich, Oswald Loretz, and Joaquín Sanmartín. Münster: Ugarit-Verlag, 2013.
LHBOTS	Library of Hebrew Bible/Old Testament Studies
LD	Lectio Divina
MC	Mesopotamian Civilizations
NABRE	New American Bible Revised Edition
NIBCOT	New International Biblical Commentary on the Old Testament
NRSV	New Revised Standard Version
OBO	Orbis Biblicus et Orientalis
Od.	*Odyssey*
OTG	Old Testament Guides
OTL	Old Testament Library
ORA	Orientalische Religionen in der Antike
RA	*Revue d'assyriologie et d'archéologie orientale*
RB	*Revue biblique*
RBS	Resources for Biblical Study
RevistB	*Revista bíblica*

RSV	Revised Standard Version
SAACT	State Archives of Assyria Cuneiform Texts
SHCANE	Studies in the History and Culture of the Ancient Near East
ScrTh	*Scripta Theologica*
SemeiaSt	Semeia Studies
StPohl	Studia Pohl
VT	*Vetus Testamentum*
VTSup	Supplements to Vetus Testamentum
WAW	Writings from the Ancient World
WMANT	Wissenschaftliche Monographien zum Alten und Neuen Testament
ZAH	*Zeitschrift für Althebräistik*
ZAW	*Zeitschrift für die Alttestamentliche Wissenschaft*

1
Prayer and Weeping

This book originated as part of a larger project investigating weeping in ancient literature.[1] I became fascinated by weeping when, in the course of researching grief, I discovered that there was a significant body of scientific research attempting to understand this complex human behavior that is shaped by both biology and culture.[2] This research provides a valuable corrective to cultural assumptions, individual bias, and misleading anecdotes or introspection. As I have worked on weeping in prayer, I have become similarly fascinated by prayer itself. According to one researcher, infant weeping and adult prayer are one and the same thing, which might explain my dual interests. According to John C. Wathey, "prayer is

[1] David A. Bosworth, *Infant Weeping in Akkadian, Hebrew, and Greek Literature*, CHSB 8 (Winona Lake, IN: Eisenbrauns, 2016); Bosworth, "Weeping in Recognition Scenes in Genesis and the *Odyssey*," *CBQ* 77 (2015): 613–33; Bosworth, "The Tears of God in the Book of Jeremiah," *Bib* 94 (2013): 24–46; Bosworth, "Weeping in the Psalms," *VT* 62 (2013): 36–46; and Bosworth, "Daughter Zion and Weeping in Lamentations 1–2," *JSOT* 28 (2013): 217–37.

[2] See esp. Ad Vingerhoets, *Why Only Humans Weep: Unraveling the Mystery of Tears* (Oxford: Oxford University Press, 2013), which summarizes a wide range of existing research. See also Judith Kay Nelson, *Seeing Through Tears: Crying and Attachment* (New York: Routledge, 2005); Tom Lutz, *Crying: The Natural and Cultural History of Tears* (New York: Norton, 1999); Karin Grossmann, "Weinen, ein Bildungsverhalten," *Psychotherapeut* 54 (2009): 77–89; Michelle C. P. Hendricks et al., "Why Crying Improves Our Well-Being: An Attachment-Theory Perspective on the Function of Adult Crying," in *Emotion Regulation: Conceptual and Clinical Issues*, eds. Ad Vingerhoets, Ivan Nyklíček, and Johan Denollet (New York: Springer, 2008), 87–96; Maria Miceli and Cristiano Castelfranchi, "Crying: Discussing Its Basic Reasons and Uses," *New Ideas in Psychology* 21 (2003): 247–63; Michael Trimble, *Why Humans Like to Cry: Tragedy, Evolution, and the Brain* (Oxford: Oxford University Press, 2012); Ad Vingerhoets and Randolph Cornelius, eds., *Adult Crying: A Biopsychosocial Approach* (New York: Routledge, 2001); and Chip Walter, *Thumbs, Toes, and Tears and Other Traits that Make Us Human* (New York: Walker, 2006).

the adult manifestation of infantile crying."[3] He summarizes his argument in five points:

1. Human infants are born helpless and will die if separated from their parents.
2. Infants and parents have an innate neural circuitry that creates an emotional bond that typically encourages parental care.
3. The infant's neural circuitry constitutes an innate model of the infant's world, most importantly including an image of its mother as a loving agent who wants to satisfy the infant's needs and does so in response to infant cries. The innate model also provides a feeling of certainty that this loving agent exists.
4. This infant neural circuitry persists into adulthood, but normally lies dormant.
5. This dormant circuitry gives rise to religious experience especially under conditions of intense stress that evoke feelings of need and helplessness.[4]

The religious experience to which Wathey refers is a sense of God's presence, or the sensation of a loving and merciful presence associated with a sense of security and joy.[5] Many people have had memorable moments in which they sense God's nearness, the proximity of an all-loving and encompassing protective presence. Wathey understands these experiences as the (re)activation of infantile neural circuitry designed to help human neonates survive their extreme vulnerability and dependency. Adults, like the babies they once were, have an implicit faith in a protective, caring other who will help them in their neediness. Within the context of this relationship, both the infant and the adult may cry to elicit needed care. For the adult, this cry may be elucidated with words of prayer and petition. Wathey claims that infant cries and adult prayers derive from the same evolved neural substrates.[6]

Based on my own research in various areas of psychology, Wathey's claim of a connection between infant cries and adult prayers appears to have merit. The first three of his five points are well grounded in attachment theory, discussed below. The latter two are possible, although Wathey oversimplifies adult religious experiences. A sense of helplessness appears to underlie most or even all weeping.

---

[3] John C. Wathey, *The Illusion of God's Presence: The Biological Origins of Spiritual Longing* (Amherst, NY: Prometheus, 2015), 182 (italics his).

[4] Paraphrased from Wathey, *Illusion*, 61–62.

[5] Wathey, *Illusion*, 26–30.

[6] Wathey, *Illusion*, 182. Wathey's reference to "the sequel, where I explore the neural circuitry of crying" appears to refer to same volume, but it is not clear where this might be (perhaps pp. 224–29 or 236–39) because the specific neural circuitry of infantile crying is not described or compared with the neural substrates of adult prayer. His claims merit more detailed and technical discussion, but the neural substrates for crying are not well understood, and those for prayer are even more obscure.

I am struck that my efforts to understand both weeping and prayer have both drawn from and led to many of the same areas of research. I originally imagined that this work would require a theory of prayer and a separate theory of weeping. Instead, I have found both prayer and weeping can be understood within the parameters of a single theory.[7]

This chapter will lay out the theory of weeping and prayer that will inform the analysis of the motif of weeping in ancient prayer texts. It will offer at least partial answers to such questions as: Why do humans weep, and why only humans? Other animals shed tears due to eye irritation, but only humans also shed emotional tears. Why would this behavior evolve at all, and why not in more species? Why do people pray and sometimes shed tears in prayer? And why do writers sometimes verbalize this nonverbal behavior in prayer texts? The present theory draws on several related aspects of psychology, and the presentation will begin with the most general level of explanation and work toward the more specific. Attachment theory offers powerful explanations for a wide variety of human behaviors, including weeping and prayer. Both behaviors represent examples of the "social sharing of emotions," a more specific area of research coherent with attachment theory. Recent work on the inner voice most of us have in our heads helps connect these two areas of research and understand both silent private prayer and public communal prayer as emotional sharing and regulation. These sections will touch on prayer and weeping to articulate their relevance, but the last section will focus on weeping. The chapter will also offer an excursus on ritual weeping and describe the present approach to analyzing the ancient texts. Briefly stated, both weeping and prayer are social behaviors by which people seek to coregulate their emotions with others, both human and divine, and to elicit help and support from them.

ATTACHMENT THEORY

Attachment theory originated as a description of how children interact with caregivers. It was intended from its inception as a larger theory of human relationship across the life span with firm grounding in evolutionary theory. Researchers from a variety of fields have contributed to the theory and the wealth of empirical

---

[7] For a helpful review of research on prayer, see Bernard Spilka and Kevin L. Ladd, *The Psychology of Prayer: A Scientific Approach* (New York: Guilford, 2013). Empirical studies involve a range of diverse theories or often lack theoretic foundations. Several studies connect prayer to emotion regulation and coping. On emotion regulation, see Shane Sharp, "How Does Prayer Help Manage Emotions?," *Social Psychology Quarterly* 73 (2010): 417–37, who finds that prayer provided significant support for women in abusive relationships.

evidence supporting it.[8] The history of the theory's origins and development have been told many times, most engagingly by Robert Karen, whose subtitle captures why the theory is so widely applicable: *Becoming Attached: First Relationships and How They Shape Our Capacity to Love.*[9] Researchers have extended and revised attachment theory in order to help explain and understand romantic, workplace, and therapeutic relationships, as well as emotional regulation. A psychologist once remarked to me that "everything goes back to attachment." I thought she was joking, but the more I read, the more I suspect she was serious. First relationships are formative. Attachment theory is not a simple explanation for every human behavior and experience, but it interacts, sometimes powerfully, with a wide range of human behaviors and experiences, including religious ones.

Humans are born with an innate attachment system, a constellation of behaviors that increase the likelihood that they will survive. These attachment behaviors include crying to elicit care from an adult. This crying behavior is preferentially directed toward known caregivers within the second half of the first year, and, as babies learn to crawl, they seek to remain in proximity to their preferred caregivers or "attachment figures." They may follow these attachment figures around or protest their absence with tears in an effort to maintain proximity. The means by which children seek closeness to their caregivers reflect a selective emotional attachment or developing bond and are therefore called "attachment behaviors." Attachment behaviors change and develop as children grow, but the attachment system never ceases to inform behavior. For example, humans of all ages weep, and attachment concerns shape this behavior across the life span.[10] At

---

[8] For an engaging introduction, see Robert Karen, *Becoming Attached: How First Relationships Shape Our Capacity to Love* (Oxford: Oxford University Press, 1998). See also Carol Gerhart Mooney, *Theories of Attachment: Introduction to Bowlbly, Ainsworth, Gerber, Brazelton, Kennell and Klaus*, Redleaf Professional Library (St. Paul, MN: Redleaf, 2010); Virginia M. Shiller, *The Attachment Bond: Affectional Ties across the Lifespan* (Lanham, MD: Lexington Books, 2017). The theory originated with the trilogy of works by John Bowlby, *Attachment*, 2nd ed. (New York: Basic, 1982); Bowlby, *Separation: Anxiety and Anger* (New York: Basic, 1973); *Loss: Sadness and Depression* (New York: Basic, 1980), which remain foundational texts. Another foundational work is Mary Salter Ainsworth et al., *Patterns of Attachment: A Psychological Study of the Strange Situation* (Mahwah, NJ: Lawrence Erlbaum, 1978; repr., New York: Routledge, 2015). For orientations to the vast body of research, see Jude Cassidy and Philip R. Shaver, eds., *Handbook of Attachment: Theory Research, and Clinical Applications*, 3rd ed. (New York: Guilford, 2016); Susan Hart, *The Impact of Attachment* (New York: Norton, 2011); Mario Mikulincer and Philip R. Shaver, *Attachment in Adulthood: Structure, Dynamics, and Change*, 2nd ed. (New York: Guilford, 2016); and Omri Gillath, Gery C. Karantzas, and R. Chris Fraley, *Adult Attachment: A Concise Introduction to Theory and Research* (London: Elsevier, 2016).

[9] Karen, *Becoming Attached.*

[10] Nelson, *Seeing.*

all ages, distress or fear activates attachment behaviors and leads people to seek their attachment figures to help them regulate their negative emotions and reestablish a sense of safety. Although a child's attachment figures are typically parents and other primary caregivers, people gradually transfer their attachment behaviors toward peers and especially romantic partners as they grow into adulthood.

The emotion regulation that happens in the attachment relationship may be understood through the two major functions of the attachment figure: to provide a safe haven and a secure base. When children feel distressed due to internal stress (e.g., hunger) or external threat (e.g., appearance of a stranger), they seek to be near their attachment figure, who can be trusted to resolve the problem (e.g., provide food or protection). Once the sense of distress has passed, the child may again return to play or exploring the environment. The attachment figure then serves as a secure base from which the child derives a sense of confidence to engage in a wide range of activities. The secure base function may be easily overlooked because the child's dependency on the parent is not obvious. If the child checks on the availability of the attachment figure only to find the figure missing, however, then the ensuing panic drives the child to seek the missing person and get help coregulating back to homeostasis (e.g., the mutual fear of a parent and child separated in a public place).

Deities also serve as attachment figures for many people. Modern psychological studies find that many Westerners relate to God as to an attachment figure.[11] Analysis of ancient Hebrew and Akkadian prayer texts suggests that deities also functioned as attachment figures for ancient people.[12] In a prayer text, the image of the deity as an attachment figure is most evident in the way the text manifests emotion regulation. While laments in the Psalter share anxieties with God as a safe haven, the psalms of trust demonstrate the powerful effects of God's secure base function. In many prayers, and especially in those reflecting emotional expression, the speaker turns to the deity as a partner for emotional sharing in ways characteristic of attachment relationships.

Attachment relationships are not all the same, and people have multiple attachment figures. Relationships are shaped by the experiences that partners have with each other. As a result of these experiences, the child develops a mental map or framework for understanding the self, others, and the world called an "internal working model." This internal working model involves two important aspects of

---

[11] Lee A. Kirkpatrick, *Attachment, Evolution, and the Psychology of Religion* (New York: Guilford, 2005), esp. 52–74.

[12] David A. Bosworth, "Ancient Prayers and the Psychology of Religion: Deities as Attachment Figures," *JBL* 134 (2015): 681–700.

attachment theory that are relevant to religion and prayer: individual differences and emotional regulation.

Internal Working Models and Individual Differences

Individuals differ in their attachment experiences, and these differences become encoded in their internal working models that tend to persist into adulthood. Given consistent interactions with caregivers through childhood, the patterns of relationship become embedded in a person's implicit memory, operate unconsciously, and resist change. Early childhood experiences can therefore shape adult personality characteristics. Researchers have identified four major types of attachment styles grounded in different experiences of attachment relationships. Securely attached children have reliable and sensitive caregivers who help them regulate their emotions and provide consistent and responsive care. As a result, these securely attached children develop internal working models of themselves as lovable and loved, of others as trustworthy, and relationships as satisfying sources of security and support. They receive appropriate help with coregulating their emotions from caregivers. By contrast, insecurely attached children develop working models of themselves as unloved and unlovable, others as unreliable and untrustworthy, and relationships as sources of anxiety. These models develop from experience of caregivers who are inconsistent, absent, dismissive, or emotionally unavailable and therefore do not provide adequate help with emotion regulation. Insecurely attached people may be avoidant or anxious. The avoidant strive to minimize their attachment needs and become self-sufficient; the anxious hyperactivate their attachment behaviors (e.g., seeking) in an effort to gain the supportive response they seek. A final category of disorganized people includes those who develop no organized strategy for navigating relationships with their caregivers and often come from backgrounds involving abuse or other risk factors.[13] These differing attachment styles correlate with crying behavior. Some evidence indicates that anxiously attached individuals weep more frequently than secure people, and that avoidantly attached individuals weep less frequently.[14] Theory would predict this result because weeping is an attachment behavior, and because these attachment styles are distinguished by hyper- and hypoactivation of the attachment system, respectively.

---

[13] Shiller, *Attachment Bond*, 34, 198. Shiller notes that disorganized attachment has sometimes been regarded as diagnostic of abuse, which is an error. Disorganized attachment has been documented in children who were not abused, but whose caregivers suffered trauma or loss, or who spent sixty or more hours per week in nonmaternal daycare.

[14] Joyce Maas, Anja Laan, and Ad Vingerhoets, "Attachment, Emotion Regulation, and Adult Crying," in *Emotion Regulation and Well-Being*, ed. Ivan Nyklíček, Ad Vingerhoets, and Marcel Zeelenberg (New York: Springer, 2011), 181–95.

Internal working models of others, both human and divine, develop along four major paths: memory, beliefs, goals, and plans.[15] Memories include specific recollections of episodes and interactions, as well as the person's interpretations of these events. For example, models of deities are grounded in past experience, such as a prayer answered or a sense of God's presence. These experiences may be vicarious and presented through storytelling and collective memory. For example, YHWH is often recalled in Scripture as the God who brought Israel up from Egypt, and this memory informs the hope that God may perform similarly salvific acts in the future. General beliefs, attitudes, and expectations also shape internal working models. They reflect beliefs such as "God is merciful," attitudes such as "prayer is effective," and expectations such as "God will forgive me." People bring various goals to their relationship interactions; these may vary over time and influence internal models. For example, a theologian whose child is in surgery may invoke a working model of God as a powerful father figure in the sky who grants favors but may turn to a more "theologically correct" image of God in a less distressing context. The overarching goal is to feel safe and secure, and that may mean drawing near to God in prayer (e.g., Ps 42:2–3) or avoidantly seeking distance (e.g., Ps 39:14). People pursue their attachment goals through different strategies, which are influenced by early experiences and learned cultural norms (e.g., "boys don't cry"). For example, crying in infancy may result either in needs being met or in punishment or abandonment, and these different experiences shape the role of weeping as a strategy in future interactions. Crying as a strategy in prayer implies an internal working model of God as someone who responds to tears with empathy and support (e.g., Gen 21:17; 2 Kgs 20:3–6; Ps 6:7–10).

Internal working models and the attachment styles that arise from them tend to become fixed and persist into adulthood. They then influence relationships generally, not only those with childhood caregivers. Evidence of continuity and change of attachment styles across the life span tends to confirm the theory that working models are preverbal models formed in early childhood that inform subsequent relational interactions including (subconscious) choice of relationship partners. People seek experiences that tend to confirm their internal working models. Experiences that should contradict their models tend to be interpreted through a confirmatory lens, such as when clear evidence of another's sincere love is suspected as a manipulation (or vice versa).

Emotion Regulation

In recent decades, scholars have focused on the role of emotion regulation in shaping behavioral patterns and causing internal working models to persist over the

[15] Gillath, Karantzas, and Fraley, *Adult Attachment*, 78–80.

life span. Attachment theory has become "one of the most influential conceptual frameworks for understanding emotion regulation."[16] Indeed, the influence of early attachment relationships persists because of their influence on emotion regulation.[17] One trauma researcher and therapist describes the realization of the importance of attachment and emotion regulation in trauma in this manner:

> When Post-Traumatic Stress Disorder (PTSD) first made it into the diagnostic manuals, we only focused on dramatic incidents like rapes, assaults, or accidents to explain the origins of the emotional breakdowns in our patients. Gradually, we came to understand that the most severe dysregulation occurred in people who, as children, lacked a consistent caregiver. Emotional abuse, loss of caregivers, inconsistency, and chronic misattunement showed up as the principle contributors to a large variety of psychiatric problems. One of the most important discoveries in psychology, neuroscience, and psychiatry has been that failure in establishing secure early attachment bonds leads to a diminished capacity to regulate negative emotions.[18]

---

[16] Philip Shaver and Mario Mikulincer, "Adult Attachment and Emotion Regulation," in *Handbook of Emotion Regulation*, ed. James Gross, 2nd ed. (New York: Guilford, 2014), 237.
[17] Shiller, *Attachment Bond*, 53–55. Allan N. Schore has developed an emotional regulatory focus within attachment theory to describe human development, trauma, and recovery. See Schore, *Affect Regulation and the Origin of the Self: The Neurobiology of Emotional Development*, Norton Series on Interpersonal Neurobiology (New York: Taylor & Francis, 1994); Schore, *Affect Dysregulation and Disorders of the Self*, Norton Series on Interpersonal Neurobiology (New York: Norton, 2003); Schore, *Affect Regulation and the Repair of the Self*, Norton Series on Interpersonal Neurobiology (New York: Norton, 2003); and Schore, *The Science of the Art of Psychotherapy*, Norton Series on Interpersonal Neurobiology (New York: Norton, 2012). Analogously, the polyvagal theory provides further evidence for the importance on emotional coregulation in humans (and other mammals); see Stephen W. Porges, *The Polyvagal Theory: Neurophysiological Foundations of Emotions, Attachment, Communication, Self-Regulation*, Norton Series on Interpersonal Neurobiology (New York: Norton, 2011) and Porges, *The Pocket Guide to the Polyvagal Theory: The Transformative Power of Feeling Safe*, Norton Series on Interpersonal Neurobiology (New York: Norton, 2017). For another important work on attachment theory and emotion regulation, see Peter Fonagy et al., *Affect Regulation, Mentalization, and the Development of the Self* (New York: Other, 2002). For an accessible summary of many of these issues, see Jonathan Baylin and Daniel Hughes, *The Neurobiology of Attachment-Focused Therapy: Enhancing Connection and Trust in the Treatment of Children and Adolescents*, Norton Series on Interpersonal Neurobiology (New York: Norton, 2014).
[18] Bessel A. van der Kolk, foreword to *The Polyvagel Theory: Neurophysiological Foundations of Emotions, Attachment, Communication, Self-Regulation*, by Stephen W. Porges (New York: Norton, 2011), xi–xii. See also van der Kolk, *The Body Keeps the Score: Brain, Mind, and Body in the Healing of Trauma* (New York: Viking, 2014).

A statistic offers one way to illustrate the importance of early experiences for later outcomes: although only about 30 percent of Western adults are insecurely attached, they account for about 75 percent of people seeking professional psychological services.[19] Internal working models interact with emotion regulation to shape a person's development. Abusive or neglectful caregivers leave children with negative images of themselves and others, as well as relationships that continue into adulthood and create patterns of emotion dysregulation that disrupt lives. Similarly, many people develop internal working models of God that may be helpful or harmful for emotion regulation. The "God image" or "God concept" that psychologists examine amounts to an internal working model of God that shapes a person's capacity to regulate emotion in prayer.[20]

An emotionally well-regulated person responds adaptively to experience. In a well-regulated state, we access helpful memories as we adapt to changing circumstances. When dysregulated, our minds turn to memories and emotions that are less helpful, even sabotaging, and we may become fixated in an emotional state that may not be appropriate to our current situation. Consider, for example, a person whose anger derives less from the present than from past experiences or general difficulties regulating emotion, someone who flies into a rage over small provocations. An analogy with physiology and its concept of homeostasis may be helpful, especially since emotions correlate with physiological measures such as heart rate and respiration. Homeostasis is a stable equilibrium among interdependent parts. In emotion regulation and physiology, a person may experience hyper- or hypoarousal without experiencing dysregulation, provided that the arousal does not exceed the person's limits of tolerance. For example, our heart and respiration rates frequently vary depending on our level of activity, but the physiological system is well regulated by adaptively adjusting to the needs of the moment. When the system does not adapt or reaches the limits of tolerance, the results may be disease or death (e.g., a heart attack while shoveling snow). In emotion regulation, the stakes are no less. People who are emotionally dysregulated, temporarily or chronically, may have violent interactions dangerous to themselves and others, suffer mental illness, or lead socially isolated or dysfunctional lives due to difficulties maintaining relationships.

---

19 Marian J. Bakermans-Kraneburg and Marinus H. van Ijzendoorn, "The First 10,000 Adult Attachment Interviews: Distribution of Adult Attachment Representations in Clinical and Non-Clinical Groups," *Attachment and Human Development* 11 (2009): 223–63, esp. 230.

20 Ralph W. Hood Jr., Peter C. Hill, and Bernard Spilka, *The Psychology of Religion: An Empirical Approach*, 4th ed. (New York: Guilford, 2009), 97–99 and Kirkpatrick, *Attachment*, 81–85.

A vignette may illustrate what emotion regulation and dysregualtion look like and how they are transmitted from parent to child. Imagine that a baby who likes to pick up and smash objects has gotten hold of a valuable and breakable figurine. The parent sees the impending danger of a broken figurine and potentially bleeding baby and reacts by shouting at the baby to stop. The baby, shocked at this negative reaction, puts the figure down and begins to cry. The well-regulated parent safely retrieves the figurine and quickly shifts to consoling the child and helping the baby regulate out of its feelings of shame and anxiety. A dysregulated parent continues to berate the baby even after the problem has been solved. The child plunges deeper into negative emotions and never receives help regulating back to homeostasis.[21] Attachment researchers have long observed that parents who are coping with their own unresolved traumas are unable to respond sensitively to their babies. Becoming a parent and caring for a small child can cause parents to relive forgotten childhood experiences that can interfere with their ability to provide care. Unfortunately, parents are more likely to be blamed than offered the help they need.

The precise boundaries between regulated emotional arousal and dysregulation may be difficult to define or discern. For the purposes of analyzing prayer, I understand prayers of petition as responses to dysregulation and a consequent feeling of being out of control. Lee A. Kirkpatrick observes the uncanny resemblance between the three situations that drive people to seek their attachment figures and those that drive them to prayer: (1) "illness, injury, fatigue"; (2) "separation or threat of separation from attachment figures"; and (3) "environmental events that provoke fear or distress."[22] Many petitionary prayers make one or more of these motives explicit. Some psalms and many Akkadian prayers respond to the problem of illness. Illness and other adverse life events are often attributed to the guilt of the sufferer and/or anger of the deity, and many prayers seek to restore the valued but threatened divine-human relationship. Most striking, entire categories of Akkadian prayer are devoted to assuaging the anger of a deity and often involve language that explicitly seeks to regulate the petitioner's anxiety by mollifying the deity's anger. Social conflict also appears as a motive to turn to prayer in an effort to seek a sense of control within a chaotic environment, and the fear of divine abandonment lurks in many prayers and informs the requests of the petitioners for the deity to pay attention to their troubles.

---

[21] For this example, see Daniel Hill, *Affect Regulation Theory: A Clinical Model* (New York: Norton, 2015), 88, 122–23.

[22] Kirkpatrick, *Attachment*, 61.

SOCIAL SHARING OF EMOTION

Many Westerners think of weeping as an individual cathartic behavior; they believe that crying is good for mental and physical health, and that holding back tears can be harmful. This cathartic notion derives from Western folk psychology that imagines emotions as analogous to flowing fluids that, if blocked, build up potentially explosive pressure. Emotional expression, including weeping, provides a release or catharsis that relieves destructive and unhealthy pressure leading to improved mood and mental health. This model of emotion lends itself to Western ideas about humans as independent agents with emotional lives that may be lived largely in private.

Study of emotion generally and weeping in particular does not support the cathartic model. Weeping is a social behavior, and emotions are not like fluids. Study of "the social sharing of emotion" generally correlates well with the research on weeping, which is a specific and powerful form of emotional sharing.[23] Emotional experiences tend to be shared with trusted relationship partners. This sharing, including weeping, increases emotional and physiological arousal rather than the calm predicted by the cathartic theory. This fact may seem both obvious and puzzling. Our experience indicates that emotions cannot be exorcized through simple expression. Consider how expressing love does not dissipate that love. Also, if expression could eradicate emotion, then we would lose "the vital fruits of our experience" because emotion enhances memory.[24] So why does the

---

[23] Bernard Rimé, *Le partage social des émotions* (Paris: Presses universitaires de France, 2005); Rimé, "Emotion Elicits the Social Sharing of Emotion: Theory and Empirical Review," *Emotion Review* 1 (2009): 60–85; Rimé, "Mental Rumination, Social Sharing, and the Recovery from Emotional Exposure," in *Emotion, Disclosure, and Health*, ed. James Pennebaker (Washington, DC: American Psychological Association, 1995), 279–91; Margaret S. Clark and Eli J. Finkel, "Does Expressing Emotion Promote Well-Being? It Depends on Relationship Context," in *The Social Life of Emotions*, ed. Larissa Tiedens and Colin Wayne Leach (Cambridge: Cambridge University Press, 2004), 105–26; Christelle Duprez, "Motives for the Social Sharing of an Emotional Experience," *Journal of Social and Personal Relationships* (2014): 1–31; Antonietta Curci and Bernard Rimé, "The Temporal Evolution of the Social Sharing of Emotions and Its Consequences on Emotional Recovery: A Longitudinal Study," *Emotion* 12 (2012): 1404–14; Bernard Rimé et al., "The Social Sharing of Emotions in Interpersonal and in Collective Situations: Common Psychosocial Consequences," in *Emotion Regulation and Well-Being*, ed. Ivan Nyklíček, Ad Vingerhoets, and Marcel Zeelenberg. (New York: Springer, 2011), 147–63; and Bernard Rimé, Susanna Corsini, Gwénola Herbette, "Emotion, Verbal Expression, and the Social Sharing of Emotion," in *The Verbal Communication of Emotions: Interdisciplinary Perspectives*, ed. Susan Fussell (Mahwah, NJ: Earlbaum, 2002), 185–208.

[24] Bernard Rimé, Gwénola Herbette, and Susanna Corsini, "The Social Sharing of Emotion: Illusory and Real Benefits of Talking about Emotional Experiences," in *Emotional*

cathartic theory persist in the face of this experience, and why do we persist in sharing emotional experiences if it offers no catharsis?

There are many benefits to sharing emotional experiences, even if catharsis is not one of them. There are also corresponding problems with not sharing emotional experiences. The term "social sharing" implies one or more other people, and this social context supplies the benefits of sharing and the corresponding ills that arise from isolation. Emotions are "upheavals of thought" that can shatter our assumptions about ourselves and our world.[25] This consequence can be isolating because our symbolic worlds are shared within a community that gives them meaning and value. By sharing these emotional experiences, we seek reintegration into the community and help making sense of our experience. Talking about emotional experiences can be a powerful means of reinforcing relationship. Listeners typically express interest in emotional stories and become emotionally aroused themselves. They may offer empathy, help with making sense, and provide practical assistance, which can make a distressed person feel cared for and safe. By contrast, memories that are not shared are "associated with (1) greater search for meaning, (2) greater efforts at understanding what had happened, and (3) greater attempts at 'putting order in what happened.'"[26] The cathartic theory thus survives in part because there are real benefits to sharing emotional experiences and real harms from not doing so. These benefits, however, do not include the dissipation of the emotion itself or relief from its emotional weight. The benefits derive from the interpersonal dimension of expression, hence "emotional sharing" is a more apt term than "emotional expression."

People do not share their emotional experience indiscriminately but prefer trusted relationship partners.[27] Even these trusted intimates can disappoint. Our pleas for help may be met with avoidance or anger from people too busy with their own problems to think about ours. Well-intentioned people often seek to help but do not know how. An extensive research literature on social support offers lessons in how (not) to love our neighbors.[28] Overt offers of support can make people feel dependent, helpless, and indebted, and less visible forms of support can be more

---

Expression and Health: Advances in Theory, Assessment, and Clinical Applications, ed. Ivan Nyklíček, Lydia Temoshok, and Ad Vingerhoets (New York: Brunner-Routledge, 2004), 35.

[25] Martha Nussbaum, *Upheavals of Thought: The Intelligence of Emotions* (Cambridge: Cambridge University Press, 2001) took the title for her book on emotions from Marcel Proust.

[26] Rimé at al., "Social Sharing," 37.

[27] Rimé, "Emotion," 71–72, 79 and Clark and Finkel, "Does Expressing Emotion Promote Well-Being?"

[28] Gregory Pierce and I. G. Sarason, eds., *Handbook of Social Support and the Family* (New York: Springer, 1996) and Shelley Taylor, "Social Support: A Review," in *The Oxford Handbook of Health Psychology* (Oxford: Oxford University Press, 2012), 192–217.

effective by avoiding these negative feelings. Like Job's friends, we often react selfishly to the pain of others. We may be more interested in preserving our own cherished assumptions about the world than in helping the person whose similar beliefs have been shattered by experience. Psychologists speak of "just world belief" or "just world theory" to refer to the human propensity to believe that the world is fundamentally fair.[29] Our need to believe in the goodness or fairness of the world motivates our tendency to blame victims for the bad things that happen to them. Just world belief allows us to maintain a sense of control over our lives, because it allows us to believe that we can avoid suffering by our good or smart conduct. Bad things happen to people because they make mistakes. This blame may be rude and overt or come through in discourse that otherwise seems empathetic. For these reasons, people choose carefully the partners with whom they share their emotional memories and sometimes regret their decisions.

In addition to its interpersonal benefits, the social sharing of emotion builds community and collective memory on a larger scale. Sometimes, the community building happens immediately, as when a leader gives shape and expression to communal feeling. These emotions may center around a specific event (e.g., a terrorist attack) or a commonly shared experience or fear (e.g., job loss). At other times, the collective memory of events and experiences may build through smaller-scale sharing. Rituals provide a common framework for communal sharing and shaping of emotions that also form collective memories.[30]

---

[29] Adrian Furnham, "Belief in a Just World: Research Progress over the Past Decade," *Personality and Individual Differences* 34 (2003): 795–819; John E. Edlund, Brad J. Sagarin, and Brian S. Johnson, "Reciprocity and the Belief in a Just World," *Personality and Individual Differences* 43 (2007): 589–96; Isabel Correia et al., "When Do People Derogate or Psychologically Distance Themselves from Victims? Belief in a Just World and Ingroup Identification," *Personality and Individual Differences* 53 (2012): 747–52; and Isabel Correia, Jorge Vala, and Patrícia Aguiar, "Victim's Innocence, Social Categorization, and the Threat to the Belief in a Just World," *Journal of Experimental Social Psychology* 43 (2007): 31–38.

[30] G. Bellelli, G. Leoni, and A. Curci, "Emocion y memoria collectiva: El recuerdo acontecimientos públicos," *Psicología Política* 18 (1999): 101–24; Carlos Martín Beristain, José Luis González, and Darío Páez, "Memoria collectiva y genocido político en Guatemale: Antecedentes y efectos de los procesos de la memoria colectiva," *Psicología Política* 18 (1999): 77–99; J. K. Herranz and N. Basabe, "Identidad nacional, ideología política y memoria colectiva," *Psicología Política* 18 (1999): 31–47; Carlos Martín Beristain, Darío Páez, José Luis González, "Ritual, Social Sharing, Silence, and Collective Memory Claims in the Case of the Guatemalan Genocide," *Psicothema* 12 (2000): 117–30; and James W. Pennebaker and Amy L. Gonzales, "Making History: Social and Psychological Processes underlying Collective Memory," in *Memory in Mind and Culture*, ed. Pascal Boyer and James B. Wertsch (Cambridge: Cambridge University Press, 2009), 171–93.

The research on the social sharing of emotions coheres with research specifically focused on weeping. Studies find that the results of weeping vary considerably based on individual variables such as age, gender, and extroversion and the social context of the crying episode, such as the immediate motivation for the tears and the reaction of others who see them. Like other forms of emotional expression, weeping increases physiological and emotional arousal, but, in favorable social environments, this arousal may elicit support, which can make a distressed person feel cared for and safe. Incompetent social support, however, may cause the weeper to feel blamed or intensify feelings of helplessness or inadequacy. Fear of this outcome drives people to seek privacy when they feel the urge to weep.[31]

The social sharing of emotion provides perspective on prayer as well as weeping. Many prayer texts involve a human sharing emotion with a deity. Laments or petitions display this sharing most obviously, as when the petitioner's pain serves as motivation for the deity to empathize and help (i.e., offer social support).[32] But hymns of gratitude and psalms of trust likewise share emotion and build relationship. In some cases, the prayer has both a divine and a human audience. For example, Lamentations explicitly addresses both God and people by employing the voice of both a narrator and Zion (e.g., Lam 1:1–11a, 11b–22). Some Akkadian prayers similarly include a narrative voice describing the petitioner as well as the first-person petitioner's voice (e.g., Dialogue between a Man and His God, 1–11, 12–16). Even when the text does not include both of these voices, prayers envision human audiences for the transaction between the deity and the person praying (e.g., Ps 6).

The research on social sharing of emotions shows how social and interdependent we are, and tears may have evolved precisely to tighten social bonds and

31 Vingerhoets, *Why Only Humans Weep*, esp. 79–138.

32 Brent Strawn has connected laments with "disclosure" of trauma, or what I call "social sharing"; see Strawn, "Trauma, Psalmic Disclosure, and Authentic Happiness," in *Bible through the Lens of Trauma*, ed. Elizabeth Boase and Christopher Frechette, SemeiaSt 86 (Atlanta, GA: SBL Press, 2016) 143–60 and Strawn, "Poetic Attachment: Psychology, Psycholinguistics, and the Psalms," in *The Oxford Handbook to the Psalms*, ed. William Brown (Oxford: Oxford University Press, 2016), 404–23. He draws on James W. Pennebaker, *Opening Up: The Healing Power of Expressing Emotions*, rev. ed. (New York: Guilford, 1997) and Judith Hermann, *Trauma and Recovery* (New York: Basic, 1992). Christopher Frechette, "Destroying the Internalized Perpetrator: A Healing of the Violent Language against Enemies in the Psalms," in *Trauma and Traumatization in Individual and Collective Dimensions: Insights from Biblical Studies and Beyond*, ed. Eve-Marie Becker, Jan Dochhorn, and Else K. Holt (Göttingen: Vandenhoeck & Ruprecht, 2014), 71–84 also develops a psychologically informed proposal for interpreting vengeance language in the Psalms.

deepen human dependency and cooperation.[33] The motivation to share emotional experience is not as simple as the practical benefits outlined above. More fundamentally, we seek to regulate our emotional lives with other people. Indeed, we are dependent on others for the quality of our emotional lives, which correlates with the quality of our lives more generally, including our mental and physical health, as well as our happiness. Bernard Rimé, a leading researcher on the social sharing of emotions, has sought to integrate several research traditions that all point toward the same conclusion: Western cultural ideas about human autonomy are largely wrong, and we remain highly relational throughout our lives.[34] Scientists generally agree that emotion regulation is a social process in young children. After adolescence, however, researchers tend to speak of "self-regulation" and "autonomy." But adults continue to share emotional experiences with others long after adolescence. Rimé suggests that the tendency to adopt a different theoretical model to describe adult emotion regulation derives from long-standing Western cultural bias that regards humans as independent agents and dependence as infantile and shameful. Evidence amply demonstrates that adults continue to seek out trusted others with whom to share emotional experiences and regulate emotions. Apart from cultural bias, why do psychologists maintain such a strong theoretical distinction between dependent children and independent adults?

THE INNER VOICE, OR THE DIALOGIC MIND

The divergent explanations of emotion regulation in children and adults make a kind of intuitive sense. Young children obviously depend on others in ways that adults appear not to. Adults appear able to regulate their emotions by themselves for periods of time when they do not have immediate access to trusted relationship partners. The isolated adult, however, is not alone. People often regulate their emotions and behaviors through the "inner voice," or the silent discourse that takes place in the mind. The inner voice has been the subject of periodic research.[35] The "private speech" of children (i.e., spoken speech not directed at anyone) becomes increasingly silent as children grow older and learn that talking aloud to no one is discouraged. Private speech has been one window into the silent inner voice, including its origins and development. For our purposes, there are three critical points about the inner voice: it originates in the social context, it is dialogic, and it regulates emotions and behavior.

Lev Vygotsky famously presented the social origins of the inner voice and his pioneering work inspired some of the early research in children's private speech,

---

[33] Walter, *Thumbs*, 165–79.

[34] Rimé, "Emotion."

[35] For an excellent introduction, see Charles Fernyhough, *The Voices Within: The History and Science of How We Talk to Ourselves* (New York: Basic, 2016).

as well as a resurgence of this work when his writings began to appear in English in the 1960s.[36] The fact that our inner voice is tied to a specific language provides one clue that its origin is social.[37] As Vygotsky and others have found, private speech derives specific content from the conversations surrounding the child and speech directed at the child. When researchers eavesdrop on children's private speech, they often hear children repeating phrases or whole speeches that they have heard from others. This external social origin of the inner voice gives rise to its dialogic nature. The social and dialogic aspect of the inner voice appears when one asks who is speaking and who is listening. The existence of the voice already implies two people or selves who mirror the social reality of conversation in the social world. The inner voice may originate from one aspect of the self addressing another. Some scholars speak of this as the "I" (present self) addressing the "you" (future self) about the "me" (past self).[38] The dialogic self appears in ancient Hebrew prayers with such expressions as "bless YHWH, O my נפש" in which the psalmist addresses one aspect of the self from another aspect. The spoken prayer reflects inner dialogue within the self. As noted above, however, these voices originate from outside the individual, from the social environment. Furthermore, there are multiple inner voices, not just one, and they can engage one another in dialogue (i.e., the נפש can talk back). These voices appear as aspects of the socially derived self: the empathetic friend, the helpful coach, the critical parent, etc. The dialogue that happens silently inside one's head derives from spoken discourse

---

36 Lev Vygotsky, *Thought and Language*, ed. and trans. Eugenia Hanfmann, Gertrude Vakar, and Alex Kozulin (Cambridge, MA: MIT Press, 2012); Vygotsky, *The Vygotsky Reader*, ed. René van der Veer and Jaan Valsinger (Oxford: Blackwell, 1994); and Peter Lloyd and Charles Fernyhough, eds., *Lev Vygotsky: Critical Assessments*, 4 vols. (London: Routledge, 1999).

37 Note that the social origin of the mind is not limited to the linguistic form of the inner voice. Rather, linguistic forms of relating depend on preexisting, nonlinguistic means of intersubjectivity. See Beatrice Beebe and Frank M. Lachmann, *The Origins of Attachment: Infant Research and Adult Treatment*, Relational Perspective Book Series (New York: Routledge, 2014), esp. 27–29.

38 Norbert Wiley, *Inner Speech and the Dialogical Self* (Philadelphia, PA: Temple University Press, 2016), 9 et passim. His discussion of the inner voice draws on the tradition in social theory rather than the psychological and empirical work that informs Fernyhough, *Voices*. Wiley sometimes mentions Vygotsky but depends more on Mikhail Bakhtin, Charles Sanders Pierce, and George Herbert Mead. Similarly, Margaret S. Archer's work focuses on theory and her own interviews with subjects to discern how the inner dialogue connects structure (external environments) and agency (interior life); see Archer, *Structure, Agency, and the Internal Conversation* (Cambridge: Cambridge University Press, 2003); Archer, *Making Our Way through the World* (Cambridge: Cambridge University Press, 2007); and Archer *The Reflexive Imperative in Late Modernity* (Cambridge: Cambridge University Press, 2012).

heard outside the head. The internal working models of other people that we carry around in our minds have voices of their own that can interact with the voices of the various aspects of the self. Sometimes we cannot easily distinguish the voices of self and others within our minds. For example, cognitive behavioral therapy (CBT) often seeks to modify dysfunctional "self-talk" that underlies some mental health problems.[39] CBT assumes that thoughts shape behavior, and that we can shape and reshape our thinking.[40] Despite the name, CBT engages emotion as well as cognition and behavior in attempts to help patients suffering various kinds of dysfunctions to revise their core beliefs, emotional lives, internal dialogues, and behaviors.[41] Destructive self-talk may derive from a derogatory parent whose words have been internalized by the child and the source forgotten. In other cases, the external voice may be more consciously recognized, as when we engage in dialogue with an absent loved one within our minds. The spouse, for example, may not be present, but a well-developed internal representation of the spouse is always available to the self.

Just as the voices of other people can enter the mind and become inner voices that can help shape regulation (or dysregulation), so also deities can enter the mind and become voices and dialogue partners. As people develop internal working models of a deity, that deity may develop a voice derived from various sources, such as religious leaders, liturgies, parental instruction, and scriptural texts. Such sources sometimes speak in the voice of the deity or state what the deity thinks or feels.[42] Through exposure to the divine mind and voice, the internal working model of the deity may at times have a voice that may speak to or with the person. This divine self becomes an audience that shapes the speech directed to the deity

---

39 Tullio Scrimali, *Neuroscience-Based Cognitive Therapy: New Methods for Assessment, Treatment and Self-Regulation* (Malden, MA: Wiley-Blackwell, 2012), 54: "Internal dialogue has great importance in determining our behavior and appears to be central in psychopathology, being at the basis of the numerous systems of diverse mental disorders."

40 Donna M. Sudak, *Cognitive Behavioral Therapy for Clinicians* (Philadelphia, PA: Lippincott Williams and Wilkins, 2006), 10–11.

41 David F. Tolin, *Doing CBT: A Comprehensive Guide to Working and Behaviors, Thoughts, and Emotions* (New York: Guilford, 2016).

42 The first-person words of Jesus routinely conclude sections of Sarah Young, *Jesus Calling Bible Storybook* (Nashville, TN: Tommy Nelson, 2012) and, in some editions of the New Testament, words spoken by Jesus are printed in red. Children and adults involved in religious communities frequently receive messages that shape their internal working models of divinity, messages that sometimes include divine speech. The text in Exodus–Numbers presents laws in the direct speech of God, and in Deuteronomy as mediated through Moses. The prophets commonly present the direct speech of God. These scriptural presentations of divine speech contribute to internal working models of God and the associated divine inner voice.

in prayer. As evident from cognitive behavioral therapy, prayer can contribute to the person's emotion regulation or dysregulation depending on the patient's internal working models of self, others, and the deity.

The precise experience of the inner voice varies considerably among individuals, and the voice(s) serve various functions such as memory rehearsal, fantasy construction, problem solving, and regulation of emotion.[43] Children use private speech at times when they most need help solving problems, and their private speech serves a regulatory function. Adults also speak aloud and silently to themselves, and this speech is often regulatory. For example, an athlete may draw on the internalized words of a coach to improve his or her performance during a competition. Inner speech may be used for modeling future scenarios for devising strategies for navigating relationships or solving problems, which are regulatory functions. Verbal prayer, whether silent or aloud, participates in the social nature of humans and the dialogism of human speech. People turn to prayer in significant measure for the purpose of regulating their emotional lives, with goals such as alleviating anxiety or elevating joy, and these prayers are inevitably dialogic.

Several biblical scholars speak of "dialogism" as developed from the writings of Mikhail Bakhtin. He righty saw that "reality is utterly, fundamentally, relational."[44] Even an internal utterance of a speaker is shaped by the anticipated voice of the listener as well as other voices, whether people close to the speaker or aspects of the speaker's self. "In other words, Bakhtin decomposes what appears to be one voice into several."[45] Many biblical scholars have fruitfully deployed Bakhtinian ideas about dialogism to read biblical texts as multivoiced compositions.[46] The present study supplements Bakhtinian dialogism with psychological research and social theory about the inner voices to show that the self is dialogic. The self is not only in relation with others but is relational within itself. There is dialogue both within and beyond the individual mind. Some prayer texts reflect the multiple

---

[43] Fernyhough, *Voices*, 49.

[44] Barbara Green, *Mikhail Bakhtin and Biblical Scholarship: An Introduction*, SemeiaSt 38 (Atlanta, GA: Society of Biblical Literature, 2000), 30; Mikhail Bakhtin, *The Dialogic Imagination: Four Essays*, trans. C. Emerson and M. Holquist (Austin: University of Texas Press, 1981); and Bakhtin, *Problems of Dostoyevsky's Poetics*, ed. and trans. Cheryl Emerson (Minneapolis: University of Minnesota Press, 1984).

[45] Wiley, *Inner Speech*, 168.

[46] See, e.g., Green, *Mikhail Bakhtin*; Carol Newsom, *The Book of Job: A Contest of Moral Imaginations* (Oxford: Oxford University Press, 2003); Roland Boer, ed., *Bakhtin and Genre Theory in Biblical Studies* (Atlanta, GA: Society of Biblical Literature, 2007); Carleen Mandolfo, *God in the Dock: Dialogic Tension in the Psalms of Lament*, JSOTSup 357 (Sheffield: Sheffield Academic Press; New York: Bloomsbury T&T Clark, 2002); and Mandolfo, *Daughter Zion Talks Back to the Prophets: A Dialogic Theology of the Book of Lamentations*, SemeiaSt 58 (Atlanta, GA: Society of Biblical Literature, 2007).

voices that may be present in the mind of the person praying, whether as external voices heard in a liturgy or internal voices not heard with ears. The contrast sometimes drawn between private and public prayer assumes a greater divide than may be appropriate. The inner voices are shaped by what is heard in the social environment, so the private prayer is informed by public prayer. Someone who creates a new prayer draws on the social experience of prayer refracted through the inner voices and therefore develops a prayer that is new, but that is inevitably shaped by previously known prayers. Whether praying publicly or privately, a person at prayer is often a person in dialogue with socially created inner voices that may include a voice of a deity based on an internal working model of that deity shaped by culture and personal experience. In the course of this dialogue, people often regulate their emotional lives, whether seeking relief from anxiety or elevating joy and gratitude.

Prayer as emotion coregulation with a deity appears in prior scholarship, although without the explicitness and specificity outlined above. Hermann Gunkel recognizes that "the goal of the complaint song is *to obtain something from YHWH*. In order to avoid missing this goal, the one praying strives *to move* the heart of God (*das Herz seines Gottes zu* bewegen) with everything he says."[47] Foreshadowing later attachment theory, Gunkel observes that "confidence (*Vertrauen*) in YHWH is the preferred and most frequently stated reason why the poets of the complaint songs offer their petition."[48] He observes that the prayer reflects the image of God as a safe haven and secure base, although this attachment language was not available to him, and he further describes the emotional turbulence of the petitioner and the attempt to coregulate emotion with God: "It is understandably human when the one praying becomes disconcerted (*unruhig wird*) with the long delay of help and has to wrestle internally with his trust (*Vertrauen*). He then casts his heart to God in stormy desire (*Da wirft er sich seinem Gott in ungestümem Verlangen ans Herz*)."[49] Similarly, Walter Brueggemann's categorization of psalms as reflecting "orientation," "disorientation," and "new orientation" correlate with emotion regulatory processes, although Brueggemann relies on a more cognitive perspective.[50] Attachment theory shows, for example, that mourners in grief oscillate between a

[47] Hermann Gunkel, completed by Joachim Begrich, *An Introduction to the Psalms: The Genres of the Religious Lyric of Israel*, trans. James D. Nogalski; Mercer Library of Biblical Studies (Macon, GA: Mercer University Press, 1998) 169–70; trans. of Gunkel, *Einleitung in die Psalmen: Die Gattugen der religiösen Lyrik Israels* (Gottingen: Vandenhoeck & Ruprecht, 1933), 231.

[48] Gunkel, *Introduction*, 170; Gunkel, *Einleitung*, 232.

[49] Gunkel, *Introduction*, 171; Gunkel, *Einleiting*, 233.

[50] Walter Brueggemann, *The Message of the Psalms: A Theological Commentary*, AOTS (Minneapolis, MN: Augsburg, 1984).

"loss orientation," in which their attachment system is hyperactivated, causing them to yearn for the lost loved one and ruminate on the deceased, and a "restoration orientation," in which their attachment system is suppressed, and they distract themselves from grief and engage in necessary tasks and other relationships.[51] This emotional regulation in the wake of loss resembles Brueggemann's "disorientation" and "new orientation, respectively.[52] Further, the extensive scholarly discussion of the "mood change" frequently found in individual laments has included discussion of emotion regulation. Psychological explanations for the mood change have proceeded without the benefit of contemporary research on emotion regulation and have largely fallen out of favor, replaced with preference for a cultic explanation in which a divine oracle of salvation is thought to have been interjected between the petition and thanksgiving. Until recently, scholars have also overlooked the fact that there are many more mood changes in the psalms, and they do not always move from lament to praise, but sometimes move in the other direction as well.[53] I will return to this topic in the discussion of individual laments.[54] The theory of prayer as emotion regulation coheres with much existing scholarship. Improved correlation with the extensive research on emotion regulation from other disciplines can help biblical scholars avoid errors and develop more precise theoretical frameworks for the fruitful analysis of ancient texts.

WEEPING

Two themes repeatedly emerge from research on crying as explanations for why humans weep: helplessness and social relationship. People weep in both positively and negatively valanced situations, such as separations and reunions. Research suggests that tears of joy in happy contexts (reunions, birth, victory) derive from recollections of negative emotions (e.g., grief) or a sense of helplessness. For example, Olympic medalists sometimes cry because they recollect the sacrifices and challenges involved in training or lost loved ones not present to see their victory.[55]

---

[51] Phillip R. Shaver and R. Chris Fraley, "Attachment, Loss, and Grief: Bowlby's Views and Contemporary Views," in *Handbook of Attachment: Theory, Research, and Clinical Applications*, ed. Jude Cassidy and Phillip R. Shaver, 3rd ed. (New York: Guilford, 2016), 40–62, esp. 42–43, 55–57.

[52] David A. Bosworth, "Understanding Grief and Reading the Bible," in *Mixed Feelings and Vexed Passions: Exploring Emotions in Biblical Literature*, ed. F. Scott Spencer, RBS 90 (Atlanta, GA: SBL Press, 2016), 117–38, esp. 126–29.

[53] Federico G. Villanueva, *The "Uncertainty of a Hearing": A Study of the Sudden Change of Mood in the Psalms of Lament*, VTSup 121 (Leiden: Brill, 2008).

[54] See pages 93–96.

[55] Ad Vingerhoets, "Crying: A Biosocial Phenomenon," in *Tears in the Greco-Roman World*, ed. Thorsten Fögen (Berlin: de Gruyter, 2009), 87–96.

Ad Vingerhoets has developed a list of situations that evoke tears, in which he pairs positive and negative contexts such as birth and death, wedding and relationship loss, reunion and separation, etc.[56] In both positive and negative situations, people may feel helpless or sense that they are out of control and unable to cope adequately with the situation. As they lose control of their emotional regulatory processes, they feel powerful unbridled emotions. From this sense of helplessness, a short step leads to the social or interpersonal aspect of weeping. As one loses control and feels helpless, one requires help from others. Thus, we cry when we feel that we cannot cope with a situation and turn to trusted others for support. The connection between helplessness and social bonding as motives for weeping finds strong support from attachment theory. A person is apt to weep in situations in which it is important to elicit empathy or support, and/or to reduce aggression or anger.

Weeping conferred such a powerful survival advantage on those human ancestors who wept that this trait became universal in the species. The response that tears evoke from people who see them may explain how this could have happened. In general, tears prompt empathy and social support while inhibiting aggression in those who see them. Like social sharing of emotion more generally, weeping has the power to strengthen social ties, and tight bonds among people confer survival advantages. Weeping appears to have a power that the spoken word does not, and tears speak more eloquently than verbal petitions. The power of tears may lie in their role as an honest signal.[57] The acoustic aspect of sobbing gains attention in a social setting. Tears may or may not be accompanied by sobs, but tears alone provide a powerful signal of helplessness. A study involving photographs of expressive faces, some with tears digitally removed, found that tears serve to disambiguate facial expressions. Without tears, the face of a person weeping turns out to be hard to read. Tears therefore "*resolve ambiguity of facial expression*."[58] Tears appear to serve a signaling function, meaning that they may have evolved because of their power to change the behavior of others by changing their information, and the change benefits the one who cries. (If there were no benefit to the weeper, then tears would be a cue rather than a signal.) Signals are more powerful if they are costly to the signaler. A verbal request for help may cost nothing and is easily faked. Tears, by contrast, are hard to fake, and they blur

---

56 Vingerhoets, *Why Only Humans Weep*, 91.

57 Oren Hasson, "Emotional Tears as Biological Signals," *Evolutionary Psychology* 7 (2009): 363–70 and Joseph Soltis, "The Signal Functions of Early Infant Crying," *Behavioral and Brain Sciences* 27 (2004): 443–90.

58 Robert R. Provine, "Emotional Tears and NGF: A Biographical Appreciation and Research Beginning," *Archives Italiennes de Biologie* 149 (2011): 271 (italics his).

vision, which impairs the ability to attack or defend. The effect may mollify would-be attackers or recruit help from allies in various contexts by signaling helplessness.

Evidence shows that crying does affect the behavior of those witnessing the weeping, although the consequences vary. Two main themes emerge: first, weeping may elicit empathy and support, as well as mitigate anger and aggression; second, weeping may elicit anger and aggression. Weeping therefore appears to be a risky strategy for gaining help, which may explain why people strive to restrain tears in some contexts. The widely divergent reactions to tears may be understood by analogy with an arms race. Tears powerfully evoke attention and empathy from others because they are thought to be an honest signal—costly and hard to fake. But if tears have such power, then people would be constrained to always respond to weeping with support even when that support may be expensive. Consequently, we need a means of defending ourselves from the power of weeping, and anger provides an effective defense that displaces empathy. People may respond angrily to tears if they suspect that the tears are fake or inappropriate. Whether a particular person will react to tears with empathy or anger on a given occasion is hard to predict. The response depends on a multitude of factors including the person's mood, their relationship to the weeper, the context of the weeping, and the cultural "display rules" about who may weep and when. In his study of repentance, David A. Lambert notes that "one may speak of the power of mourning rites to elicit empathy as a sort of irritant to the deity."[59] The divine reaction to mourning rites (e.g., fasting, weeping) might be better understood as stress rather than irritation. Like infant cries, mourning rites elicit stress that may manifest as either empathy or anger.[60] God communicates to Jeremiah that God will not listen to the cries of Israel (Jer 11:11) as the divine wrath has become so intense that even the intercessions of Moses and Samuel would not be heard (Jer 15:1). God has shifted away from the possibility of empathy, and only anger remains.[61]

Studies find that tears impact how others perceive the weeper's credibility. People who weep or otherwise show more emotion are perceived as more credible than those who show less affect. For example, studies of crying by rape victims found that police officers rated those victims who cried or showed negative emotions as more credible than those who did not.[62] Emotionally expressive people

---

[59] David A. Lambert, *How Repentance Became Biblical: Judaism, Christianity, and the Interpretation of Scripture* (Oxford: Oxford University Press, 2016), 17.

[60] Bosworth, *Infant Weeping*, 4–21.

[61] Bosworth, "Tears," 43.

[62] Guri C. Bollingmo et al., "Credibility of the Emotional Witness: A Study of Ratings by Police Investigators," *Psychology, Crime, and Law* 14 (2008): 29–40; Lawrence G. Calhoun, "Victim Emotional Response: Effects on Social Reaction to Victims of Rape," *British Journal*

are generally deemed more credible than those whose emotion is more controlled. Public weeping can have a significant impact on a person's reputation. In Japan, leaders freely weep at press conferences to show sincere remorse for errors, and their Japanese audiences generally accept these displays as sincere and respect the person for weeping. Tears can have a positive effect on a person's reputation.[63] Many Western countries have different rules about weeping, and leaders are not permitted to weep in this context. In other situations, however, Western leaders may weep openly. In a television interview, General Norman Schwarzkopf, who commanded allied forces in the First Gulf War, said that it was appropriate for a commander to weep in some situations, such as when he was with his troops in Saudi Arabia on Christmas Eve, but tears of a general would be demoralizing on the battlefield or in debriefing after the war.[64] His observations appear to accord with an ancient Israelite perception that David's weeping after the death of his son Absalom made his victorious troops feel shame (2 Sam 19:1–8). In literary contexts, a character hiding tears from other characters may communicate to the reader that the character has appropriately strong emotions without revealing to other characters the emotional life and therefore identity of the weeper. Joseph in Genesis and Odysseus in the *Odyssey* provide examples.[65] Because tears are perceived as an honest signal, they can shape how people are evaluated by others. Tears may make a person seem more credible and more emotional, but also potentially weak or unstable.

These evaluations translate into behaviors as witnesses to weeping respond with comfort or punishment. "The majority of the studies that have examined social reactions to crying support the attachment perspective on adult crying."[66] People tend to offer comfort to those who weep, and they distinguish between strangers and close relations. We are much more likely to offer comfort to a friend or family member than to a stranger, and this comfort extends to physical contact with close relations but almost never with strangers. This distinction implies that attachment is a key factor in weeping, and that intimates are more likely than

of Social Psychology 20 (1981): 17–21; and Louisa Hackett, Andrew Day, and Philip Mohr, "Expectancy Violation and Perceptions of Rape Victim Credibility," *Legal and Criminological Psychology* 13 (2008): 323–34.

63 Vingerhoets, *Why Only Humans Weep*, 123.

64 Vingerhoets, *Why Only Humans Weep*, 123 and "Barbara Walters Interviews General Norman Schwartzkopf," *20/20*, March 1991, YouTube, https://www.youtube.com/watch?v=A6AN7KTLKNM; https://www.youtube.com/watch?v=ohNUIVHRWWo.

65 Bosworth, "Weeping in Recognition Scenes."

66 Vingerhoets, *Why Only Humans Weep*, 125.

strangers to provide support.[67] Even though people often seek to be alone and conceal their crying, weeping is a profoundly social behavior.

PATTERNS IN WEEPING BEHAVIOR

The research on weeping has discovered several patterns in weeping behaviors that might inform our reading of ancient texts. Two separate studies have independently identified three types of weeping.[68] When a baby or small child is left alone, the child experiences three stages of emotional response to the separation that correlate with three types of crying. The same three stages have been observed in older children and adults, including cancer patients. The first stage is protest, associated with "protest crying," which involves loud wailing or screaming in an effort to change the situation by gaining attention and care. This effort to regain the attachment figure may be understood as driven by fear and/or anger. The behavior is loud and requires considerable energy. Those who hear it find the noise aversive and stressful, and they may respond with empathetic support or angry punishment or dismissal. "Protest criers often reject sympathy outright because accepting comfort of any kind implies acceptance of the loss."[69] In general, anger becomes a more likely reaction as a child grows older. As the situation of abandonment continues, the child shifts into a second stage called "despair," associated with "sad crying" and characterized by quiet tears. The anger and fear that drove the protest now give way to a sense of helplessness and despair. The person abandons hope that the situation will be reversed. In adults, this type of crying seems more likely to elicit empathy than protest crying. It is a quieter signal of helplessness and need that does not create as much stress as the noisy aversive crying of protest. This type of crying may result in reunion or in the development of a new attachment bond to replace what was lost. If the situation continues, a baby enters a third stage called "detachment," which is associated with deep sadness, depression, hopelessness, and withdrawal. This stage is not associated with weeping, although some refer to it as "inhibited" or "detached" crying or "crying on the inside."[70] If weeping is intended to elicit help when people feel helpless, a lack of tears in this stage indicate the depth of hopelessness. There is no point in weeping because there is no hope.

These three types of crying may be understood as two, since the third is characterized by a lack of crying. The underlying emotions and goals are also different.

---

[67] Vingerhoets, *Why Only Humans Weep*, 125–26.

[68] Nelson, *Seeing*, 36–41 and K. Rydé, M. Friedrichsen, and P. Strang, "Crying: A Force to Balance Emotions among Cancer Patients in Palliative Home Care," *Palliative and Support Care* 5 (2007): 51–59.

[69] Hendricks et al., "Why Crying Improves Our Well-Being," 90.

[70] Nelson, *Seeing*, 40–41 and Rydé, Friedrichsen, and Strang, "Crying."

Texts do not reliably distinguish between these two kinds of weeping, but language and imagery sometimes accentuate the voiced sobs over tears, suggesting protest crying. Protest crying may be expected in prayer because protest criers "want action rather than comfort; they want caregivers to do something about their loss."[71] The absence of explicit attention to sound may or may not indicate sad crying. The surrounding context of the prayer and its descriptions of the speaker's emotional state may further help distinguish the two types of crying and the emotional difference they represent (anger versus sadness).

Another pattern in weeping behaviors that may appear in texts concerns the timing of crying. Across cultures, people cry more in the evening than during the day. This pattern holds for both infants and adults. No one knows whether this pattern has an underlying biological component (analogous to circadian rhythms that influence sleep) or is more strictly environmental. After a day of work and socializing, accumulated stress may make evening weeping more likely than daytime weeping. Also, people are normally in the company of trusted family members in the evening, before whom their weeping is less inhibited. Alternatively, evening hours may be more associated with solitude. Survey findings also show that people are often alone in cars when they weep. Whatever the reason, people cry more in the evening hours. Ancient prayer texts sometimes reflect this correlation between evening and weeping with references to nighttime and sleeplessness.

Gender also influences weeping. Across cultures, women tend on average to weep more than men. The extent of this gender difference varies by culture, with Western cultures generally showing a greater gender distinction and central African cultures showing the least distinction.[72] The gender difference in crying behavior is not observable in infants but emerges in middle childhood and accelerates dramatically in adolescence as boys reduce their crying behavior and girls do not. This difference declines in old age as women cry less and men's behavior remains consistent. The gender difference in crying behavior appears to involve both biological and cultural influences. Women may be more prone to cry due in part to higher levels of oxytocin and prolactin, which are associated with weeping.

---

[71] Hendricks et al., "Why Crying Improves Our Well-Being," 90.

[72] Agneta H. Fischer and Antont S. R. Manstead, "The Relation between Gender and Emotions in Different Cultures" and Ad Vingerhoets and Jan Scheirs, "Sex Differences in Crying: Empirical Findings and Possible Explanations," both in *Gender and Emotion: Social Psychological Perspectives*, ed. Agneta Fischer (Cambridge: Cambridge University Press, 2000), 71–94 and 143–65, respectively.

Yet hormones do not simply determine behavior.[73] Women appear to be more frequently exposed to situations that induce tears, whether traumas beyond their control (e.g., sexual abuse) or chosen activities. Women are more likely than men to enter helping professions like nursing and hospice care, choose to watch tear-jerker media (emotional films, news items about reunions), and form close bonds with other women—both men and women report feeling more comfortable weeping in the company of a woman than a man.[74] In many ancient texts, this gender difference appears reversed. Biblical narratives and Homeric epics frequently present men weeping, with women's tears featuring much less frequently. This reversal of the expected gender difference reflects the greater interest of the narratives in male characters and the comparative sidelining of female characters. In the prayer texts under study, the person praying may be male or female, although some texts specify a male petitioner. There is not enough evidence to reliably determine whether prayer texts are more likely to reflect weeping if the deity addressed is female.

Anger and Weeping

Tears have the potential to assuage anger, which is an important consideration for the present study because many prayers seek to mollify the anger of a deity. Two entire categories of Akkadian prayers seek to "calm the heart" of a deity (*dingiršadabbas* and *eršaḫungas*),[75] and some Hebrew prayers similarly assume divine anger as the major problem to be resolved.[76] These prayers reflect contexts of penitence and attempts to repair broken relationships. Some evidence from Western populations indicate that a woman's tears in a conflict situation signal that the conflict has gone too far and reduce aggression in the other person.[77] Several biblical examples illustrate the power of tears to soften anger. Most vividly, when Josiah hears "the book of the law," he rips his garments and inquires of God, "for great is the wrath of YHWH that is kindled against us (כי־גדלה חמת יהוה אשר־היא נצתה בנו) because our ancestors did not obey the words of this book" (2 Kgs 22:11–13). Speaking for God, the prophetess Huldah confirms that YHWH is angry: "They have provoked me to anger (חכעיסני) with all the work of their hands. Therefore my wrath will be kindled against this place and it will not be quenched"

---

[73] For a classic and accessible discussion of this point, see Robert Sapolsky, "The Trouble with Testosterone: Will Boys Just Be Boys?," in *The Trouble with Testosterone and Other Essays on the Biology of the Human Predicament* (New York: Simon & Schuster, 1998), 149–59.

[74] Vingerhoets, *Why Only Humans Weep*, 187–204.

[75] See pages 57–67

[76] See pages 133–134.

[77] Carrie J. Lane, "Evolution of Gender Differences in Adult Crying" (PhD diss., University of Texas at Arlington, 2006).

(ונצתה חמתי במקום הזה ולא תכבה) (2 Kgs 22:17). She also says that Josiah will be spared punishment for his penitent tears:

> Because your heart was penitent and you humbled yourself before YHWH [יען רך־לבבך ותכנע מפני יהוה] when you heard how I spoke against this place ... and because you have torn your clothes and wept before me [ותבכה לפני], I also have heard you. Therefore, I will gather you to your ancestors and you will be gathered to your grave in peace. Your eyes will not see the disaster that I will bring on this place. (2 Kgs 22:19–20)

Josiah's tears do not save Judah, but they do save him. The text states that his weeping has a specific target audience (YHWH), and that YHWH is affected by this appeal. The text implies that if Josiah had not expressed sorrow and penance, then he would have lived to see the disaster and suffer with his people. There is even a slight hint that had all the people wept, they might have been spared. YHWH specifically mentions weeping in conjunction with a penitent heart, humiliation, and tearing clothes. Josiah specifically weeps "before me," indicating that the tears have a specific intended audience. They are not private tears but a shared emotional expression to a trusted other whose anger might be alleviated. In this case, tears are partially successful. YHWH remains angry but not at the one who wept. Similarly, Nehemiah weeps in prayer before God when he hears about the destruction of the walls and gates of Jerusalem (Neh 1:4). He also mourns, fasts, and offers a prayer confessing Israel's sins that have "offended you deeply" (Neh 1:7). In other places, weeping may seek to assuage anger, or it may be understood as a grief response to disaster, although these two goals need not be understood as separate in these cases (Deut 1:45; Judg 2:4; 20:23–26).

In the biblical examples, weeping proves at least partially successful at mitigating divine wrath. In some Homeric episodes, weeping fails entirely to motivate mercy. Dolon surrenders to Odysseus and Ajax, provides them with the intelligence about the Trojans that they request, weeps (δακρύσας, *Il.* 10.377) as he begs for mercy, and promises ransom if his life is spared (*Il.* 10.372–464). Diomedes kills him anyway. Similarly, Agamemnon kills the two sons of Antimachus in spite of their tearful pleas for mercy and ransom (κλαίοντε, *Il.* 11.136). Likewise Odysseus's unfaithful serving women weep but suffer execution anyway (ὀλοφυρόμεναι, θαλερὸν κατὰ δάκρυ χέουσαι, *Od.* 22.447). In a different context, Phoenix sheds tears (δάκρυ ἀναπρήσας, *Il.* 9.433) as he begs Achilles to lay aside his anger (χόλος, *Il.* 9.436) and return to the fight against the Trojans, but Achilles remains unmoved by his tears: "do not trouble my spirit with weeping and lamentation" (μή μοι σύγχει θυμὸν ὀδῦρόμενος καὶ ἀχεύων, *Il.* 9.612).

As the Homeric examples indicate, tears do not reliably mitigate wrath. Indeed, there is some evidence that weeping can cause anger or enhance aggression.

The sound of infant cries can motivate caregiving or abuse.[78] An analysis of rape reports found that crying by the victim during the attack correlated with a significant increase in violence by the attacker and injuries suffered by the victim.[79] Crying can and has been used for personal gain and therefore suspected as a manipulation. Since ancient times, lawyers and their clients have used tears to sway juries, by swindlers to gain money, and by the guilty to gain forgiveness. In each case, the target of the tears may prefer to resist the petition. In therapeutic contexts, the crying of certain patients (especially those with narcissistic or borderline personality disorders) can induce strong negative feelings in therapists who feel manipulated.[80] Claiming that tears are fake can neutralize the power of tears by enlivening a sense of self-protective anger rather than self-giving empathy.

The impact of weeping on the anger of another person may be variable but perhaps not entirely unpredictable. Several of the Homeric examples involve transactions between enemies on the battlefield, where there is no prior bond of trust between the people. The weeping of Dolon and the sons of Antimachus reflects their helplessness and vulnerability rather than any particular trust in the men who will kill them. Odysseus's maids might hope for mercy, but they, too, are in a helpless situation in the power of those whom they betrayed. No relational bond of trust exists that might make these tears an effective means of assuaging anger, but it is the only hope these characters see in a desperate situation. By contrast, Phoenix and Achilles have a long-standing close relationship. Phoenix is like a father to Achilles, but Achilles is angry at Agamemnon, not Phoenix, and Phoenix's tearful pleas do not assuage this wrath.

In other cases, weeping may mollify anger. Jane Austen provides a striking literary example in *Mansfield Park*. Fanny Price is a poor relation of Sir Thomas Bertram's wife who has come to live in his home as part of his family's plan to help Fanny's impoverished mother by relieving her of a child and raising the child with improved prospects. Fanny has angered Sir Thomas by refusing an offer of marriage from Mr. Crawford because she perceived Crawford's base conduct with Sir Thomas's daughters. (He later runs off with one of them after she is married to someone else.) After she refuses Mr. Crawford's proposal, Sir Thomas confronts

---

[78] Bosworth, *Infant Weeping*, 4–21.

[79] Sarah E. Ullman and Raymond A. Knight, "The Efficacy of Women's Resistance in Rape Situations," *Psychology of Women Quarterly* 17 (1993): 23–38 and Janice M. Zoucha-Jensen and Ann Coyne, "The Effect of Resistance Strategies on Rape," *American Journal of Public Health* 83 (1993): 1633–34.

[80] Vingerhoets, *Why Only Humans Weep*, 131 and Judith Kay Nelson, "Crying in Psychotherapy: Its Meaning, Assessment, and Management Based on Attachment Theory," in *Emotion Regulation: Conceptual and Clinical Issues*, ed. Ad Vingerhoets, Ivan Nyklíček, and Johan Denollet (New York: Springer, 2008), 202–14.

Fanny in an effort to persuade her into the match. His long speech chastises what he perceives as her willfulness, selfishness, and stupidity. The episode is worth quoting at length from the last part of his reprimand:

> "And I should have been very much surprised had either of my daughters, on receiving a proposal of marriage at any time which might carry with it only half the eligibility of this, immediately and peremptorily, and without paying my opinion or my regard the compliment of any consultation, put a decided negative on it. I should have been much surprised and much hurt by such a proceeding. I should have thought it a gross violation of duty and respect. You are not to be judged by the same rule. You do not owe me the duty of a child. But, Fanny, if your heart can acquit you of ingratitude—"
>
> He ceased. Fanny was by this time crying so bitterly that, angry as he was, he would not press that article farther. Her heart was almost broke by such a picture of what she appeared to him; by such accusations, so heavy, so multiplied, so rising in dreadful gradation! Self-willed, obstinate, selfish, and ungrateful. He thought her all this. She had deceived his expectations; she had lost his good opinion. What was to become of her?
>
> "I am very sorry," said she inarticulately, through her tears, "I am very sorry indeed."
>
> "Sorry! yes, I hope you are sorry; and you will probably have reason to be long sorry for this day's transactions."
>
> "If it were possible for me to do otherwise" said she, with another strong effort; "but I am so perfectly convinced that I could never make him happy, and that I should be miserable myself."
>
> Another burst of tears; but in spite of that burst, and in spite of that great black word miserable, which served to introduce it, Sir Thomas began to think a little relenting, a little change of inclination, might have something to do with it; and to augur favourably from the personal entreaty of the young man himself. He knew her to be very timid, and exceedingly nervous; and thought it not improbable that her mind might be in such a state as a little time, a little pressing, a little patience, and a little impatience, a judicious mixture of all on the lover's side, might work their usual effect on. If the gentleman would but persevere, if he had but love enough to persevere, Sir Thomas began to have hopes; and these reflections having passed across his mind and cheered it, "Well," said he, in a tone of becoming gravity, but of less anger, "well, child, dry up your tears. There is no use in these tears; they can do no good. You must now come downstairs with me. Mr. Crawford has been kept waiting too long already. You must give him your own answer: we cannot expect him to be satisfied with less; and you only can explain to him the grounds of that misconception of your sentiments, which, unfortunately for himself, he certainly has imbibed. I am totally unequal to it."
>
> But Fanny shewed such reluctance, such misery, at the idea of going down to him, that Sir Thomas, after a little consideration, judged it better to indulge

> her. His hopes from both gentleman and lady suffered a small depression in consequence; but when he looked at his niece, and saw the state of feature and complexion which her crying had brought her into, he thought there might be as much lost as gained by an immediate interview. With a few words, therefore, of no particular meaning, he walked off by himself, leaving his poor niece to sit and cry over what had passed, with very wretched feelings.[81]

This narrative constitutes an episode of weeping with multiple points of interest for the present discussion. In the novel, Fanny is repeatedly wounded by unjust accusations of ingratitude, and the note of ingratitude here spurs her weeping to a new level of bitterness that makes Sir Thomas pause in his anger. As she sees how she appears in the eyes of her benefactor, she feels helpless and worries about what may become of her. Sir Thomas knows her to be timid and nervous (in this perception he is correct) and changes his tactic for getting Fanny to acquiesce to the marriage, thinking that allowing Crawford more time to woo her will be more effective than berating her. He adopts a less angry tone and orders her to come downstairs to decline Crawford in person (again). Again, her tears lead to a change in Sir Thomas, who relents because her tear-stained face might discourage Crawford's advances.

Fanny's tears are striking for their motivation and for what they do and do not accomplish. She feels that the situation before her exceeds her capacity to cope, as in several previous episodes when Fanny cries. In this case, however, she weeps in the presence of Sir Thomas, whose gravity makes him an intimidating figure even to his own children. Fanny, who trusts no one in the family except Sir Thomas's second son Edmond, normally seeks to conceal her tears.[82] The fact that she weeps in front of Sir Thomas reflects the depth of her despair and inability to retreat from the confrontation. The effect of her tears on Sir Thomas is twofold: first, he becomes less angry and changes both his tone and tactic; second, he releases her from confronting Crawford again. Yet her tears do not accomplish everything she could wish. Sir Thomas relents on the second point "in spite of" her tears rather than because of them. He still thinks she is wrong to refuse Crawford; her weeping has not changed his mind or his goals. He will maintain his position until Fanny is vindicated when Crawford seduces and absconds with Sir Thomas's married daughter, whose husband then sues for divorce.

Her tears have a third effect on Sir Thomas: they remind him of her timid and nervous temperament. Weeping in this transaction reflects the wider reality

[81] Jane Austen, *Mansfield Park*, ed. R. W. Chapman, 3rd ed. (Oxford: Oxford University Press, 1934), 319–20 (vol. 3, ch. 1, or in some editions ch. 32).

[82] Edmond catches her crying as a child (ch. 2) and becomes the only person to show her genuine kindness.

that tears can cause a person to be perceived as unstable or weak. Austen's detailed narration shows weeping mollifying anger but not achieving the weeper's ultimate goal. In other words, Fanny's tears check Sir Thomas's anger but do not persuade him of the correctness of her position. Interestingly, many readers and critics dislike Fanny as much as Sir Thomas does in this moment. On the bicentennial of this least-favored Austen novel, several writers composed essays in defense of the book and of Fanny Price. They rightly noted that people who dislike Fanny (whom critics often deride for her weeping) and therefore the novel misread Fanny's character and therefore misunderstand the book.[83] They treat Fanny exactly as the villains in the book do.

As research on weeping and anger continues to develop, it may adequately describe the nuances narrated by Austen. Tears may evoke anger or mollify it, and the reaction hinges on a wide variety of factors. The relationship between the person weeping and the audience matters, with a previous bond of trust more likely to lead to a reduction in anger. If the one who sees the tears knows the person to be deceptive or manipulative, this information, derived from past experience, most likely motivates anger rather than empathy.

The prayers designed to mollify the anger of a deity appear to involve the complexities and uncertainties of weeping in human interactions. The prayers reflect not only the anxieties about present suffering attributed to divine anger but also fear that the deity may persist in anger. The speaker has enough confidence in relationship to the deity to approach the deity in prayer and to weep, but the deity's response is not assumed to be automatically positive.

Ritual Tears

One striking aspect of weeping that partly explains why it may evoke empathy or anger concerns volition and weeping. Weeping is a behavior that people can sometimes control and sometimes not. The control that may be exerted can tend in either direction: suppressing the urge to cry or crying without needing to do so. Sometimes people are so moved that they cannot stop the flow of their tears. Joseph twice removes himself from the presence of his brothers as the only way he can conceal his tears from them (Gen 42:24; 43:30). The second example uses

---

[83] Tara Isabella Burton, "In Defense of Fanny Price," *Paris Review*, 7/10/2014, https://www.theparisreview.org/blog/2014/07/10/in-defense-of-fanny-price/ and Paula Byrne, "Mansfield Park Shows the Dark Side of Jane Austen," *Telegraph*, 7/26/14, http://www.telegraph.co.uk/culture/books/10987048/Mansfield-Park-shows-the-dark-side-of-Jane-Austen.html. I would add that *Mansfield Park* is a fascinating read from an attachment theoretical perspective, and the blame misdirected at Fanny should land where Austen strives to place it: the adults in her life, who are themselves both victims and perpetrators of unjust systems.

explicit language of effortful emotion regulation when Joseph is moved by the sight of his brother Benjamin when the brothers come to Egypt the second time: "Joseph quickly welled up with compassion [נכמרו רחמיו] for his brother and was on the verge of crying [ויבקש לבכות], so he went into another room and wept [ויבך] there. He washed his face and came out. He gained control of himself [ויתאפק] and said, 'Serve the food'" (Gen 43:29–30). The *hithpael* of the verb אפק appears the third time Joseph cannot control his weeping and reveals himself to his brothers (Gen 45:1–3). These examples explicitly show a man unable to control his tears, which is one common experience of weeping.

Tears are not always beyond our control. Weeping may sometimes elicit anger in those who witness it because they expect that the tears should be controlled and restrained. The weeper may be blamed or ridiculed for lack of emotional control and stability. Furthermore, people can weep when they are not overcome. For example, actors can weep on cue in staged situations that are entirely fictional. Since these so-called crocodile tears are possible, people may suspect that a person weeping is a person acting, and the person acting is seeking to manipulate the audience. When one senses that one is being manipulated with emotional blackmail, anger is an understandable response that inhibits the empathy that might otherwise succumb to the manipulation. The ways in which weeping may or may not be volitional complicate how a given episode of crying is perceived by others. Is this crying person in genuine need of help, or are these tears manufactured to manipulate me into giving help that is not really needed?

This problem informs discussion of ritual weeping. In his study of ritual weeping, Gary L. Ebersole rightly critiques the view that real tears are a manifestation of spontaneous emotion and the corollary position that ritual tears are somehow fake.[84] Vingerhoets makes a helpful distinction: there is no such thing as fake tears—all tears are real in the sense that they reflect emotion—but tears may be sincere or insincere. The weeping of the actor on stage is insincere, but that does not mean the actor feels nothing. Most actors describe drawing on their own emotional memories to perform the emotions they portray on stage.[85] Ritual weeping might be sincere or insincere depending on whether there is a difference between what the weeper feels (the emotional experience of the actor) and appears to feel (the emotional experience of the character portrayed by the actor). Homer provides an insightful example in the description of people weeping over the body of Patroclus in the *Iliad*. Several different constituencies weep for different reasons, but all perform their tears as ritual lament for Patroclus. Briseis sincerely weeps for Patroclus. She is a captive woman who saw her husband and three brothers

---

[84] Gary L. Ebersole, "The Function of Ritual Weeping Revisited: Affective Expression and Moral Discourse," *HR* 39 (2000): 211–46.
[85] Vingerhoets, *Why Only Humans Weep*, 146–47.

killed and her city sacked in a raid that Achilles led and in which he made her his captive, but she weeps (κλαίουσα, *Il.* 19.287) over Patroclus's body and claws at her flesh because, she says to his body, "I weep [κλαίω] for you incessantly in death, as you were always kind" (*Il.* 19.300). The text continues: "She wept [κλαίουσ'] as she spoke, and the women also lamented [στενάχοντο] / They seemed [πρόφασιν] to lament Patroclus, but each had their own sorrows (*Il.* 19.301–2)." The text makes a clear distinction between the one woman who mourns sincerely for Patroclus and the others who only appear to do so. The other women genuinely feel and express their sorrow, but their sorrows are centered on the loss of their own family members whom Patroclus may have killed, not on the death of Patroclus himself. They did not benefit, as Briseis did, from Patroclus's kindness. He promised to make her the lawfully wedded wife of Achilles, which is not something he could do for only one woman. Shortly after this passage, the poem describes another distinction within the mourning of the Greeks: Achilles "wept [κλαίουσ'] as he spoke, and the elders also lamented [στενάχοντο] / each one thinking on what he had left behind at home" (*Il.* 19.338–39). The lines verbally parallel the prior description of the captive women lamenting their own sorrows while seeming to mourn Patroclus. Here, the elders who remain with Achilles after others have left are Agamemnon, Menelaus, Odysseus, Nestor, Idomeneus, and Phoenix (*Il.* 19.310–11). Each has been long absent from home due to the prolonged war, and, while they seem to lament in solidarity with Achilles's grief for Patroclus, they mourn like the captive women for their own sorrows. This Homeric passage indicates an understanding that people may join in public mourning seemingly for a common cause, but in fact many mourners think on other sorrows. The text does not imply that anyone's tears are fake, as everyone has pain that motivates sincere sorrow.

This evidence suggest that Vingerhoets is right to regard all tears as real even if their sincerity may be suspect. The tears of actors on stage, like those of professional mourners, may not be motivated by the loss at hand, but they are not unmotivated. In addition to the strategies that actors use to summon tears at will, those engaged in ritual mourning may also respond to emotional contagion. The actor who weeps alone on stage has a more challenging task then the one who acts opposite to another person weeping. Similarly, emotions are contagious in a group. Tears flow more easily for someone surrounded by people in tears. Jeremiah 9:16–17 refers to this emotional contagion. God says through the prophet:

התבוננו וקראו	Inquire and call
למקוננות ותבואינה	for the wailing women to come,
ואל־החכמות שלחו	the most skilled ones summon.
ותבואנה ותמהרנה	Let them come quickly
ותשנה עלינו נהי	and raise for us a dirge

ותרדנה עינינו דמעה	so that our eyes may flow with tears,
ועפעפינו יזלו־מים	and our pupils flow with water.

The crying of the wailing women motivates and facilitates the weeping of others, in this case God.[86] The weeping of the women and God may then motivate weeping in the prophets and the people. The social expectation of weeping in specific ritual contexts also lowers inhibitions that may apply outside those contexts. It also establishes social solidarity in an emotional community. Even if the precise reasons for grief vary among individuals, they weep together and thereby participate in a common emotional bond that joins them together. In Jer 9:16–21, the people might join in the weeping of God and the wailing women and thereby demonstrate sorrow for their disobedience, which might even save them from God's punishment.[87] In the Homeric example, people weep for significantly diverse reasons, and the narrator indicates the diversity that underlies the community of tears. Everyone has their own sorrow and grief, but the mourning over Patroclus allows them to express their sorrows.

It does not appear that ritual weeping is dramatically different from other weeping. Some scholars have rightly critiqued a tendency to question the authenticity of emotions expressed in ritual. Pamela E. Klassen tells an illuminating story of attending the Hindu wedding of a friend in Canada. She was warned that the "time for crying" was approaching and then saw the female kin of the bride weeping over her as they lamented the loss of their relative. She describes how she initially perceived these tears as inauthentic but, on later reflection, realized that the "time for crying" allowed an opportunity for people to express the grief and loss involved in the maturing of a child. She notes that Western weddings that have no such ritual can still be tearful affairs. The ritual space for weeping in the Hindu wedding may be seen as reflecting authentic emotion, whereas Western reluctance to admit painful emotions on what is alleged to be a happy occasion may be seen as inauthenticity.[88] Her observation returns to the issue of tears of joy, and whether this expression is a disguise used to hide the painful emotions that underlie even otherwise happy occasions. Perhaps people weep at weddings as they realize what they are losing (a child and family member) but pretend that the tears are joyfully connected to what they allegedly gain (new family and kin).

---

86 Many commentators try to claim a change of speaker to make these tears Jeremiah's rather than God's, and the LXX reads "your [pl.] eyes" to identify the people as the ones who will weep. The first person plural language is consistent with divine speech elsewhere, generally understood as the royal "we"; see Bosworth, "Tears," 35–36.

87 Bosworth, "Tears," 43–45.

88 Pamela E. Klassen, "Ritual," in *The Oxford Handbook of Religion and Emotion*, ed. John Corrigan (Oxford: Oxford University Press, 2008), 151–52.

The ritual weeping she observed may thus be more honest than the more private and individual weeping often seen at weddings without this ritual opportunity. By contrast, Niu Zhixiong recalls a similar experience of ritual weeping at his grandfather's funeral. He saw his mother and aunts weeping bitterly, then suddenly smiling with tears still on their cheeks. He concluded that the weeping was "nothing but obligation" dictated by social obligation rather than interior grief.[89] Zhixiong, like many others, draws far too strong a distinction between these motivations for weeping. The conclusions of Vingerhoets and Klassen seem much more on target. Ritual weeping extends rather than contradicts the crying behaviors seen in private life. The work of Saul Olyan on ritual mourning in the Bible maintains a consistent focus on ritual actions without addressing the emotions that underly them, but also without denying emotion or characterizing ritual as merely dishonest acting. Due to his avoidance of emotion, he has difficulty explaining the similarities between ritual mourning for the dead and similar behaviors accompanying petitions.[90] With emotion in view, the similarity seems to be the result of the similar emotion in both instances. Grief is strikingly similar whether caused by bereavement or other loss. Indeed, weeping is an attachment strategy that evolved because it helped to reinforce relationships, gain help, and restore circumstances. The behavior continues in bereavement even though the dead cannot be brought back the way an absent caregiver might be summoned by cries. Mourning and petition share a common emotional motivation and goal.

METHOD

By the ancient adage *lex orandi, lex credendi*, "the rule of prayer is the rule of belief," internal working models of deities may be reconstructed from prayer texts. The person to whom an utterance is addressed shapes the utterance itself through the speaker's relationship with the listener and the internal working model that the speaker has evolved on the basis of that prior experience. For example, Judah's speech in Gen 44:18–34 is shaped by his belief that his audience is "the equal of Pharaoh" (Gen 45:18) and his past experience with the disguised Joseph. In prayers, the textual manifestation of the divine image is not limited to explicit descriptions or titles of the deity but appears in the whole content of the prayer.

---

89 Niu Zhixiong, *"The King Lifted Up His Voice and Wept": David's Mourning in the Second Book of Samuel* (Rome: Editrice Pontificia Università Gregoriana, 2013), 9.

90 Saul Olyan, *Biblical Mourning: Ritual and Social Dimensions* (Oxford: Oxford University Press, 2004), 95. Olyan suggests that the self-abasement of mourning was transferred to other contexts (e.g., petition) where self-abasement seemed a desirable means of gaining attention. I do not suggest that this explanation is wrong, only that recognizing the emotion common to both situations may also help explain the similarity of behaviors.

Careful attention to the language of a prayer can reveal the image of the deity that the prayer assumes, or its implied audience.

The present study combs through a corpus of Akkadian and Hebrew prayers for textual mentions of weeping. For those prayers that make some mention of weeping, the above evidence suggests several questions to ask about the text: Does the language of the prayer reflect emotional coregulation between the deity and the person praying? This language might include identification of the deity as a parent or more generally reflect an internal working model of the deity as a safe haven or secure base. Does the text indicate motives for the prayer consonant with attachment theory, specifically illness or injury, (threat of) separation from attachment figures, or environmental events stimulating fear or distress? Does the prayer text reflect a dialogic self or multiple voices? Does the text offer evidence that the type of weeping is angry or sad? Is the weeping localized in the nighttime? Is the deity understood to be angry? What social consequences does the petitioner hope or expect as a result of weeping? These effects might be on the deity or other audiences. The weeping may have consequences for the weeper's reputation, but these are less likely to be discernible in a prayer text compared to a narrative text.

The above questions arise from the psychological research outlined above. This research was developed from study of modern populations of living people rather than the study of literary texts. The theories developed from evidence derived from modern people can, with caution, be applied to ancient peoples and their artifacts. Some distinctions are important to appreciate what the present study can and cannot determine. The present work assumes that the prayer texts reflect the culturally embedded minds of those who developed the prayers. But text, person, and performance are not simply the same. A prayer text that mentions weeping might be performed without any tears, and a prayer with no mention of tears might be performed with weeping. Different people may perform the same prayer differently, and one person may perform it differently at different times. Ancient prayer texts do not give direct access to any specific person, but they do reflect the culture from which they emerged and the human minds that created them. The present study is necessarily limited to the texts and therefore their implied speaker(s). The texts reflect weeping behaviors and internal working models of deities that their human authors derived from some combination of their biological and cultural inheritances.

The present study is corpus based. The study encompasses a corpus of over one thousand Akkadian prayers and the 148 Hebrew psalms, even though only those that mention weeping receive detailed analysis. Within each corpus, prayers are grouped together according to genre. Since the study is corpus based, it is possible to make observations about the frequency of the weeping motif in the corpora of prayer and analyze this data by genera. Note that the corpus is not limited to prayers that include weeping, because this would offer no opportunity to compare prayers with and without weeping. Similarly, some interesting texts that involve weeping are not included because the corpus was selected on the basis of prior scholarship unrelated to the theme of weeping. If all texts involving weeping were included, it would skew the comparisons within the corpus by skewing the corpus toward weeping and making it appear more important than it actually is. Consequently, the corpora follow delimitations identified by others.

2
Weeping in Akkadian Prayers

Some Akkadian prayers clearly reflect their emotion regulatory function. The speaker may be worried about an uncertain future, troubled by the anger of a deity, or seeking divine assistance with earthly problems. In these cases, the prayer seeks to alleviate anxiety. Sometimes, the speaker enlivens a sense of joy and gratitude in prayers often classified by modern scholars as "hymns." The present discussion of a corpus of Akkadian prayers will divide the analysis according to prayer genres, discuss each genre separately, and then conclude with observations about the corpus as a whole. The genre distinctions employed are those identified in *Reading Akkadian Prayers and Hymns*, edited by Alan Lenzi in an earlier volume of this series.[1] This volume includes a small anthology of Akkadian prayers with bibliography for further study. As noted in the discussion of each genre below, these bibliographic references serve as descriptions of prayer corpora for analysis.

By developing the corpus of prayers from Lenzi's volume, I have avoided two alternatives. First, I had at one time planned to use Benjamin Foster's anthology as the corpus of prayer but discovered that it does not represent the various genres evenly, which would limit the study and potentially provide mistaken results. I needed a much larger and more representative sample of prayers. Second, I determined not to develop my own idiosyncratic set of prayers for analysis because my own collection might skew heavily toward prayers and genres involving weeping, which would also corrupt the results. The purpose of this corpus-based study is to compare prayers with weeping to those without, but the comparison would provide misleading results if it included almost all the extant prayers involving weeping and a small fraction of those with no weeping. Lenzi's volume therefore

[1] Alan Lenzi, *Reading Akkadian Prayers and Hymns: An Introduction*, ANEM 3 (Atlanta, GA: Society of Biblical Literature, 2011). It is also available online in a PDF version that reflects a corrected edition made in 2015. The slight differences in content and pagination do not impact any of the citations in the following discussion, so the references work for either version. For the PDF, see "Ancient Near East Monographs," SBL Press, https://www.sbl-site.org/publications/books_anemonographs.aspx.

provided the basis for developing a corpus of Akkadian prayers that represents the extant texts rather than my own interests. Following this prior volume also meant including *eršaḫunga* prayers, which are really Sumerian prayers with Akkadian interlinear translations. Lenzi includes them because they resemble other Akkadian prayers.[2] This inclusion proves fortuitous because *eršaḫunga*s emerge as the most interesting prayer genre in relation to weeping and enable us to recognize the relationship between human weeping and divine anger.

In his introduction, Lenzi discusses the problems of categorizing Akkadian prayers and hymns. The distinction between prayers and hymns in the title correlates with the difference between down-regulating negative emotions (prayer, or petitions) and up-regulating positive ones (hymns, or prayers of praise). Lenzi rightly notes that the boundary between these types "is not hard and fast" because hymns may include petitions, and petitions may include praise, but the overall theme of a text can often be identified as petition or praise.[3] He understands "prayer" as a general term within which one may distinguish such genres as hymns and petitions. Lenzi starts with a broad definition of prayer as "a kind of religious or ritual speech that communicates one's concerns/petitions to a benevolent supra-human being via words."[4] He then provides a helpful discussion of the value and limitations of this definition for working with ancient Mesopotamian texts.[5] Akkadian incantations can often be distinguished from prayers because they address entities other than gods (e.g., demons, animals) and represent divine speech rather than human speech. For example, incantations to soothe crying babies routinely address the baby and, like incantations generally, conclude by claiming that the words of the ritual were given by one or more deities.[6] The present work focuses on weeping in prayer, not incantations. Lenzi elaborates on the problem of modern versus ancient classifications. The ancient scribes often added rubrics or superscriptions to the texts that might be used to differentiate various genres. The scribes, however, did not reliably label texts and sometimes used these labels in ways that confound modern attempts to make sense of them. For example, the term *šiptu* often marks the start of an incantation and indeed is typically translated as "incantation." The term also appears at the start of many *šuilla*s, which are

---

[2] Lenzi, *Reading Akkadian Prayers and Hymns*, 12 n. 29.

[3] Lenzi, *Reading Akkadian Prayers and Hymns*, 9.

[4] Lenzi, *Reading Akkadian Prayers and Hymns*, 9.

[5] Lenzi, *Reading Akkadian Prayers and Hymns*, 8–23.

[6] See David A. Bosworth, *Infant Weeping in Akkadian, Hebrew, and Greek Literature*, CHSB 8 (Winona Lake, IN: Eisenbrauns, 2016), 33–53. One of the incantations speaks about the baby rather than to the baby but has no clear addressee (49–50). For full edition of all the related incantations, see Walter Farber, *Schlaf, Kindchen, Schlaf!: Mesopotamische Baby-Beschwörungen und -Rituale*, MC 2 (Winona Lake, IN: Eisenbrauns, 1989).

prayers rather than incantations.[7] The genres demarcated in *Reading Akkadian Prayers and Hymns* reflect a mix of ancient and modern classifications that constitute helpful analytic categories. For each genre, I have looked at a representative corpus of examples to see whether weeping is mentioned. Of these genres, weeping appears in some *šuillas*, *dingiršadabbas*, *eršaḫungas*, and hymns. I will briefly note other genres and speculate on why weeping is absent from these prayers, but the focus will be on those prayers (and genres) in which the speaker refers to weeping.

ŠUILLAS

The *šuilla* has been the most studied of all types of Akkadian prayer since the early days of Assyriology. For all the discussion of this large category of texts, no edited anthology of *šuillas* has been published for decades.[8] Lenzi is developing a digital edition of all the *šuillas* online.[9] Christopher Frechette notes that about 110 *šuillas* are known in almost 300 exemplars, for which he provides a bibliographic list.[10] He also lists comparative features for 46 *šuillas* that are complete or nearly complete, and these *šuillas* form the corpus for the present study.[11] "*Šuilla*" is the most common rubric found with Akkadian prayers. The Sumerian term means "lifted hand(s)" and refers to a gesture commonly seen in Mesopotamian iconography that indicates greeting. Some scholars suggest that the *šuilla* rubric refers to prayer generally and thereby minimize the gestural reference of the term. By this logic, they include a wide variety of incantation prayers as *šuillas* even though they do not bear the rubric or resemble the literary form of texts with the rubric.[12] Others, however, follow Werner Mayer's suggestion that the modern category of *šuilla* should respect its native use by including only those texts that actually have or likely (could have) had the *šuilla* rubric.[13] He thinks that *šuillas* are distinct from other incantation prayers in that they have a general or unspecific purpose as

---

7 The term might be better rendered as "ritual wording" because it applies to both prayers and incantations, but the translation "incantation" has become firmly established in Assyriology; see Lenzi, *Reading Akkadian Prayers and Hymns*, 16 n. 39.

8 Leonard W. King, *Babylonian Magic and Sorcery, Being "The Prayers of the Lifting of the Hand"* (London: Luzac, 1896) and Erich Ebeling, *Die akkadische Gebetsserie "Handerhebung"* (Berlin: Akademie-Verlag, 1953).

9 Alan Lenzi, "Corpus of Akkadian Shuila Prayers Online," http://www1.pacific.edu/~alenzi/shuilas/catalog.html.

10 Christopher Frechette, *Mesopotamian Ritual-Prayers (Šuillas): A Case Study Investigating Idiom, Rubric, Form, and Function*, AOAT 379 (Münster: Ugarit-Verlag, 2012), 249–75 (appendix 3).

11 Frechette, *Mesopotamian Ritual-Prayers*, 277–82 (appendix 4).

12 Frechette, *Mesopotamian Ritual-Prayers*, 111–13.

13 Werner Mayer, *Untersuchungen zur Formensprache der babylonische "Gebetsbeschwörigen"*, StPohl 5 (Rome: Biblical Institute Press, 1976), 7–8.

opposed to other prayers that respond to specific concerns. However, some *šuilla*s manifest specific concerns (e.g., hostile magic). Rather than assuming an original generic *šuilla* prayer which might be modified with specific language for particular applications, Frechette "takes the fact [that] so many exemplars of Akkadian *šuilla* prayers include interpolations reflecting specific concerns as indicative of their function rather than contrary to it."[14] Through comparison of their literary features with other prayers, he proposes that the distinctiveness of *šuilla*s lies in their emphasis on greeting the high deity addressed. *Šuilla*s ask the high god or goddess to reconcile the petitioner to his or her own personal god. Many misfortunes were understood as rooted in a disrupted relationship with the personal deity responsible for protecting the person, and high gods could be called upon to help repair that relationship and restore the life of the petitioner.

*Šuilla*s may be classified into three categories based on the language of the text and the type of ritual expert who performed it. Texts in the Emesal dialect of Sumerian were associated with the *kalû*, or cult singer. *Šuilla*s performed by the *āšipu*, or exorcist or incantation priest, sometimes have a further rubric, *mis pî,* that specifies their use within the ritual to animate images of deities, and these prayers are in Sumerian. The final category of *šuilla*s consists of Akkadian texts also associated with the *āšipu* but focused on individual concerns. Frechette identifies the forty-six best-preserved *šuilla*s that constitute the corpus of Akkadian *šuilla*s analyzed for the present study. Each attests the *šuilla* rubric.

NUSKU 13

Nusku 13 is a short *šuilla* with a brief mention of weeping as something that will not or should not happen. The *šuilla* appears in the context of a *namburbi* ritual for lighting strike. (Nusku, also known as Gibil, was associated with light and fire.)[15] The prayer mentions the deity's wrath (*ezzu*, line 92), enumerates several offerings being made to Nusku, and then says:

104 *ḫa-diš mu-ḫur lìb-ba-ka li-nu-uḫ ka-bat-ta-ka lip-šaḫ*	Take it with joy. May your heart be at rest, may your liver be calm.
105 *ana* É *te-ru-bu bi-ki-tú la ta-šak-kan*	In the house that you entered, do not establish weeping.
106 *it-ta-ka da-me-eq-tú lib-ba-ši-ma*	May a good sign from you appear.

[14] Frechette, *Mesopotamian Ritual-Prayers*, 8.

[15] The text is edited with commentary in Stefan Maul, *Zukunftsbewältigung: Eine Untersuchung altorientalischen Denkens abhand der babylonisch-assyrischen Löseritual (Namburbi)* (Mainz: von Zabern, 1994), 127–51. The *šuilla* encompasses lines 92–109 of Maul's edition.

The prayer connects the offerings to the calming of the deity's emotions (heart and liver). "The house that you entered" most likely refers to the house that was struck by lightning.[16] The petition that the god not establish weeping in that house refers to the evil that the lightning strike portends. The *namburbi* seeks to ward off this vague potential evil, which could cause people in the household to weep. The *šuilla*, like the *namburbi* ritual within which it appears, is designed to prevent this outcome. It is motivated by anxiety about the future, and the weeping describes a potential painful future rather than a present reality of suffering. The prayer is motivated by a fear-inspiring environmental event (a lightning strike). The petitioner seems to turn to Nusku as the agent of the event rather than as an attachment figure but engages in coregulation, seeking to reduce anxiety by assuaging the god's evident anger. The prayer refers to possible future weeping, which is not further described as sad or angry. No present weeping plays a role in calming the deity, although the prospect of future tears may deter the Nusku's anger. The text does not involve multiple voices.

ISHTAR 2

Ishtar 2 is a well-preserved *šuilla* that includes the motif of weeping twice. Scholars have outlined its structure in diverse ways due in part to transitional sections that are difficult to divide precisely. The prayer begins and ends with hymnic praises of Ishtar (lines 1–41, 103–5). The central body of the prayer consists of two petitionary sections (42–55, 79–102) that frame a lament (56–78).[17] The first forty-one lines of the prayer praise Ishtar for her power and mercy. Weeping first appears in the petition following the introduction (lines 42–55) and again in the complaint immediately following the petition (56–78). The first reference appears in several lines beginning with the word *aḫulap*, which literally means "(it is) enough" and is the word that a deity speaks to indicate that the petitioner has suffered enough, and that the deity now has mercy. In the introduction, four lines begin with "your *aḫulap*" (27–30), referring to Ishtar's mercy. These lines are introduced by recollecting to Ishtar that "you look upon the wronged and afflicted, you guide them

---

16 Maul, *Zukunftsbewältigung*, 150.

17 This outline follows Anna Elise Zernecke, "A Shuilla: Ishtar 2: 'The Great Ishatar Prayer'," in Lenzi, *Reading Akkadian Prayers and Hymns*, 257–58 and Zernecke, *Gott und Mensch in Klagegebeten aus Israel und Mesopotamien: Die Handerhebungsgebete Ištar 10 und Ištar 2 und die Klagepsalment Ps 38 un Ps 22 im Vergleich*, AOAT 387 (Münster: Ugarit-Verlag, 2011), 150–51. Annette Zgoll, *Die Kunst des Betens: Form und Funktion; Theologie und Psychagogik in babylonisch-assyrischen Handerhebungsgebeten zu Ištar*, AOAT 308 (Münster: Ugarit-Verlag, 2003), 69 identifies the same sections but with slightly different division: 1–41, 42–55, 56–92, 93–100, 101–105. Mayer, *Untersuchungen*, 28–29 n. 60 has yet another variation: 1–40, 41–55, 56–78, 79–92, 93–100, 101–105.

aright every day" (26). Later, in the lament (56–78), the speaker identifies himself as one of those afflicted, so this praise of Ishtar's mercy prepares for the request for mercy. Similarly, the four lines in the introduction beginning "your *aḫulap*" anticipate the six lines in the petition beginning "*aḫulap*" (45–50). In this context, the initial "my *aḫulap*" (*ahulapīya*, 45) refers to the word of mercy that the goddess would pronounce for the benefit of the speaker:

42 *ana-ku al-si-ki an-ḫu šu-nu-ḫu šum-ru-ṣu* IR$_3$-*ki*	I appeal to you, your tired, wearied, suffering servant.
43 A.MUR-*in-ni-ma* ^{d}GAŠAN.MU *le-qe-e un-ni-ni-ia*	Look at me my lady and accept my supplication.
44 *ki-niš nap-li-sin-ni-ma ši-mé-e tés-li-ti*	Look faithfully upon me and listen to my prayer.
45 *a-ḫu-lap-ia qí-bi-ma ka-bat-ta-ki lip-pa-áš-ra*	My *aḫulap* speak for me, and let your liver be reconciled to me,
46 *a-ḫu-lap* SU-*ia na-as-si šá ma-lu-ú e-šá-a-ti u dal-ḫa-a-ti*	*aḫulap* for my suffering body, which is full of confusion and trouble,
47 *a-ḫu-lap lìb-bi-ia šum-ru-ṣu šá ma-lu-ú dím-ti u ta-né-ḫi*	*aḫulap* for my suffering heart, which is full of tears and sighs,
48 *a-ḫu-lap te-re-ti-ia na-as-sa-a-ti e-šá-a-ti u dal-ha-a-ti*	*aḫulap* for my wretched, confused, and troubled omens,
49 *a-ḫu-lap* É-*ia šu-ud-lu-pu šá ú-na-as-sa-su* ÉR.MEŠ	*aḫulap* for my sleepless house, which laments with weeping,
50 *a-ḫu-lap kab-ta-ti-ia šá uš-ta-bar-ru-ú dím-ti u ta-né-ḫi*	*aḫulap* for my liver, which perseveres (in) tears and sighs.
51 ^{d}*Ir-ni-ni-i-tu*$_4$ *la-ab-bu na-ad-ru lìb-ba-ki li-nu-ḫa*	Irninitu, aggressive lion, let your heart be at rest with respect to me!
52 *ri-i-mu šab-ba-su-ú ka-bat-ta-ki lip-pa-áš-ra*	Furious wild bull, let your liver be reconciled to me.
53 SIG$_5$.MEŠ IGI.II-*ki lib-ša-a e-li-ia*	May your kind eyes be on me.
54 *ine bu-ni-ki nam-ru-ti ki-niš nap-li-sin-ni ia-a-ši*	With your bright face look kindly upon me!
55 *uk-ki-ši ú-pi-šá* ḪUL.MEŠ *šá* SU.MU ZÁLAG-*ki nam-ru lu-mur*	Drive away the evil magic concerning my body! Let me see your bright light![18]

Both sections referring to *aḫulap* (27–30, 45–50) begin with language about Ishtar "looking" (*naplusu*, N of *palāsu*): the first connects her look with divine help, while the second seeks help from her. These lines refer several times to the heart (*libbu*, 47, 51) and liver (*kabattu*, 45, 50, 52) of both Ishtar and the petitioner. Both organs represent seats of emotion. The first *aḫulap* line asks that Ishtar's liver be reconciled (*napšuru*) to the speaker (dative suffix -*a*), a request repeated in line 52. The last

[18] Translations of Ishtar 2 modified from Zernecke, "Shuilla," 282–84.

aḫulap line refers to the liver of the petitioner, which continues in tears and sighs (*dimti u tānēḫi*, 50). The verb *šutabrû* (Št of *bitrû* with subjunctive -*u*, "to continue, persevere") emphasizes the constancy of the speaker's tears and sighing. The dysregulated liver/feelings of the goddess correspond to a dysregulation in the speaker. The speaker seeks to calm Ishtar in order to alleviate his own turbulence, so that the two relationship partners return to a happy homeostasis. The same idea and even some of the same words appear in reference to the hearts of the goddess and the petitioner. The petitioner complains that his heart is full (*malû*) of tears and sighing in line 47 (like his liver in line 50). The petitioner's tears are thus twice connected to sighing and to the two primary organs associated with emotion: heart and liver. His heart is furthermore modified as *šumruṣu*, "suffering, afflicted, in pain."

The emotional agony described through the heart and liver contributes to a portrait of the speaker in desperation, and both of these lines reflect physiological effects of emotional pain, often accompanied by an unpleasant sensation in the viscera. Each of the five *aḫulap* lines refers to an aspect of the petitioner's suffering. In addition to the tears and sighing of the heart and liver, the "wretched body" (*zumrīya nassi*) is full of confusion and trouble. This line may refer to another physical manifestation of emotional pain—or, more broadly, mental anguish—because *zumru* may refer to the body or the whole person. The remaining two *aḫulap* lines refer to troubled omens, which are understood to cause anxiety, and the household plunged into weeping. In this third reference to weeping in the passage, the petitioner describes his house as sleepless or troubled (*šudlupu*) because it laments with weeping. House (*bītu*) here refers to the household that is plunged into weeping due to the suffering of the petitioner, which may encompass the whole family. Like his own heart and liver, the members of his household are dysregulated due to his suffering.

The passage involves several requests for Ishtar to look at the speaker.[19] These requests indicate that the weeping has a specific audience, and Ishtar's regard should repair the petitioner's problems (e.g., line 41: "The one who is not well becomes well seeing your face"). Lines 51–52 provide the first indication in the prayer that Ishtar's wrath is the main problem. The speaker compares Ishtar to a wild and aggressive lion (*labbu nadru*) and an angry wild bull (*rīmu šabbasû*) and asks that her heart be calm and her liver/feelings reconciled to him (dative suffixes). The prayer seeks to soothe Ishtar's anger, an emotional state of turmoil connected to her heart and liver, the same organs associated with the speaker's "tears and

19 Anna Elise Zernecke, "How to Approach a Deity: The Growth of a Prayer Addressed to Ištar," in *Mediating Between Heaven and Earth: Communication with the Divine in the Ancient Near East*, ed. C. L. Crouch, Jonathan Stökl, and Anna Elise Zernecke, LHBOTS 566 (New York: Bloomsbury, 2014), 130 identifies Ishtar's "looking" as central to the prayer.

sighs." If Ishtar's organs return to a happy homeostasis, then the petitioner, too, will experience a corresponding relief.

The speaker returns to the motif of weeping in the lament (56–78) that outlines the suffering that has motivated the prayer. The complaint begins with the question "How long?" and speaks of enemies looking malevolently at the petitioner, a contrast with Ishtar's benevolent gaze. Enemies and persecutors weaken the speaker, who finds new ways to express his sense of dysregulation:

62 *a-sab-bu-u'ki-ma a-gi-i šá up-pa-qu* IM *lem-na*	I toss like a wave that an evil wind amasses.
63 *i-šá-a'it-ta-nap-raš lìb-bi ki-ma iṣ-ṣur šá-ma-mi*	My heart flies and flutters like a bird of the sky.
64 *a-dam-mu-um ki-ma su-um-ma-tu*$_4$ *mu-ši u ur-ra*	I moan like a dove night and day.
65 *na-an-gu-la-ku-ma a-bak-ki ṣar-piš*	I burn and weep bitterly.
66 *ina u*$_8$*-ú-a a-a šum-ru-ṣa-at ka-bat-ti*	In "woe" and "alas" my liver is suffering.
67 *mi-na-a e-pu-uš* DINGIR.MU *u* ^{d}*iš-tár*-MU *a-na-ku*	What indeed have I done to my god and goddess?
68 *ki-i la pa-liḫ* DINGIR.MU *u* ^{d}*iš*$_8$*-tár*-MU *ana-ku ep-še-ek*	I am treated as if I did not fear my god and goddess.

The image of an evil wind churning up a wave captures the speaker's experience of enemies making his life miserable. The turbulent water mirrors the petitioner's dysregulated state, and the wind constitutes its external cause. The language resembles Marduk's use of wind to generate waves that annoy Tiamat in *Enūma Eliš* (I.107–8). The beating heart imagined as a fluttering bird identifies a specific physiological symptom: the petitioner's heart beats rapidly and perhaps irregularly. Here again the heart and liver stand for the interior physiological disruption and the disturbing feelings of negative sensations within the viscera, feelings familiar to any reader although hard to describe in specific language. The poetry of lament favors images and terms for internal organs to speak of these sensations that vividly evoke fear and anxiety.

The bird image for the heart prepares for the dove in the next line, a frequent image of constant sorrow. Weeping and doves often appear together in poetry (Ishtar 2.64–65; *Eršaḫunga* 1.15b 4′–5′; *Dingiršadabba* 11.1 12–14) since the soft cooing of the dove sounds mournful to human ears. Ancient Near Eastern authors and audiences likely imagined the Eurasian collared dove (*streptopelia decaocto*) or Oriental turtle dove (*streptopelia orientalis*) when reflecting on the sounds these references to doves evoked for them. Both species, like the many other species of dove in Asia and beyond, have similar soft cooing calls. The Eurasian collared dove has recently expanded its range through most of the North American continent after colonizing Florida from the Bahamas, where they had been released.[20] The cooing is the male dove seeking a mate, and the song may begin before dawn and continue into the night. This incessant and prolonged mournful tune provides a suitable analogy for a human's perpetual and audible weeping. Ancient Mesopotamians would have been familiar with doves, which have been kept in dovecotes since the dawn of civilization.[21] Most dove species happily build nests in human structures. The emphasis on the constancy of lament ("day and night") underscores the continuous suffering of the petitioner also present in the sleeplessness of line 49 and the perseverance in line 50.

The meaning of *nangulāku* is uncertain, but the term appears in reference to stars as shining and emotions in contexts of complaint. It may refer to symptoms of an illness, and it may mean "glowing" or "burning."[22] If the astral context implies a steadiness or consistency in a star's shining, the occurrence here may emphasize the constancy of the speaker's bitter weeping. The previous line clarifies the continuous nature of the crying in its audible aspects (voiced sobbing like a dove's moaning), and the present line may specify the continuous flow of tears from the eyes like light from the stars. The petitioner returns again to his liver/feelings as "suffering."

The petitioner turns to Ishtar as a safe haven in a time of distress. The prayer is motivated by a range of miseries involving social conflict and bodily symptoms deriving from the anger of personal deities (lines 67–68, 77, and 85–86). The vague language of the prayer fits a wide variety of circumstances involving illness and external events. The petitioner understands the negative experience as the consequence of Ishtar's anger, and the prayer reflects coregulation in which the petitioner expects weeping to mollify divine wrath. Both weeping passages suggest the quiet crying characteristic of despair rather than the loud angry crying of protest. In the first passage, the only reference to noise is "sighing." In the second, the petitioner moans like a dove, and the sound of a dove strikes human ears as low and mournful rather than loud and shrieking. This sad type of crying seems suitable to the prayer because the petitioner claims to have been suffering a long time, and sad crying follows the initial protest crying. Both passages associate weeping with nighttime, which is consistent with the finding of contemporary research that people cry more in the evening hours than during the day. In the first passage, the petitioner complains that his house has become a sleepless house of weeping. The

---

[20] To hear a recording of the Eurasian Collared-Dove's call, visit Cornell Lab of Ornithology, "All About Birds," https://www.allaboutbirds.org/guide/Eurasian_Collared-Dove/sounds.

[21] Andrew D. Blechman, *Pigeons: The Fascinating Saga of the World's Most Revered and Reviled Bird* (St. Lucia: University of Queensland Press, 2006), 11–12.

[22] Zernecke, "Shuilla," 272 and Zgoll, *Die Kunst*, 65.

second refers to moaning like a dove night and day, which emphasizes the constancy of weeping.

In addition to the well-preserved Neo-Babylonian version discussed above, Ishtar 2 also exists in a thirteenth-century BCE version from Boğazköy. This older version (Text F) consisted of 50 lines compared to the 105 of the later version (Text A). Anna Elise Zernecke observes that the basic structure of the two versions is the same, but that the additional lines in Text A are so unevenly distributed that the two prayers are quite different.[23] The opening praise is nearly the same in both (37 lines became 41 lines), but the later sections of petitions and lament are much expanded in the later version such that the praise constitutes 74 percent of Text F but only 39 percent of Text A. The first appearance of weeping described above (lines 45–50) appears only in Text A. Many of these lines (45–50) parallel lines from the praise section (27–30), which are common to Texts A and F. The text of the first petition has thus been expanded on the basis of a passage from the invocation.[24] The reference to weeping in the lament section of Text A has a slender basis in the older Text F. Text F has one broken line (2‴) that reads "night and day" and likely corresponds to line 64 of the later version: "I moan like a dove night and day." The older version then asks Ishtar to look (*naplisānī-ma*, line 3‴), parallel to the later version's line 92. The later version takes up the moaning dove image and immediately adds language of weeping, followed by many more lines of lament, which are in turn followed by the second petition section. The evidence of the growth of Ishtar 2 shows that the motif of weeping was both introduced in a place where it did not previously exist and expanded in a place that only alluded to weeping. The growth of the weeping motif reflects the disproportionate growth of the prayer in the lament sections.

Ishtar 10

Ishtar 10 is a well-preserved *šuilla* that includes weeping. The prayer identifies the wrath (*zenû*, 11) of the personal god as the cause of petitioner's lamentation (*nissatu*, 12). The speaker asks Ishtar, also presumed to be angry, to calm herself and show mercy. Between the address (1–6) and thanksgiving (39–42), the lament divides into two parts (8–18, 19–38), marked by the name "Ishtar" that starts line 19 and coincides with a shift of focus from the speaker's misery to the petition proper.

---

[23] Zernecke, "How to Approach a Deity," 127–28.

[24] Zernecke, "How to Approach a Deity," 132. The term *aḫulap* is missing from the older version in the invocation, but the lines are otherwise parallel, and the later version established a clearer parallel between the passages with the addition of *aḫulap*, referring to Ishtar's *aḫulap* in lines 27–30 and the petitioner's *aḫulap* in lines 45–50.

Explicit reference to weeping concludes the first of these two sections. I reproduce lines 12–18 along with the beginning of the petition (19–27):[25]

11 *iš-tu* ^{d}*iš*$_8$*-tár u ì-lí be-li iz-nu-ú* UGU-*ia*[26]	Because (my) goddess and my god, my lord, are angry at me,
12 *e-ru-ub ni-is-sa-tu*$_4$ *ú-ṣi ku-ú-ru*	I enter, wailing! I leave, depression!
13 *su-ú-qu a-ba-aʾ-ma e-ger-ru-ú-a dam-qu*	I go along the street, my audible omen was not good:
14 *et-bé ùʾ-i ú-šab ta-né-ḫu*	I stood up—woe! I sat down—sigh!
15 *la ṭa-ba-am-ma ak-lum mur-ru-ra-ku ki mar-ti*	Food is not good to me, I am as bitter as gall.
16 *ina ma-a-a-al mu-ši gi-lit-ti u par-da-a-ti*	On my bed for the night, my terror and my terrifying (dreams).
17 *a-dam-mu-um ki-ma* TU^{mušen} *mu-ši u ur-ra*	I moan like a dove night and day,
18 *ina di-im-ti bu-ul-lu-la-ku ina* SAḪAR.ḪI.A *bal-la-ku*	with tears I am covered, with dust I am smeared.
19 ^{d}15 *a-šar ta-ru-ru za-mar tap-pa-áš-šá-ra*	Ishtar, where you curse, you will loosen for me quickly.
20 *ag-gu lìb-ba-ki i-re-em-mu di-i-ni*	Angry one, may your heart have mercy on my case
21 ^{d}15.MUL.MEŠ *a-šar ta-ru-ru za-mar tap-pa-áš-šá-ra*	Ishtar of the Stars, where you curse, you will loosen for me quickly.
22 *ag-gu lìb-ba-ki i-re-em-mu di-i-ni*	Angry one, may your heart have mercy on my case.
23 *ta-a-a-ra-ti u re-mé-na-a-tú*	You are one who turns, you are one who has mercy,
24 *en-né-né-e-ti u mu-pa-áš-ra-a-ta*	you are gracious, you are forgiving.
25 *nu-ḫi-im-ma* ^{d}GAŠAN *ka-bat-ta-ki lip-pa-aš-ra*	Be calm, mistress, may your liver be reconciled,
26 *lìb-ba-ki ki-ma* AD *u* AMA *ana aš-ri-šu li-tu-ru*	may your heart be like a real father and mother,
27 ŠÀ *ilu-ti-ki da-ri-ti lip-pa-áš-ra*	may the heart of your eternal divinity be reconciled.

The speaker describes a constant state of misery. He is persistently depressed and does not eat or sleep. Instead, he moans like a dove night and day, suggesting both the sorrowful quality of his weeping and its constancy. The next line moves from the audible quality of the dove's moaning and the human sobbing it implies to the visible signs of human weeping. The speaker describes himself as covered in tears mixed with dust. The verb *balālu* generally means "to mix, smear" in the G-stem

25 For the edited text, see Zgoll, *Die Kunst*, 107–26.

26 For variants, see Zgoll, *Die Kunst*, 110.

or "to coat, smear" in the D-stem. The verb appears twice in this line, first in reference to tears (D stative), then in reference to dust (G stative). The contrast between the D and G stems is not strong. The D-stem is typical with tears, as in *bu-ul-lul ina di-ma-ti i-bak-ki* [*ṣar-piš*], "stained with tears, he weeps bitterly."[27] The G stative often means "to be spotted, variegated."[28] The speaker presents to Ishtar a dust- and tear-stained face. Dust and tears go together because ancient Near Eastern mourners often covered themselves with dust as a visible sign of their distress (cf. *Gilgameš* XII 100, 149). An incantation against demons describes the grief and panic at a lunar eclipse, and someone "smears himself" (*ub-tal-li-lu*) with dust.[29] In Ishtar 10, dust serves as a visible sign of distress, reinforcing the impact of the tears. Also, as tears disambiguate facial expressions, the dust may disambiguate the tears. The presence of dust must mean that the tears are connected to grief due to serious distress. These are not the happy tears of a reunion or watering due to mere eye irritation. The elaborated motif of weeping encompassing moaning like a dove and being covered in a mix of tears and dust provides the climax and conclusion of the speaker's description of his misery and prepares for the transition to petition.

The tears and sobbing of the petitioner should move Ishtar to help. The beginning of the petition makes repeated references to Ishtar's heart and liver, asking that the goddess abandon her wrath, forgive, and show mercy like a real father or mother. The twice-repeated line "Angry one, let your heart have mercy in my case" (lines 20 and 22) identifies Ishtar's anger as a problem that needs to be turned to mercy. The petition includes praise of Ishtar as one who turns, has mercy, and is gracious and forgiving by way of adding persuasive force to the request that she show mercy. The speaker asks her to be calm and her liver and heart to "forgive" (*lip-pa-aš-ra*, 27, 25).

The language explicitly seeks to use the speaker's pitiful misery to assuage the anger of Ishtar, which, in turn, would improve the petitioner's well-being. Language of calm (*nâḫu*) and loosening (*pašāru*) suggest return to a homeostasis in which the goddess harbors no anger toward the speaker. As a result, the speaker imagines that Ishtar's favor will transform his social life from the bad reputation he suffers

---

27 *CAD* 2:44a and W. G. Lambert, "Three Literary Prayers of the Babylonians," *AfO* 19 (1959): 52. *CAD* notes similar uses of the D-stem with other bodily substances like semen and dung. It sometimes appears with dust in magical recipes; see Bosworth, *Infant Weeping*, 40 (3.53–54) and 47–48 (29.17–18).

28 *CAD* 2:41b.

29 Markham Geller, *Evil Demons: Canonical* Utukkū Lemnūtu *Incantations*, SAACT 5 (Helsinki: Neo-Assyrian Text Corpus Project, 2007), 16.70. The text is broken where the subject of the verb would be expected. The word for "dust" survives in Sumerian but not in the Akkadian interlinear translation.

(line 13) to a favorable reception among his superiors, inferiors, family, and friends (32–38). The prayer appears motivated by a legal case and reputation rather than such evils as illness. The text reflects how social relationships can dramatically impact emotional life, and the speaker seeks vindication as a means of restoring happiness. In the structure of the petition, tears are instrumental for gaining the sympathy and support of Ishtar and mollifying the divine anger at the root of the problem. Like Ishtar 2, the text locates weeping at night and uses dove imagery that implies quiet sad weeping rather than protest weeping.

Summary

Of the forty-six *šuilla*s that constitute the present corpus, three of them (7 percent) mention weeping. Ten of the forty-six specifically describe the deity addressed as angry, and all three that mention weeping fall within this subset of prayer mentioning divine wrath. Thus, 30 percent of the prayers involving divine anger include weeping, and 100 percent of the prayers including weeping involve divine anger. Both Ishtar *šuilla*s describe sad and constant weeping with the image of a dove, while the Nusku prayer does not describe the potential future weeping in any detail. The Nusku prayer also appears different in that Nusku does not seem to be a safe haven in times of distress but appears to be the target of the prayer because the lightning strike indicates his anger. In the Ishtar prayers, by contrast, the petitioner seems to turn to the goddess as a source of comfort, or safe haven. The motives for all the prayers correspond with reasons people turn to attachment figures, namely fearsome external events and circumstances and illness. In the Ishtar prayers, weeping is part of the effort to down-regulate the goddess's wrath and alleviate the petitioner's. In the Nusku prayer, the weeping is a future possibility that may dissuade Nusku from anger.

*ERŠAḪUNGA*S

The Sumerian rubric *eršaḫunga* means "lament to rest the heart (of a deity)." These laments are designed to appease the anger of a deity and therefore the problems that the deity's anger has created for the petitioner. *Eršaḫunga*s are directed toward the high gods, belong to the corpus of the cult singer (*kalû*) rather than the exorcist (*āšipu*), and do not begin with EN, 'incantation'. These three features distinguish them from *dingiršadabba*s, which are discussed later in this chapter. The prayers ask the deity to say "enough" (*aḫulap*), meaning that the petitioner's suffering has been sufficient. Although they are Sumerian prayers, *eršaḫunga*s are included here because they have Akkadian interlinear translations (the focus here) and resemble Akkadian *dingiršadabba*s. Lenzi's volume includes *eršaḫunga*s for these reasons.[30]

[30] Lenzi, *Reading Akkadian Prayers and Hymns*, 12 n. 29.

Also, *dingiršadabbas* should be studied in conjunction with *eršaḫungas* given their nearly common purpose to calm angry deities.

Eršaḫungas have a relatively consistent structure: opening, lament, petition, intercession, conclusion. The opening seeks the deity's attention by various means, and this section shows significant variability. The lament then describes the petitioner's symptoms and sometimes includes confessions of sin with claims of ignorance. It may conclude or transition to the petition with descriptions of ritual acts such as kneeling or kissing. The petition asks for healing and restoration of the relationship. It may include the request that the deity speak the word "enough" (*aḫulap*), which would signify the deity's determination that the penitent had suffered enough, that the deity's heart is appeased, and that the petitioner's suffering is at an end. The section often ends with promises to praise the deity and then transitions to the intercession. In the intercession, the speaker calls on various deities to intervene in order to appease the heart of the deity addressed in the prayer as a whole. An *eršaḫunga* concludes with a petition asking that the deity be merciful like a real mother or father. As in Akkadian prayers more generally, two voices are often evident in *eršaḫungas*: those of the petitioner and an intercessor who speaks about the petitioner. The suffering of the petitioner may be described in the first person or third person.

Stefan Maul has edited over 140 *eršaḫungas*, of which 27 are sufficiently complete for analysis and inclusion in the present corpus.[31] In these prayers, the petitioner and the deity are seeking to coregulate their emotions. The human speaker seeks to assuage the deity's anger at his own misbehavior and the concrete consequences of this anger for him (e.g., illness). By calming the anger of the deity, the petitioner relieves his own anxiety and sense of shame and restores the

---

[31] Stefan Maul, *"Herzberuhigungsklagen": Die sumerisch-akkadischen Eršahunga-Gebete* (Wiesbaden: Harrassowitz, 1988). Three additional *eršaḫungas* have been published since Maul's edition; see Maul, "Zwei neue 'Herzberuhigungsklagen,'" *RA* 85 (1991): 67–74 and M. J. Geller and Christian Bauer, "CT 58, No. 70: A Middle Babylonian Eršahunga," *BSOAS* 55 (1992): 528–32. These texts are fragmentary and not included in the present corpus. The one published by Geller and Bauer includes weeping, but the immediate context of the word for "his tears" is lost. Maul does not provide a unique number for each prayer he edits. His abbreviation Ešḫ refers to manuscripts (often joins of multiple fragments), and some *eršaḫungas* exist in multiple manuscripts. He organizes the prayers by deity addressed; e.g., all the prayers to gods are in part 1, and prayers to goddesses are in part 2, each part further divided by deity (e.g., prayers to Enlil are in part 1.2). I have used letters to identify the six prayers to Enlil as 1.2a–1.2f. I identify each prayer by this numeration (e.g., 1.2b) and use no letters if there is only one prayer to that deity. The prayers that constitute the corpus of *eršaḫungas* for the present study are: 1.1, 1.2a, 1.2b, 1.2c, 1.2e, 1.2f*, 1.3a, 1.3b., 1.3c, 1.5a, 1.6a, 1.6b, 1.6c, 1.6d*, 1.7a, 1.7d*, 1.10a, 1.11, 1.14*, 1.15b*, 1.15c, 1.16*, 2.1a, 2.1b., 2.1d*, 2.3*, 2.6. Asterisks indicate that weeping is mentioned.

relationship with the deity. The intercessor voice expresses common cause with the petitioner and asks the deity to witness the sufferer's plight, forgive his sins, and stop being angry.

The first "heart appeasing lament" in Maul's edition (1.1) illustrates the emotion regulatory function of the *eršaḫunga*.[32] Although it does not include weeping, it makes frequent references to the heart of the deity (here, Anu) in this intercessor's voice:

11 [...*in ma-ru-uš-ti-šu áš*]*-ra-ak iš-te-né-ʾì*	[...in his distress, he] always seeks your places.
12 [...*ina ma-ru-u*]*š-ti-šu áš-*[*r*]*a-ak iš-te-né-ʾì*	[...in his dist]ress he is constantly seeking your place.
13 *áš-ru-ka* [*iš-te*]*-ne-ʾì a-ḫa-ti iš-te-ne-ʾì*	He is [constantly seek]ing your place, (your) precincts he is constantly seeking.
14 ŠÀ-*ka ez-zu a-na áš-ri-šu li-tu-ra*	May your angry heart return to its place,
15 ŠÀ-*ka ag-gu a-na áš-ri-šu li-tu-ra*	may your wrathful heart return to your place,
16 [*nu*]*-u*[*g-gat*] *lìb-bi e-dir-ti-ka a-na áš-ri-šu* [*li-tu-ra*]	[may the anger] of your darkened heart [return] to its place,
17 [*ina ik-ri*]*-bi u t*[*a*]*ṣ-li-ti ana áš-ri-šu* [*li-tu-ra*]	[by pray]er and offering [may it return] to its place.

The text continues to ask forgiveness and concludes with the standard concluding formula:

38 [*libbaka*] *ki-ma lìb-bi um-me a-lit-te a-na áš-ri-šu li*!(TU)*-tu-ra*	[May your heart] return to its place like the heart of a real mother,
39 [*kima um-me a*]*-lit-ti a-bi a-lid-*[*d*]*i* [*a-na áš-ri-šu*] *li-tu-ra*	let it return [to its place] [like a real] mother, like a real father.

This conclusion expresses the hope that the deity will be like the petitioner's mother or father and show mercy, end the punishment, and forget anger. The conclusion assumes a model of parents as merciful and invites the deity to be similarly merciful. It thereby presents an understanding of the human-divine relationship as analogous to the child-parent relationship, in which the child experiences sensitive and responsive caregiving. Children often have the experience of irritating or angering their parents, sometimes for reasons that they do not understand. Ideally, parents overcome their anger and help their children regulate out of their sense of fear and shame. The parental aspect of the deity does not appear suddenly at the end but informs the prayer throughout. The persistent

---

32 Maul, "*Herzberuhigungsklagen*," 73–81.

seeking after the deity reflects the desire of the distressed person to be close to an attachment figure.

Eršaḫunga 1.2f

The text of *Er* 1.2f to Enlil (IVR² 21*n2, Ešḫ n9) presents Enlil as restless and sleepless (10).[33] Enlil directly attacks the petitioner and causes his crying:

12 *be-lum šá* ŠÀ-*šu e-liš la i-nu-ḫa-*[*am*]	Lord whose heart above is not at rest,
13 *be-lum šá* ŠÀ-*šu šap-liš la i-pa-ši-ḫa-am*	lord whose heart below is not calm,
14 *e-liš u sap-liš la i-nu-ḫa-am*	above and below it is not at rest,
15 *šá ú-qad-di-da-an-ni ú-qa-at-ti-an-ni*[34]	who makes me bow down and finishes me.
16 *ina qa-ti-ia a-šu-uš-ti iš-ku-na*[35]	In my hand he places affliction,
17 *ina zum-ri-ia pí-rit-tam iš-ku-na*	in my body he places terror,
18 *bur-mi-i-ni-iá di-im-tam ú-ma-al-li*	the iris of my eye he fills with tears,
19 *lìb-bi šá qí-da-a-tim ta-ni-ḫa ú-ma-al-li*	my bent down heart he fills with sighing.

The prayer next transitions to asking Enlil's "pure heart" to be calm and at rest (20–21). The prayer mentions several things Enlil does to the petitioner along with inducing tears. Sighing often appears with weeping,[36] but this text also mentions affliction (*ašuštu*), terror (*pirittu*), and being bent over. Enlil makes the speaker "bow down" (D of *qadādu*), and the speaker complains that his heart is "bent down" (*qaddu*). Enlil's heart is not at rest, which explains why he afflicts the petitioner, who is bent over either in pain and exhaustion or in petition and supplication. The speaker talks about Enlil in the third person while complaining that the god "finishes me" (*uqattiʾanni*), meaning that he brings him close to death. The variant reading communicates a similar idea: Enlil causes him to be ill. In line 16, the term *ašušti* means "affliction, grief." The variant *arurti* means "famine, hunger." By either reading, Enlil causes the petitioner to suffer by placing grief or hunger in his hand (*qātu*, a play on words if one follows the *uqattiʾanni* variant in the previous line). Similarly, Enlil places terror in the speaker's body. Enlil's agency in the person's suffering appears also in his weeping and sighing. The deity fills the speaker's irises with tears and his heart with weeping. The role of Enlil in the person's weeping indicates the importance of Enlil's anger at the petitioner. The speaker approaches Enlil not hoping for relief from suffering unrelated to Enlil but

---

[33] Maul, *"Herzberuhigungsklagen,"* 112–21.

[34] Variant: *mar-ṣi-*[*iš*...], 'ill'.

[35] Variant: *a-ru-ur-*[*ti iš-ku-na*], 'famine, hunger'.

[36] For references to tears and sighing, see Ishtar 2 (see pages 43–48 in this volume); *Er* 1.14 and 1.15b (see pages 58–62 in this volume); Ešḫ 94 fragment in Maul, *"Herzberuhigungsklagen,"* 338; and Ešḫ 45 in Maul, *"Herzberuhigungsklagen,"* 233.

as the very cause of his suffering. His tears, then, are not a manifestation of the physical pain of his illness and misery but derive from Enlil's anger and the threat it poses to the person. The language of the lament clearly identifies Enlil as the source of the problem, so the prayer seeks to assuage the wrath of the god.

The reference to weeping appears near the end of the lament section, and the lament and petition make many references to the heart of Enlil (fourteen times in seventeen lines), along with one reference to the heart of the petitioner (line 19). These two hearts, divine and human, depend on one another for emotion regulation throughout the prayer. Enlil's heart is in turmoil because of the petitioner's sin, and the petitioner's heart is bent over because of Enlil's punishment. The petitioner seeks Enlil's forgiveness so that both hearts may be at rest. The petition section ends in line 26 with an image of emotion regulation: *ana pu-uš-šu-uḫ šà-šu* ^{d}MIN *ina te-ès-li-ti li-*[*iz-zi-zu-šu*], "For calming Enlil's heart he remains at prayer." The implication appears to be that the petitioner will not cease praying until he finds relief, understood as the calming of Enlil's heart, which in turn will calm the petitioner's heart. Illness motivates the prayer. The prayer maintains the voice of the petitioner throughout; no intercessory voice appears to speak of the petitioner in the third person. The prayer mentions tears but no sound, suggesting sad rather than angry weeping. The text does not mention nighttime weeping. The prayer anticipates that the sad weeping will appease the anger of Enlil.

ERŠAḪUNGA 1.6D

Eršaḫunga 1.6d to Adad (Ešḫ n22–n23) likewise attributes the petitioner's suffering to divine agency.[37] The surviving text also explicitly identifies Adad as angry:

6′ [*anaku a*]*-rad-ka ma-ḫar-ka kám-sa-ku*	[I,] your servant, kneel before you,
7′ [*be-lum p*]*u-luḫ-ta-ka gal-lit-tum ma-a-ta u ni-ši tar-me*	[lord,] with your fearsome terror you cast down land and people.
8′ [*be-lum tugal*]*-lit-an-ni ma-ru-uš-tum te-pu-šá-an-ni*	[Lord, you ter]rify me, you do evil to me.
9′ [. . .*ki-m*]*a a-le-e ik-tùm-an-ni*	[. . .like] an *alû*-demon you overpower me.
10′ *ina i-*[*ni*]*-ia* [*di*]*-im-tum ul ip-par-ku*	In my eyes, tears do not cease,
11′ *ina bi-*[*kit(i) (u)*] *ta-ni-ḫi u*$_4$*-me-šam uš-ta-bar-ri*	in my wee[ping and] sighing daily I persevere.
12′ *a-di ma-*[*ti(m)*] *be-lì ina er-nit-ti-ka ma-tim tas-pu-un*	How l[ong] my lord? In your victory you flattened the land.
13′ *be-lum* ŠA*-ka gal-tum šá-mu-ú li-ni-iḫ-ḫu*	Lord, may heaven rest your disturbed heart.

37 Maul, "*Herzberuhigungsklagen*," 161–65.

14′ dIŠKUR *ka-bat-t*[*a-ka*] *a-dir-tim er-ṣe-tim li-šap-*[*šiḫ*]	O Adad, may the earth cause [your] darkened mo[od] to re[lent]

The broken petition section expresses hope that heaven and earth can calm Adad's heart along with the petitioner's ritual offerings. Adad is the direct cause of the petitioner's suffering, and the prayer is explicit in its address to Adad: "you do evil to me" (line 8). The speaker also likens the deity to a demon. The text reflects an understanding of deities as protecting people from evil, but evils could happen because an angry deity withdraws that protection and allows the person to be attacked by a demon.[38] The language of this prayer presents the god as directly responsible for evil, so the anger of Adad is experienced as active animosity rather than passive neglect. The language about weeping specifically emphasizes the constancy of this aggressive divine behavior: tears do not cease and weeping is a daily behavior. The continuous aspect of the weeping appears also in the next line, where the speaker says he daily "perseveres" in weeping and sighing. The Št lexical form of *barû* or *bitrû* appears in other *eršaḫunga*s (e.g., 1.7d, 1.14) and Ishtar 2 (line 50).[39] In *eršaḫunga*s, the verb almost always describes persevering in tears and sighing. The one surviving example of the verb with other vocabulary still involves emotional misery ("lamentation and burning of heart") and, like all other examples, occurs with the term "daily," which intensifies the meaning of the verb (1.6b).[40] Adad, who roars (line 2) and casts down land and people (line 7), terrifies and overpowers the petitioner, whose response is a steady stream of tears that should disarm the deity's anger and move his heart to compassion. The deity is aggressive and demonic. All the surviving lines express the voice of the petitioner, and no intercessor's voice appears. The weeping appears more sad than angry, and no voiced sound appears, only tears and sighing. Although the text includes no specific reference to nighttime, it does describe the weeping as constant. The weeper says that he kneels in a submissive posture. The vague language and broken text makes the motivation for the prayer obscure; it might involve illness or social conflict.

---

38 Jean Bottéro, *Religion in Ancient Mesopotamia*, trans. Teresa Lavender Fagan (Chicago, IL: University of Chicago Press, 2001), 185–88.

39 *CAD* 2:280 (*bitrû*) and *AHw* 123 (*berû/barû*). See also Erš 93 and Erš 94 (both fragments) in Maul, *"Herzberuhigungsklagen,"* 337–38.

40 Maul, *"Herzberuhigungsklagen,"* 150.

Eršaḫunga 1.7d

Eršaḫunga 1.7d to Marduk (Ešḫ n26) preserves only the end of the lament section and start of the petition.[41] The lament concludes with an elaborate description of the petitioner's weeping. The interlinear Akkadian translation reads:

8′ *[a-bak]-ki it-ḫu-sa ul a-kal-[la]*	[I am weep]ing, sobbing, I cannot stop.
10′ *[ina ma-a]-a-al mu-ši ta-ni-ḫa iš-šak-[na]*	[on my] bed at night, sighing is appointed.
12′ *[ina nu-b]é-e u qu-bé-e u₄-me-šam uš-ta-bar-ri*	[In wailing] and lament daily I persevere.
14′ *be-lum ríg-mì ṣar-piš ad-di-ka ši-man-ni*	O lord, I cry out to you bitterly! Hear me!

Here weeping is associated with sobbing, sighing, wailing, lament, and crying out. The meaning of the term *naḫāsu* remains uncertain, but it describes sobbing, wailing, lamenting, or other activity closely associated with crying.[42] It appears with crying also in 1.14 line 21 and 1.15 line 2′. Sobbing seems most likely in these contexts because it is a behavior that the speaker cannot control, like the tears indicated by *bakû*. In the prayer itself, the speaker must have sufficient control to articulate the words, but he describes inarticulate and uncontrolled weeping behaviors that frequently overwhelm him. The crying out may refer either to the voiced sobs of uncontrollable weeping or to the prayer itself. The other terms refer to behaviors that appear more volitional (sighing, wailing, lamenting), but the first reference stresses the petitioner's loss of emotional control. The durative has here a modal sense of "I cannot stop."[43] People can sometimes control their tears, but weeping is sometimes uncontrollable, and the heavy sobs that the language seems to describe suggest involuntary loss of emotional control due to extreme distress and helplessness. The following two lines locate this crying in bed at night and during the day. The constancy of weeping illustrates the petitioner's deep distress and dysregulation. The prayer should reach Marduk and mollify the god with its representation of the petitioner's extreme need. The petitioner continues to beg "Hear me!" (line 14′) and "Hear my prayer!" (16′), and he says, "I your petitioner kneel before you" (18′), adopting a position of submission and petition. The prayer indicates that the speaker cries frequently or continuously, both night and day. Only the voice of the petitioner appears, although the broken text may have had an intercessory voice in parts that have not survived. The speaker raises a loud noise, which may suggest more angry weeping than other quieter examples of

---

41 Maul, *"Herzberuhigungsklagen,"* 174–79.

42 *CAD* 11.1:132b. Maul, *"Herzberuhigungsklagen,"* 176 renders it "das Schluchzen?," meaning "the sob(bing)."

43 Thus Maul, *"Herzberuhigungsklagen,"* 176: "kann ich nicht zurückhalten!"

weeping. Night is mentioned as a time for weeping. The specific motive for the prayer is unclear, but it involves some adversity attributed to divine wrath.

ERŠAḪUNGA 1.14

Eršaḫunga 1.14 to Mandanu is relatively well preserved in two manuscripts (SBH n30, Ešḫ n37).[44] As in several other *eršaḫunga*s, the wrath of the deity is assumed rather than explicitly stated. The lament section focuses on the petitioner's tears in language familiar from 1.7d:

18 [*i-bak*]-*ki it-ḫu-sa ul i-kal-la*	[He is weeping,] he cannot stop sobbing.
19 [*i*]-*ni-ia bi-ki-tum ú-ma-al-la*	My [e]yes he fills with weeping.
20 [*ina*] *ma-a-a-al mu-ši ta-ni-ḫi ú-mel-la-an-ni*	[On] (my) bed at night, he fills me with sighing,
21 [*ina*] *bi-ki-tum*! *u ta-ni-ḫi uš-ḫ*[*a*]*r-x-x-an-ni*	[with] weeping and sighing he makes me collapse.

The first line is almost exactly the same as 1.7d line 8 except that these verbs are in the third rather than first person. A narrator's voice describes the petitioner as weeping (durative) and unable to stop sobbing. The third person perspective is clear from the last verb, which is readable, and can therefore restored in the first verb, which is partly broken. This third-person language marks the start of the lament section (the previous litany is in the first person), which switches back to the first person after this line. As in 1.7d, the line describes the petitioner as unable to gain control of himself, which may explain why a different voice describes the petitioner's plight. Although the text mentions weeping, sighing, and sobbing, it does not mention tears. The speaker complains that Mandanu fills his eye with weeping rather than tears. The following line locates the bed at night as a place and time for sighing and likewise identifies the deity as the cause of the speaker's suffering. Mandanu has filled the person with sighing and his eyes with tears, meaning that the deity is the active agent causing the crying. The next line continues to point to Mandanu as the cause of the weeping and sighing, because the deity makes the speaker collapse under the weight of this emotional pain. Maul restores the broken verb as *uš-ḫar-*[*ši-ša-*]*an-ni*, from *naḫaršušu* (Š, "to cause to collapse"). It could also be read as *uš-ḫar-*[*mi-ma-*]*an-ni* with the same meaning (*naḫarmumu* also means "to collapse") or even *uš-ḫar-*[*mi-ṭa-*]*an-ni* (Š of *naḫarmuṭu*, "to melt or dissolve something").[45] The meaning "dissolve" may make sense in connection with water and weeping, although tears are conspicuously absent in this passage. The sense of "collapse" captures the exhaustion that depression and

---

44 Maul, *"Herzberuhigungsklagen,"* 206–13.
45 Maul, *"Herzberuhigungsklagen,"* 212.

weeping creates. As in 1.7d, the weeping behaviors are located in bed at night; "daily" weeping is not explicitly mentioned, although it is implied in the durative verbs and the petitioner's inability to stop sobbing.

The intercessory voice speaks next and presents the petitioner as someone who "carried the appointed offering" (line 22), "offered you prayer" (23), and "gazes at you faithfully" (23). The intercessory voice asks that prayers and offerings speak to Mandanu, and that the heart of the deity be at rest like heart of a mother or father. The standard plea for the heart to be at rest, along with the deity's active attack on the petitioner, indicates the anger of the deity. The continuous and uncontrolled weeping of the petitioner, sometimes described by another voice, seeks to mitigate this wrath and restore the petitioner's circumstances. The text seems to describe a sad type of crying and identifies night as a time for weeping. The motivation for the prayer is vague as the prayer does not describe a specific problem created by divine anger.

ERŠAḪUNGA 1.15B

Although *eršaḫungas* are typically prayers to high gods, *Er* 1.15b is to a personal god (Ešḫ n38–n42).[46] Personal gods were associated with families. Individuals typically inherited a personal god who functioned as a divine parent and protector who kept demons and misfortunes away and facilitate success. People enjoyed close relationships with personal gods, but these deities could abandon their protégés as a result of unethical behavior or cultic neglect, leaving them exposed to misfortune.[47] Maul edits *eršaḫungas* to personal gods, but only two are complete enough to include in the present corpus, and 15b is the only one that includes weeping.[48] The text exists in several copies, one of which Maul thinks was not an *eršaḫunga* because it begins with ÉN, "incantation." An earlier prayer was evidently repurposed as an *eršaḫunga*.[49] The lament section describes the petitioner's misery in the voice of a third person. The petitioner speaks in the first person after the lament in the petition. The fragmentary opening refers to angry gods whose hearts are evil, preparing the purpose of the prayer, which is recapitulated at the end: "let your angry heart be calm" (line 21′). The lament develops the motif of weeping in some detail:

---

[46] Maul, *"Herzberuhigungsklagen,"* 216–28. For translations, see Benjamin R. Foster, *Before the Muses: An Anthology of Akkadian Literature*, 3rd ed. (Bethesda, MD: CDL, 2005), 723–24.

[47] For a thorough discussion of the personal god, see Karel van der Toorn, *Family Religion in Babylonia, Syria and Israel: Continuity and Change in the Forms of Religious Life*, SHCANE 7 (Leiden: Brill, 1996), 66–147.

[48] For all six, see Maul, *"Herzberuhigungsklagen,"* 213–36.

[49] For discussion of the various copies, see Maul, *"Herzberuhigungsklagen,"* 215–16 and 223-24.

1′ [*ina ṣu-ru-up*] *lìb-bi ina bi-ki-ti le-mu-te*	[In burning] of heart, in evil weeping,
2′ *ina ta-ni-ḫi wa-ši-ib*	in sighing, he is dwelling.
3′ *ina qu-ub-bé-e mar-ṣu-ti ṣú-ru-up lìb-bi*	In the lamentation of illness and burning of heart,
4′ *ina bi-ki-ti* ḪUL-*ti ina ta-ni-ḫi lem-ni*	in evil weeping, in evil sighing,
5′ *ki-ma su-um-ma-ti i-dam-mu-um šu-up-šu-uq mu-ši u ur-ri*[50]	like a dove he moans, he is in difficulty night and day.
6′ *a-na* DINGIR-*šú re-mi-ni-i ki-ma lit-ti i-na-ga-ag*[51]	To his own god like a cow be bellows.
7′ *ta-ni-ḫa mar-ṣa-am iš-ta-na-ka-an*[52]	Bitter sighing he constantly suffers.
8′ *a-na* DINGIR-*šu ina un-ni-ni ap-pa-šu i-la-ab-bi-in*	To his god with supplication he prostrates himself.
9′ *i-bak-ki nu-ḫu-sà ul i-kal-la*	He is weeping; he cannot hold back his sobbing.

One manuscript has an alternative reading for lines 3′–4′:

3′ [*ina qubbe marṣuti ṣú*]*-ru-up lìb-bi ina bi-ki-ti l*[*e-mutti?*]	[In the lamentation of illness,] burning of heart, in evil weeping,
4′ *ina ṣú-ru-up lìb-bi ina bi-ki-ti u ta-ni-ḫi* [*a-ši-ib*]	in burning of heart, in weeping and sighing [he dwells.]

The relatively elaborate description of the petitioner's weeping compared to other *eršaḫungas* may be due to its address to a personal god. A personal god might be regarded as a more trusted intimate before whom emotional displays are less inhibited. But there may be no particular significance to this difference from other *eršaḫungas*, or the difference may derive from an earlier form of the prayer before it was repurposed as an *eršaḫunga*. The text associates weeping with sighing and characterizes both as evil. The text repeatedly notes the constancy of the petitioner's weeping: he "dwells" in sighing, experiences difficulty "night and day," constantly suffers sighing (Gtn of *šakānu*, "to make present"), and does not sleep. The actions of the petitioner are described with particles or durative forms, which emphasize the ongoing quality of the actions of dwelling in sighing, moaning like a dove, bellowing to his god like a cow, prostrating himself, weeping, sighing, and being unable to stop. The voice of the narrator repeatedly emphasizes the continuous nature of the petitioner's suffering.

50 One MS reads accusatives.

51 Or: *i-šá-as-si*, "he calls, shouts."

52 Or: *mar-ṣi-iš uš-tan-na-aḫ*, "he constantly suffers bitterly."

Unlike other examples, this prayer also speaks to the petitioner's "burning heart" and "lamentation of illness." The prayer does not mention hearts often, but the hearts of both the petitioner and the personal god appear. At the opening of the prayer, the angry god has an evil heart (line 1); at the end of the prayer, the petitioner asks that it may be like the heart of a real mother or father in the standard conclusion (22′–23′). The petitioner is twice described as having a "burning heart" (*ṣurup libbi*), the second time in connection with "lamentation of illness," suggesting that the petitioner suffers from sickness attributed to divine wrath. The deity's evil (*lemnu*) heart corresponds to the "evil weeping" and "evil sighing" of the petitioner. The god's heart is later described as "angry," and this anger explains why the petitioner suffers and now prays for the deity's heart to be calm ("let your angry heart be calm," 21′). The "angry" heart of the god creates the "burning" heart of the petitioner, which motivates weeping and sighing. They need to coregulate to the peaceful connection they formerly enjoyed.

The prayer compares the petitioner to two animals: a moaning dove and a bellowing cow. These animal images emphasize the sad vocalizations of the petitioner. The moan of a dove is a mating call that strikes human ears as sad and appears with weeping (Ishtar 2.64–65; *Er* 1.15b 4′–5′; *DŠ* 11.1 12–14; *Ludlul Bēl Nēmeqi* I 107–10). The bellow of a cow, by contrast, really does express bovine grief. A happy cow is a quiet cow. Two common reasons a cow bellows both involve relationship: to locate a missing calf or to locate the herd.[53] In both cases, the cow is cut off from vitally important relationships and resorts to vocalization as a means of restoring proximity and relationship. The cow's bellow is part of the attachment system of the cow, just as weeping is part of the attachment system of humans. In other contexts, a text may focus on the vocalization of the baby animal rather than the mother as here. In the Dialogue between a Man and His God, the narrator describes the petitioner weeping before his personal god like a donkey foal separated from its mother.[54] This animal vocalization is therefore an apt analogy for the petitioner's cries.

The prayer includes the voices of both the petitioner and the intercessor. The intercessor presents the image of the weeping petitioner, but the petitioner speaks in the immediately following lines, evidently through to the ending, with its plea

---

[53] J. M. Watts and J. M. Stookey, "Vocal Behavior in Cattle: The Animal's Commentary on Its Biological Processes and Welfare," *Applied Animal Behavior Science* 67 (2000): 15–33. More recently, researchers have parsed cattle calls more precisely through electronic analysis of voice prints and demonstrated that cattle calls are individually distinctive; see Mónica Padilla de la Torre et al., "Acoustic Analysis of Cattle (Bous Taurus) Mother-Offspring Contact Calls from a Source-Filter Theory Perspective," *Applied Animal Behavior Science* 163 (2015): 58–58.

[54] See pages 67–69.

that the personal god may be like a mother or father. The text represents the sad type of weeping, clarified with appropriate animal imagery. Night is mentioned with day as a time for weeping. The language clearly reflects coregulation of emotion between the petitioner and deity with some help from an intercessory voice. The petitioner's illness motivates the prayer, and the petitioner's weeping contributes to the persuasive power to assuage divine anger.

ERŠAḪUNGA 1.16

Eršaḫunga 1.16 is a prayer to any god (IVR^2 10), or "a god I do not know" (line 4).[55] The text appears to reflect a situation in which the petitioner is experiencing illness and other symptoms that might be explained as the punishment of an angry deity. In a world populated by a wide range of deities, the petitioner has not been able to identify what he or she has done wrong that may have offended the deity. The opening line (in Akkadian, line 2) asks: *šá be-lim nu-ug-gat* ŠÀ-*šu ana aš-ri-šu li-tu-ra*, "May the angry heart of the lord return to its place." The prayer frequently places the unknown god in parallel with an unknown goddess, because the gender of the angry deity is unknown:

4 *i-lum ša la i-du-ú (li-tu-ra)*	May the god I do not know return to his place.
6 ^{d}*iš-tar ša la i-du-ú (li-tu-ra)*	May the goddess I do not know return to her place.

The nature of the offense is also unknown. Although the supplicant admits to violating unspecified taboos, he pleads innocence and later claims not to know what crime he has committed:

33 *ik-kib* DINGIR-*ia ina la i-[de-e a-kul]*	[I broke] my god's taboo in ign[orance.].
35 *an-zil* ^{d}*iš-ta-ri-ia ina la i-de-e ú-kab-bi-is*	I crossed my goddess's bounds in ignorance.
…	…
43 *an-ni e-pu-šu ul i-[de]*	The wrong I did I do not kn[ow.]

The petitioner knows about the anger of some god or goddess because he experiences the consequences of divine wrath: a deity has burned or tormented him (*uṣarripanni*, 55), made him sick (*marṣiš ušemanni*, 53), and appointed affliction for him (*ašuštu iškuna*, 57). These manifest signs of divine displeasure have led to social isolation:

---

[55] Maul, *"Herzberuhigungsklagen,"* 236–46. Translation modified from Charles Halton in Lenzi, *Reading Akkadian Prayers and Hymns*, 447–64.

59 *áš-ta-né-ʾe-e-ma mam-ma-an qá-ti ul i-ṣa-bat*	I constantly sought, but no one would grab my hand.
61 *ab-ki-ma i-ta-te-ia ul iṭ-ḫu-u*	I wept, but no one came close to me.
Rev.	Rev.
2 *qu-bé-e a-qab-bi mam-ma-an ul i-ši-man*^{an}*-ni*	I would speak a lament, but no one would hear me.
4 *uš-šu-ša-ku kàt-ma-ku ul a-na-ṭa-al*	I am distressed. I am alone. I cannot see.
6 *ana* DINGIR-*ia réme-ni-i at-ta-na-as-ḫar un-ni-ni a-qab-bi*	I search constantly for my merciful god, I speak a petition.
8 *ša* ^{d}*iš-tar-ia še-pa-ša [ú-na-á-šaq ina* IGI-*ki] ap-ta-[na-ši-il]*	[I kiss] the feet of my goddess, I keep crawling before you.]

The verb forms emphasize the constancy of the petitioner's attachment behaviors. Durative forms describe both the petitioner's pleas for help and their lack of success in lines 52 and 2. His inability to see is also durative in line 4, as is his speaking a petition in line 6. The frequency of his seeking behavior is further underscored with the Gtn and Ntn forms in the durative in both lines 59 (*aštaneʾʾe*) and rev. 6 (*attanasḫar*). Both verbs indicate constant searching after a person. The simple G stems of both verbs (*šeʾû*, *saḫāru*), however, can also mean "to go around" or "to scrutinize," respectively.[56] Thus the stems selected clarify the sense of the verb and indicate the frantic nature of the seeking behavior through its frequentive aspect. Similarly, the petitioner's crawling appears in the Gtn form in line 8 to indicate the frequency of this self-abnegation and supplication. His distress and loneliness are described with stative forms. The pervasive use of durative forms and several Gtn forms contrasts with the simple G preterite forms in line 61: "I wept, but no one came close to me." The preterites convey the sense that weeping was a strategy attempted once or a few times and then abandoned due to its failure, in contrast to the other behaviors that the supplicant still employs despite ongoing lack of success. Not only do these preterites contrast with the verbs in the present passage, but they also break from the usual employment of the motif of weeping, which emphasizes the continuity of the petitioner's tears. The difference in tense corresponds to the difference in function: the weeping is a past act directed toward an unsympathetic human audience rather than a present process directed toward a divine audience.

The petitioner constantly seeks help and solace, but he finds none. It is not specified whether he experiences rejection from people, deities, or both. Behaviorally, the petitioner weeps, laments, and seeks. The weeping and lamenting are methods of seeking help. The petitioner has searched for help and sounded the alarm with weeping and lamenting, but no one will offer help or consolation. He

---

56 *CAD* 15:52 and *CAD* 17.2:358–63.

even crawls around at the feet of the unknown deity, an expression that implies submission, humiliation, and desperate begging. The whole prayer is in the voice of the petitioner. The crying might be of the sad or angry kind, but the context suggests the panic of a child separated from a parent, or protest crying. The prayer does not mention nighttime.

ERŠAḪUNGA 2.1D

Eršaḫunga 2.1d to Ishtar (Ešḫ n73) employs the weeping motif after a long but mostly broken opening.[57] The texts exalts Ishtar as "creator of everything, guide of every creature / mother goddess whose side no god can draw near" (10′–12′). The petitioner humbly concludes, "Let me speak a petition" (16′), and launches into the lament:

18′ *[b]e-el-ti ul-tu u*$_4$*-um ṣe-eḫ-re-ku ma-aʾ-diš šal-pú-ti ṣa-am-da-ku*	My mistress, from the day I was young, I was tightly yoked to my ruination.
20′ *[a-ka-la] ul a-kul bi-ki-tum kur-ma-ti*	[Food] I do not eat, weeping is my ration.
22′ *[mê ul áš-ti] dim-tú maš-ti-ti*	[Water I do not drink,] tears are my drink allowance.
24′ *[libbi ul…] ka-bat-ti ul im-mi-ir*	[My heart does not…] my liver is not cheerful.
26′ […] *e-tel-liš ul e-[ti-iq]*	[…] like a lord, I do not [pass on].
2 […] *mar-ṣi-iš a-dam-mu-um*	[…] bitterly I am moaning.
4 […] *ma-a-da šum-ru-ṣa-at ka-bat-ti*	[…] my liver torments me much.

The petitioner complains in his own voice (the Sumerian text is third person) that he has suffered ruin from his youth. He says that he has been "very tied to my ruination." The verb *ṣamādu* may mean "to tie up, bind, yoke," or generally to connect two things together.[58] The intensive adverb *mādiš* in this context would seem best captured by "tightly." The petitioner is tightly connected to his ruin (*šalputtu*), a term derived from the Š stem of *lapātu*, "to destroy, ruin, plunder."[59] The stative form indicates the speaker's long-standing difficulties. As usual, the prayer is vague enough to apply to many circumstances. In some sense, the petitioner has experienced a life filled with adversity.

The motif of weeping and tears as food and drink seems to highlight either the petitioner's fasting or the frequency of his weeping episodes (cf. *Dš* 9 25′–26′; *Dš* 11.5. 101–2). If the weeping and tears are understood as substitutes for food, then the petitioner weeps and fasts. If the petitioner still eats, then the weeping episodes are as regular and frequent as eating and drinking. The distress is like

---

[57] Maul, "*Herzberuhigungsklagen*," 289–95.

[58] *CAD* 16:89–92.

[59] *AHw* 1.536–37 and *CAD* 17.1:261–62.

hunger and thirst: it can never be definitively satisfied. Weeping does not end the suffering; there is no catharsis. The term *kurummatu* (*kurmatu*) refers to a food ration or allowance provided by the state to dependent people or domestic animals.[60] It suggests that the petitioner has indeed suffered a hard life and depends on handouts to survive. The term *maštītu* may refer simply to a drink, but in this context likely refers to a drink ration analogous to the food ration, reinforcing the dependence of the petitioner.[61] The image of rationing highlights the petitioner's dependence and lack of autonomy. Weeping and tears are assigned to him; he has not freely chosen them. In his helpless and miserable condition, he regularly weeps and may also fast to gain the attention of Ishtar.

The remainder of the lament is broken and the rest of the prayer missing, but the surviving text refers to the heart and liver as organs of emotion. The petitioner's liver is not cheerful, and it torments him. The description of the heart is broken. The end of the prayer, now missing, almost certainly asks Ishtar's heart to be calm and return to its place, according to the standard ending of *eršaḫungas*. The whole surviving prayer is in the voice of the petitioner, who seeks to improve his life by assuaging the wrath of Ishtar. It reflects a sad crying and makes no mention of night. The weeping contributes to the power of the prayer to assuage Ishtar's wrath.

ERŠAḪUNGA 2.3

Eršaḫunga 2.3 to Aya (Ešḫ n74–n75) preserves part of the lament with the motif of weeping:[62]

13 *ina i-ni-šu šá dim-tim šak-[na-a taq-r]ib-tú* [...]	with his eyes which [are f]ull of tears [an off]ering [...]
14 *ina pa-ni-šu e-šu-tim*	with his face troubled,
15 *ina ú-suk-ki-šu šá dim-tim la ib-ba-lu4*	with his cheeks on which tears do not dry,
16 *ina šap-ti-šú šá la-ga-a na-da-a*	with his lips on which dirt is cast,
17 *ina-qa-ti-šú šá ina rap-pi šu-un-ḫa*	with his hands that are shackled are weary,
18 *ina ir-ti-šu šá ki-ma ma-li-li qú-bi-i i-ḫal-lu-lu4*	with his breast with/like a flute he sounds a lament.

The surviving part of the lament is entirely in the third person as an intercessor describes the petitioner's condition. The prayer continues with the third person language until line 24, where it switches to first person at the end of the petition and through the surviving part of the intercession. The stative *šaknā* here means

60 *CAD* 8:573–79.

61 *CAD* 10.1:393–94.

62 Maul, *"Herzberuhigungsklagen,"* 296–302.

that the petitioner's eyes are constantly full of tears. Similarly, the tears are still wet on his cheeks, because ongoing weeping refreshes them. His face also appears troubled, and his lips are dirty because he has cast dirt on himself as part of his supplication. Most of the description focuses on the appearance of the person, especially his tear-stained face, but the last line of the lament notes the noise of his lament, comparing the voiced sounds from his breast with the doleful tune of a flute. While some texts liken the sounds of the petitioner to a moaning dove, this prayer compares it to a musical instrument in its association with lamenting tunes. The image describes the sad type of weeping expected to mollify divine anger. The prayer is in the voice of a petitioner who may also be the first-person speaker making offerings in lines 25–27.

SUMMARY

What distinguishes *eršaḫungas* that include weeping from those that do not? Mostly how complete the lament section of the prayer is. Of the twenty-seven prayers in the corpus, eight include weeping (22 percent). Weeping appears only in the lament section of *eršaḫungas*. If one eliminates from the corpus those prayers whose lament sections are missing, then sixteen prayers remain in the corpus, and 50 percent of them include weeping. This proportion increases again if one restricts the corpus further to the eleven examples where the lament section is intact (69 percent). Weeping appears to be an almost standard element of an *eršaḫunga*. The formulaic conclusion is recognizable in spite of the fragmentary nature of the texts because the wording is identical in all surviving examples and appears in the same location (the very end). The weeping motif, by contrast, may appear near the start, middle, or end of the lament section. The weeping motif also appears in a wide variety of linguistic manifestations and is never quite the same twice. Weeping therefore appears frequently in *eršaḫungas*, although it may not be a standard (i.e., required) element. Both the petitioner's voice and the intercessor's voice express the weeping motif, which often occurs with related crying terms (wailing, lamenting, sighing, moaning), emotional vocabulary (heart, liver, angry, terror) and postures of self-humiliation (bowing down [1.2f], kneeling [1.6d], prostration [1.15b], crawling [1.16]). The weeping described is consistently of the sad type, although *Er* 1.7d (with its loud noise) and 1.16 (with its frantic seeking behavior) reflect something closer to protest crying, suggesting more anger or panic. The precise motivations for the prayers are typically vague, but *eršaḫungas* clearly address divine anger, and illness seems to be a common problem. The standard conclusion asking the deity's heart to be merciful like a real father or mother betrays the explicit attachment relationship between petitioner and deity. The petitioner seeks to coregulate with the deity as an attachment figure. The petitioner's suffering and anxiety will be alleviated as the prayer mollifies the anger of the deity.

DINGIRŠADABBAS

Dingiršadabbas are prayers for calming the anger of a personal god.[63] In addition to the high gods worshipped by the whole community, Mesopotamian people also worshipped their own personal deities. These personal deities cared for their human protégés by keeping them healthy and enabling their successes. The personal deity was typically a family god whose reverence was transmitted through generations, and wives might adopt the personal deities of their husbands. The relationship with the personal deity might be damaged by failure to pay proper respect to the god or through some kind of sin. In these cases, the personal deity might become angry and abandon the person, exposing them to a variety of misfortunes and illnesses, sometimes explained as demonic attacks from which the personal deity would normally protect the person. Someone who experienced adversity might attribute their affliction to the wrath of the personal god and turn to that god in prayer to make amends. The *dingiršadabba* was designed for this purpose. Alternatively (or in addition), one could ask high gods for help repairing the relationship with the personal god, as in some *šuillas*, such as Ishtar 2.[64] The divine sphere was populated with a range of deities and demons, and the personal god could help a person negotiate good relationships in order to enjoy health and happiness. In this way, these family deities resemble parents who help their children grown into a network of relationships.[65]

The Old Babylonian text known as Dialogue between a Man and His God offers some insight into *dingiršadabbas*, the relationship with the personal god, and weeping.[66] The poem opens with a narrative description of the suffering of a young man who approaches his personal god in petition:

1 *eṭ-lu-um ru-u-iś a-na i-li-šu i-ba-ak-ki ú-te-ne-en-ne-en* IG-*x* [*x x*] *x x-šu*	A young man is weeping to his god like a friend, constantly praying [...]
2 *ḫa-mi-iṭ* ⸢*li*⸣-*ib-bu-uš du-ul-la-šu ma-ru-iṣ-ma*	His heart is on fire, his toil troublesome.
3 *i-ta-aʾ-da-ar ka-ba-at-ta-su i-ni-in-ḫi*	His liver is grieving from suffering.
4 *i-ni-iš-ma ik-ta-mi-us i-pa-al-si-iḫ*	He is weak and bent over, he is prostrate.

---

63 Margaret Jaques, *Mon dieu qu'ai-je fait?: Les digîr-šà-dab(5)-ba et la piété privée en Mesopotamie*, OBO 273 (Göttingen: Vandenhoeck & Ruprecht, 2015), 3: "Les diĝiršadaba se démarquent des autres prières par leur destinataire: les šuilla et la plupart des eršaḫuĝa sont adressées à un dieu nommé à qui un individu expose ses souffrances et qu'il supplier de s'apaiser, alors que les diĝiršadaba sont exclusivement destinées au dieu personnel."

64 Mayer, *Untersuchungen*, 16–17 thinks the *dingiršaddaba* is a type of *šuilla.*

65 van der Toorn, *Family Religion*, 66–147.

66 Jaques, *Mon dieu*, 4–9.

5 *ik-bi-us-sú-um-ma du-ul-la-šu ba-ka-i-iš ig-ra a*[*b*...]	His toil has become too heavy for him, he has drawn n[ear] to weep.
6 *ki-ma bu-ri-im pa-ar-si-im* <*ša*> *i-me-ri i-na-ag-ga-ag*	He brays like the weaned foal of a donkey,
7 *iš-⸢ta⸣-pu ma-ḫa-ar i-li-*[*(im)*] *re-ši-šu*	he has become loud in the god's presence, his chief,
8 *ri-mu-um pi-šu-ú la-al-la-ra-ma ri-gi-*[*im-šu*]	a bull is his speech, [his] voice two lamenters.
9 *be-li-iš-šu qú-ba-am ub-ba-la ša-ap-ta-š*[*u*]	His lips bear a lament to his lord,
10 *be-li-iš-šu du-ul-li iḫ-bu-tu i-ma-an-nu*	to his lord he recounts the toil he has gone through
11 *in-ḫi i-na-ḫu-⸢ú⸣ i-pa-aš-ša-ar eṭ-lu-u*[*m*]	the man explains the suffering he is enduring.[67]

The text then begins to quote the man's speech, which is the most broken passage in the text. The introductory narrative may provide a native Mesopotamian understanding of a *dingiršadabba*. The man approaches his personal god in prayer "like a friend" (*ru-i-iš*) because of his suffering, seeking relief.[68] The man "weeps to his god" (*a-na i-li-šu i-ba-ak-ki*), an expression indicating that his weeping is persistent and constant (durative verb) and directed to an audience. Similarly, line 5 emphasizes that the man "draws near [to his god] in order to weep" (the *-iš* ending on an infinitive indicates purpose).[69] The approach to the deity in a time of stress reflects the petitioner turning to the god as a safe haven. The man trusts the god enough that, far from hiding tears from the deity, he specifically seeks the deity as a target for emotional sharing and as a friendly audience for his tears. The connection with the attachment system also appears in the comparison of the man to a weaned donkey that brays. Like many other mammals, the young donkey calls out in protest at separation from its mother. The sound is loud and plaintive, and it motivates the mother to return to the foal just as a human infant cry gets caregiver attention. The loudness of the man's complaint appears again in the

---

67 The translation is modified from W. G. Lambert, "A Further Attempt at a Man and His God," in *Language, Literacy, and History: Philological and Historical Studies Presented to Erica Reiner*, AOS 67 (New Haven, CT: American Oriental Society, 1987) 187–202.

68 Some scholars understand the *-iš* ending as comparative "like a friend." See Jaques, *Mon dieu*, 8; Lambert, "Further Attempt," 194; Foster, *Before the Muses*, 148; and Jacob Klein, "Man and His God: A Wisdom Poem or Cultic Lament?," in *Approaches to Sumerian Literature: Studies in Honor of Stip (H. L. J. Vanstiphout)*, ed. P. Michalowski and N. Veldhuis, CM 35 (Leiden: Brill, 2006), 123–43, esp. 133–34. Others think it means "for a friend" and imagine three persons in the dialogue: the man, his god, and his friend; see Jean Nougayrol, "Une version ancienne du 'juste souffant'," *RB* 59 (1952): 239–50, esp. 243.

69 *GAG* §67 and John Huehnergard, *A Grammar of Akkadian*, HSS 45, 3rd ed. (Winona Lake, IN: Eisenbrauns, 2011), 311.

comparison to a bull and two lamenters. The sound may be loud sobbing like the cry of the infant or, as the next lines suggest, a more articulate complaint formed in intelligible language rather than sobs. The petitioner's complaint contains some language familiar from *dingiršadabbas*: "I do not know what sin I have committed" (line 13). The fragmentary prayer has the desired result. The god responds favorably: "mercy is granted to you" (55) and "for you the gate of prosperity and life is open, / go in and out of it and prosper" (66–67). The text indicates that the personal god is the creator of the person (58) and has guards who can be appointed to watch over the person (59).[70] As Margaret Jaques notes, "the personal god has a special rapport with an individual. He is his creator and his protector."[71] All humans are children of the divine due to the involvement of deities in the creation of new life, and personal gods seem particularly implicated in the generation of the family.[72] The Dialogue between a Man and His God provides insight into Mesopotamian beliefs about personal gods and therefore the *dingiršadabbas*.

Jacques has recently produced an edited version of the *dingiršadabbas*. The Sumerian examples consist of *DŠ* 1–*DŠ* 6. The bilingual texts consist of *DŠ* 7–*DŠ* 10. The Standard Akkadian version is *DŠ* 11, which consists of several collected prayers. I here separate them out into *DŠ* 11.1 through *DŠ* 11.10. The corpus for the present study consists of the prayers for which there is Akkadian text.[73] Jaques discerns a four-part structure in the Sumerian and bilingual *dingiršadabbas*: questions, protestation of innocence, supplication, and request for calming. This organization is less evident in the Akkadian texts. For example, the Sumerian and bilingual prayers routinely begin with the question "What have I done?," but the Akkadian prayers show a variety of opening lines. This specific question, "What have I done?," also appears in *Er* 2.1a[74] and the *šuilla* Ishtar 2.67,[75] both addressed to Ishtar.[76] The most distinctive aspect of the opening of a *dingiršadabba* is the lack of divine epithets. The prayers do not use any divine names, only "my [personal]

---

[70] van der Toorn, *Family Religion*, 98–99.

[71] Jaques, *Mon dieu*, 3: "Le dieu personnel a un rapport privilégié avec un individu. Il est son créateur et son protecteur."

[72] van der Toorn, Family Religion, 97–98 and David A. Bosworth, "Ancient Prayers and the Psychology of Religion: Deities as Attachment Figures," *JBL* 134 (2015): 694.

[73] Asterisks indicate prayer including the weeping motif. Parentheses indicate the inclusive line numbers for the various prayers in *DŠ* 11. *DŠ* 11.8–11.10 are from sections B and C with independent line numbers; see Jaques, *Mon dieu*, 83–86. The corpus consists of *Dingiršadabbas* 7, 8, 9*, 10, 11.1 (1–22)*, 11.2 (23–39), 11.3 (40–53), 11.4 (54–70), 11.5 (71–108)*, 11.6 (109–20), 11.7 (121–75), 11.8 (B 1–9), 11.9 (10–32), 11.10 (C 1–19).

[74] Maul, "*Herzberuhigungsklagen*," 280.

[75] See page 44.

[76] Jaques, *Mon dieu*, 137.

god" (*ilī*), and do not employ the epithets characteristic of *šuilla*s to named deities.[77] Lenzi argues that this contrast reflects the difference in social distance between humans and high gods and humans and their personal gods.[78] Instead, *dingiršadabba*s enumerate general aspects of personal gods such as their role in creating human life ("builder of all humanity you are" [11.4. 55] and "who brings my seed into being" [11.3. 41]) and protecting the person ("who guards my life" [11.3 41]). The protestations consist primarily of economic metaphors in which the speaker claims to be innocent, for example by not retaining sheep and cattle for himself. Within the context of protestation, the motif of the speaker's house becoming a house of weeping appears in several Sumerian and bilingual *dingiršadabba*s but not in any standard Assyrian texts. Weeping also appears in the supplication section in the form of the image of tears as sustenance. These images parallel those found in *eršaḫunga*s, but the *dingiršadabba*s use more fixed metaphors in paired lines or couplets.[79] The requests for calming that conclude the prayers by asking the deity to become calm and stop being angry may also include weeping ("I am held in tears like a reed thicket; lift your face [to me]" *Dš* 9 28).

DINGIRŠADABBA 9

Weeping appears twice in *Dš* 9.[80] After the initial claim of innocence, the speaker transitions to the protestation of innocence mixed with supplication as he notes how he is treated as one who is guilty:

13′ *áš-šá-tú ta-áš-qu-la-ma-r*[*a*...]	My wife you have taken....
14′ *i-li ina ni-iš qa-ti-ia* [...]	My god, in the lifting of my hands [...]
15′ *bi-ti ana* É *dim-ma-tim i-tur-ma*	(My) house has turned into a house of weeping.
16′ *i-li ana-ku ka-ma-ak-šu ina libbi-šú tu-še-ši-b*[*a-an-ni*]	My god, I am a prisoner to it, you have made [me] dwell in it.
17′ *ki-ma me-e a-šar al-la-ku ul i-*[*di*]	Like water, I do not know where I am going.
18′ *ki-ma e-lip-pi i-na ka-ar in-nem-mi-du ul i-*[*di*]	Like a boat, I do not know what quay I will dock at.

The image of the house of weeping appears in the Sumerian *dingiršadabba*s 1, 2, 3, 4, as well as this bilingual text, but not in the standard Assyrian versions. Two Sumerian texts (*Dš* 1 and 2) add a line including "dwelling of sobs" parallel to

[77] Jaques, *Mon dieu*, 134 and Mayer, *Untersuchungen*, 39–45.
[78] Alan Lenzi, "Invoking the God: Interpreting Invocations in Mesopotamian Prayers and Biblical Laments of the Individual," *JBL* 129 (2010): 303–15.
[79] Jaques, *Mon dieu*, 179–80.
[80] For the text, see Jaques, *Mon dieu*, 53–60.

"house of tears," but the other two closely resemble the bilingual version here. Jaques classifies the house of weeping motif among the motifs that serve the protestation of innocence.[81] The verb "turned" indicates that the present state of sorrow is a major change from former happiness. The Sumerian has a causal verb indicating that the god is deemed responsible for this transformation. The reference to the house as a prison suggests illness. The prison motif is part of the house of weeping, but the reference to the wife and son appears as a separate motif that Jaques classifies as contributing to the supplication.[82] The supplication is characterized by imperative verbs, which appear in the Sumerian version of this motif ("Let my wife lean on me, let my son lean on me"). The Akkadian translation does not retain the imperative verbs and therefore appears as a continuation of the protestation. The term *šaqālu*, "to pay" does not fit the context, and the dictionaries correct it to *saqālu*, "to take away" (?).[83] The underlying Sumerian term is translated with a wide variety of Akkadian terms in different contexts.[84] While the Sumerian line requests that the speaker be strong and well so that the family may rely on him, the Akkadian version interprets the line as a complaint that the family has also been afflicted. Given the reference to the house as a prison, which appears in a context of illness in *Ludlul Bēl Nēmeqi* (II 92), it seems that the whole household is sick, no one can leave, and former felicity has become suffering and weeping.[85]

Later in the prayer, the speaker asks the god for help and returns to the theme of weeping in the hope of gaining the attention and help of the deity:

25′ *a-kal a-ku-lu₄ ina ta-ni-ḫi ina šu-un-ni-ia*	The food I eat with sighing my second time
26′ *me-e áš-tu-u ina ta-ni-ḫi ina šu-un-ni-ia*	the water I drink with sighing my second time
27′ *ki-ma ap-pa-ri i*[*na i-di-ip-ti*] *tak-la-an-ni ki-niš nap-il-sa-an-ni*	You kept me like a marsh in wind, regard me reliably.
28′ *ki-ma ṣu-ṣe-e i*[*na dim-ma-ti ka-la-ku re-ši-ka i-šá-a*	I am held in tears like a reed thicket. Lift your face (to me).
29′ [*m*]*u-pa*[*l-sa-ta*] *ki-niš nap-li-sa-an-ni*	You are one who looks. Regard me reliably.

---

[81] Jaques, *Mon dieu*, 157–60.

[82] Jaques, *Mon dieu*, 160–63.

[83] *CAD* 15:168; *AHw* 1027; and Jaques, *Mon dieu*, 161–62. She translated the Sumerian line as "Que mon épouse se penche(?)! Que mon enfant se penche(?)!" The Akkadian she renders: "Tu as emporté(?) mon épouse, tu as emporté(?) mon enfant."

[84] Margaret Jaques, *Le vocabulaire des sentiments dans les textes sumériens: Recherche sur le lexique sumérien et akkadien*, AOAT 332 (Münster: Ugarit-Verlag, 2006), 8–9.

[85] Jaques, *Mon dieu*, 59, 157–60.

30′ *i-li be-lí mu-pa*[*l-sa-ta*] *ki-niš nap-li-sa-an-ni*	God, king, you are one who regards me reliably.
31′ *ina nap-lu-si-ka a-wi-lum* [*šu*] *i-bal-luṭ ki-niš nap-li-sa-an-ni*	When you look at a man, he lives, regard me reliably.
32′ *a-wi-il* [*tappalasu awīlum*] *šu-u i-bal-luṭ ki-niš nap-li-sa-an-ni*	The man whom you look at, that man lives, regard me reliably.
…	…
35′ [(…) *libbi ili-ia ana aš̌ri-šu li*]-*tur*	[(…) let the heart of my god re]turn [to its place.]

The Sumerian a-nir (Akk. *tanīḫu*, moaning) is often parallel to ér (*bikītu* or *dīmtu*).[86] *Er* 2.1d 19′–22′ has a similar image employing weeping instead of moaning.[87] The reference to a marsh in the wind appears also in *Er* 1.15b 16′–17′.[88] The marsh image continues in the explicit mention of tears: the speaker is kept in tears like a reed thicket is kept in water. The verb "I am held" indicates that the speaker would escape the tears if he could but feels constricted, as in the reference to the house of weeping being like a prison (line 16′). The reeds provide an image of something similarly held, because plants cannot change their location at will. In conjunction with the prior line about wind, the waters here may be turbulent, which enhances the image of emotional distress. By contrast, some Akkadian incantations for soothing crying babies employ water imagery to represent the calm of a sleeping baby: "be like swamp water, sleep like a baby gazelle, be secure like well water."[89] Like human emotion, water may be calm and at rest or churning and turbulent. The specific image of the speaker held in tears like a reed emphasizes the sense of being stuck, trapped, and unable to repair the situation that is driving constant weeping. The wider use of water imagery manifests the emotions of the prayer and echoes this reference to tears. The theme of ignorance and anxiety about the future manifests in the line "I am like water, where I am going I do not know / like a boat, I do not know what quay I will dock at" (lines 17–18).[90] Water images also unpack the plea "I have slipped! Seize my hand! / In calm water, be my boat-pole. / In deep water, be my rudder. / In the day of the storm do not turn me away" (lines 19–23). The image of being on a boat on the water evokes anxiety and the need for a sense of control. The usual instruments of control (boat-pole, rudder) may be useless in a storm, which churns the water and the emotions of the boatman. These waters become tears as the speaker sees himself stuck in misery like a reed in water. Water and tears are more loosely connected in the speaker's

[86] Jaques, *Le vocabulaire*, 493–94.
[87] Maul, *"Herzberuhigungsklagen,"* 290.
[88] Maul, *"Herzberuhigungsklagen,"* 220.
[89] Bosworth, *Infant Weeping*, 39–40 (and, similarly, 48) and Farber, *Schlaf*, 41–43.
[90] Jaques, *Mon dieu*, 163–65.

reference to drinking water with moaning (26′), because an informed reader knows that moaning is often parallel to weeping or tears.

The last several lines end with the plea "look faithfully upon me" (lines 29–34), which stands in parallel to several other expressions that similarly request divine attention and help such as "seize my hand" (20) and "lift your face (to me)" (28). The last line summarizes what all these pleas ask for: "Let the heart of my god return to its place" (35). The concluding reference to the god's heart is the most explicit indication that the petitioner understands the deity to be angry. Unlike the *šuilla*s to Ishtar, this prayer does not provide explicit detail about the presumed emotional state of the deity. The personal god is somehow responsible for the various sufferings of the speaker, and anger appears to be the most likely explanation. Consequently, the speaker elaborates on his misery and weeps in an effort to mollify divine wrath and gain the god's empathy and help. Thus, the prayer represents coregulation. The weeping appears sad, and the major complaint concerns the petitioner's sense of helplessness and loss of control expressed through images of prison and being held in place. The prayer is in the voice of the petitioner throughout.

DINGIRŠADABBA 11.1

Dingiršadabba 11.1 addresses the high gods Ea, Shamash, and Marduk, which makes it unusual for a *dingiršadabba*.[91] The petitioner quickly mentions his parents and describes his suffering, concluding with reference to his crying:

8 GIN$_7$ MUŠEN *nu-uḫ-ḫu-tu ab-ru-ú-a*	Like a bird, my wings are cropped,
9 *ú-šem-miṭ kap-pi-ya i-tap-ru-šá ul a-li-ʾ*	he tore my wings, I can no longer fly.
10 *mun-ga iṣ-ṣa-bat i-di*-MU	Paralysis has seized my arms,
11 *lu-ʾ-ti im-ta-qut* UGU *bir-ki*-MU	debility has fallen on my knees.
12 *a-dam-mu-um* GIN$_7$ *su-um-mat mu-ši u ur-ra*	I moan like a dove night and day.
13 *na-an-gu-la-ku-ma a-bak-ki ṣar-piš*	I am fevered, I am weeping bitterly.
14 *di-im-tú na-an-ḫu-za-at ina* IGI^{II}.MU	Tears well up in my eyes.

The petitioner then asks the gods to remove the sins of his father and mother from him. In this case, the early mention of the parents who created him prepares for the later analysis of the parents' sin as the cause of the suffering described metaphorically between these references to parents. The verb *naḫuzu* may be the N-stem of *aḫāzu*, meaning "to propagate," or more likely from *naḫāsu*, "to sob,

91 For the text, see Jaques, *Mon dieu*, 66–67.

lament, wail."[92] The petitioner is like a dove, moaning night and day. Here, the dove image connects with the metaphor a few lines earlier of the petitioner as a bird with its wings cropped so that it cannot fly. This image also comports with the language of imprisonment (line 2), paralysis (10), and weakness (11). The dove image evokes a soft, mournful sound suggestive of sad crying, which persists day and night. This sad crying contributes to the coregulation of the prayer that seeks to change the deity and therefore the petitioner. The voice of the petitioner speaks throughout the prayer; there is no intercessory voice.

DINGIRŠADABBA 11.5

Dingiršadabba 11.5 is the only Akkadian prayer that shows the same organizational structure as the Sumerian and bilingual examples.[93] The prayer includes many of the same water motifs present in *Dš* 9 and other *dingiršadabbas*. The speaker claims not to have consumed by himself the bread and water he found (lines 83–86), claims ignorance like water and a boat (90–91), and asks the deity to be his boat-pole and rudder (94–95). The motif of weeping appears as a variant to the occurrence of tears in *Dš* 9:

98 NINDA *ut-tu-ú ina ta-ni-ḫi a-ta-kal*	The bread I have found I have eaten in sighing.
99 A *ut-tu-ú ina ta-ni-ḫi al-ta-ti*	The water I have found I have drunk in sighing.
100 GIN7 *a-ri-id ap-pa-ri ina ru-šum-de na-da-ku*	Like one going down in the marsh, I fell in the mud.
101 *mu-up-pal-sa-ta ki-niš nap-li-sa-an-ni*	You who look, look faithfully at me.
102 *ki-ma ṣu-ṣe-e di-im-ma-tu tu-um-tal-la-an-ni / re-ši-ia šu-uq-qí*	Like a quagmire, you have filled me with tears, lift my head.
103 *mu-up-pal-sa-ta ki-niš nap-li-sa-an-ni*	You are one who looks (benevolently), regard me reliably.
104 LÚ *tap-pal-la-as-ma* LÚ *šu-ú i-bal-luṭ*	You look at a man and that man lives.

The references to the marsh and falling in the mud add to the extensive water imagery in the prayer familiar from *Dš* 9. The complaint that the god has filled him with tears like a quagmire continues the marsh imagery. It also intensifies the image by identifying the god as the cause of his weeping, whereas previously the god was not responsible for the petitioner falling. The expression resembles the tear motif in *Dš* 9: "like a quagmire, I am held (*ka-la-ku*) in tears," where *Dš* 11.5 changes the verb: "like a quagmire, you fill me (*tu-um-tal-la-an-ni*) with tears." In

---

92 For further discussion, see the Literary Prayer to Marduk below (pages 82–84). See also Jaques, *Mon dieu*, 95–96.

93 For the text, see Jaques, *Mon dieu*, 74–78.

the second example, the role of the deity is more explicit. The passive construction in *DŠ* 9 implies that the deity holds the petitioner, an implication explicit in the underlying Sumerian. In *DŠ* 11.5, the speaker identifies the deity as the one who has filled him with tears and asks the deity to "lift my head." The lifting of the head means a general show of favor rather than a literal head-lifting, but the literal sense adds to the quagmire image in this context. By literally lifting the head, the deity can save the speaker from drowning in the quagmire. The quagmire, however, represents tears, so the request for favor (lifting of the head) asks that the cause of the tears be removed. The parallel expression in *DŠ* 9 asks "lift your head to me," which also asks for favor and relief. As in *DŠ* 9, so also in *DŠ* 11.5, after the mention of tears, the petitioner repeatedly begs the god to "look at me," which implies seeing the petitioner's suffering and tears and therefore relenting from anger and letting the divine heart return to its place (line 108). Like *DŠ* 9, the prayer does not explicitly identify the god as angry, but the behavior of the god (rejecting the petitioner and causing him pain) is best explained and understood as wrath. The deity's anger has caused the petitioner's tears, and these same tears may help assuage that wrath by generating empathy. The prayer thereby represents coregulation. The text describes tears but no sound, so the weeping appears sad rather than as protest crying. The weeping contributes to the persuasive power of the prayer, which does not include the voice of an intercessor.

Summary and Note on Hittite Prayers

Since *eršaḫunga*s and *dingiršadabba*s seek to mollify the anger of a deity, one might expect them both to employ the weeping motif with equal regularity. Or one might expect the *dingiršadabba*s to employ weeping more frequently because the personal god would seem to be a more intimate relationship partner than a high god. In fact, however, weeping is much more common in the *eršaḫunga*s than in *dingiršadibba*s. Of the ten Akkadian *dingiršadabba*s, only two include weeping, and one of them is the introductory prayer to the high gods. One of the three bilingual texts includes weeping. Although weeping may have been present in some of the more broken texts, the surviving corpus suggests that it was relatively rare compared to the frequency in *eršaḫunga*s, although more common than in *šuilla*s. If the prayer to high gods is included, then three of the thirteen prayers (24 percent) include weeping; if it is eliminated, then two of twelve prayers (17 percent) include weeping. Although the Sumerian prayers are not part of the present study, four of the six Sumerian *dingiršadabba*s include weeping, and the other two are broken. As this type of prayer developed from its Sumerian origins, use of the weeping motif seems to have declined. The difference in weeping frequency between the Sumerian and Akkadian *dingiršadabba*s suggests that the prayer tradition developed over time as Sumerian language and culture was displaced by Akkadian language and culture. The difference in weeping frequency between the *eršanḫunga*s and *dingiršadabbas* may therefore be the result of this change of time and language rather than any difference in the deities addressed (high gods versus personal gods). Both Sumerian and Akkadian *dingiršadabbas* present a single voice speaking the prayer. The prayer texts and rubric indicate that the petitioner in these prayers seeks to coregulate emotion with a deity. The motive for the prayers is often vague and fits a variety of distressful circumstances, especially illness.

Jaques's edition of the *dingiršadabbas* includes an edition of Hittite prayers to the sun god for appeasing a personal god by Daniel Schwemer.[94] The three prayers are known as Prayer of a Mortal, Prayer of Kantuzili, and Prayer of a King in Itamar Singer's translation of Hittite prayers.[95] Of these three, one (Prayer of a King) includes weeping and draws on language familiar from the Mesopotamian *dingiršadabbas*: "My house has become a house of tears" (lines 65″–66″). Another one (Prayer of a Mortal) has a similar expression but without the weeping: "My house has become a house of anguish" (154). This new edition of the Hittite texts facilitates further study of these prayers that clearly draw on Mesopotamian traditions and incorporate them into a Hittite cultural matrix.

*NAMBURBI*S

Namburbi rituals ward off the evil portended by an omen (the Sumerian term means "undoing of it"). These omens could be anything observed that had ominous significance in the Mesopotamian belief system, such as the behaviors of various animals (e.g., seeing a snake or lizard in a house), lightning strike, or lunar eclipse. A superstitious person in the modern West may become concerned about a black cat crossing his or her path. Similarly, ancient Mesopotamian people who saw omens that revealed the will of the gods became concerned about the evil that these omens presaged. The *namburbi* ritual was designed to ward off this evil and thereby alleviate the anxiety of those worried about the omen. The ritual was not expected to resolve the manifestation of the portent, only the portended evil itself (e.g., it would not drive a snake from the house, but only ward off the evil predicted by the snake's presence). Maul has edited fifty *namburbi* rituals that form the corpus for the present study.[96] Although the ritual clearly has emotion regulatory functions, and emotion regulation appears in many texts, the texts never mention

---

[94] Daniel Schwemer, "Hittite Prayers to the Sun-God for Appeasing an Angry Personal God: A Critical Edition of *CTH* 372–74," in *Mon dieu qu'ai-je fait? Les diĝir-šà-dab₍₅₎-ba et la piété privée en Mesopotamie*, ed. Margaret Jaques, OBO 273 (Göttingen: Vandenhoeck & Ruprecht, 2015), 349–93. The volume also includes Charles Steitler, "A Glossary of the Hittite Prayers to the Sun-God (*CTH* 372–74)" (421–55).

[95] Itamar Singer, *Hittite Prayers*, WAW (Atlanta, GA: Society of Biblical Literature, 2002), 30–39.

[96] Maul, *Zukunftsbewälitgung*.

weeping except for the request in a *šuilla* embedded in a ritual that the deity not establish weeping.[97] The lack of weeping in this category of texts may reflect literary convention, or it may be indicative of the kinds of contexts that evoke emotion but not tears. Unlike prayers of penitence, the speaker in *namburbi* incantations does not seem aware of a rupture in relationship with the divine and may not feel acute emotional distress and helplessness. The evil is a future potential, not a present reality.

*IKRIBU*S

As an Akkadian word, *ikribu* can mean prayer, but it is also a more technical term for a prayer that a diviner recites in the course of a divination sacrifice (extispicy). The prayer is connected to each step in the ritual, and the diviner recites it while performing the ritual. As a result, the prayer reads like a kind of self-talk or prayerful expression of the inner voice. The prayer involves both narration of actions and requests for what the diviner hopes to discover when opening the animal and examining the liver. The prayers typically address Shamash and Adad as gods of judgment and divination, respectively. The best current edition of this genre of prayer involves text and commentary on an Old Babylonian ritual and provides the corpus for the present study.[98] No reference to weeping appears in the corpus. The overall ritual is motivated by some anxiety about the future that the gods may resolve by granting knowledge through extispicy. The focus of the prayer, however, remains on the ritual actions and shape of the innards, so the language of the prayer is not emotional.

*TAMĪTU*S

A *tamītu* is a prayer that asks a question of the gods Shamash and Adad and petitions them for an answer in preparation for an extispicy ritual. The priest would then sacrifice the sheep (while reciting an *ikribu*), extract the liver, and read the answer. The texts were standardized and sufficiently vague that they could be reused for various occasions. The questions cover a wide range of topics, including whether a person is telling the truth, the outcome of a river ordeal, and lunar eclipses. The most frequent topics concern personal safety and the success of military missions. W. G. Lambert has collected and edited *tamītu*s, and his edition forms the corpus of approximately forty-three *tamītu*s, some fragmentary, for the

---

97 See discussion of Nusku 13 on pages 42–43 in this volume.

98 Ivan Starr, *The Rituals of the Diviner*, BMes 12 (Malibu, CA: Undena, 1983). For the Standard Babylonian rituals, see Heinrich Zimmern, *Beiträge zur Kenntnis der babylonischen Religion* (Leipzig: Hinrichs, 1901), 190–219.

present study.[99] *Tamītus* invariably begin with the address "Shamash, lord of judgment, Adad, lord of the inspection" and may then name the person for whom the question is being asked, the question itself and its specifications or limitations (temporal frameworks, restrictions), language to persuade the deities to help, and a conclusion.[100]

The motif of weeping is not attested in the *tamītus*. These prayers may involve emotional language, but only at some remove because the speaker is the priest who will perform the extispicy speaking about the person who is requesting the ritual, typically as a means of coping with anxiety about the uncertain future. For example, one lengthy and well-preserved *tamītu* asks about the well-being of a client for the remainder of the year, covering many issues of health and safety. The client is described as constantly anxious about the possibility that he may die: "the decreed evil end of his days, which he constantly dreads (*i-ta-nam-da-ru*) and fears (*ip-ta-na-al-la-ḫu*), will not overtake NN, will it?" (331–32). The Gtn verb forms emphasize the constancy and therefore likely severity of the client's anxiety that motivates the oracle question. The emotional language that appears in *tamītus* describes the present state of the client (as above) or an imagined future state (from the same *tamītu*: "will he be satisfied, beaming, and happy?" (311). The client is spoken about rather than speaking, but the emotion regulatory function of the ritual appears clear from the nature of the questions and the descriptions of the client. Within this emotional context, weeping could be mentioned either as the present state of a nervous client or as an imagined future state (e.g., grief and mourning, which normally involve weeping, are mentioned in the same *tamītu*, line 329). The fact that weeping does not appear in any of the *tamītus* may be an accident of preservation or reflect the nature of the *tamītu* prayer. These prayers are prosaic, but other Akkadian prayers that refer to weeping are poetic. Also, the person directly petitioning the deities is the priest, who stands at a remove from the emotion of the client, who is not directly involved in the ritual.

LETTER PRAYERS

Old Babylonian letter prayers are written by individuals to a deity.[101] Individuals composed letters to deities that fit the modern definition of prayer but were not grouped with ritual prayers by the Mesopotamians themselves. Unlike other

---

99 W. G. Lambert, *Babylonian Oracle Questions*, MC 13 (Winona Lake, IN: Eisenbrauns, 2007).

100 For more detailed description of the structure of *tamītus*, see Lambert, *Babylonian Oracle Questions*, 14 and Lenzi, *Reading Akkadian Prayers and Hymns*, 51–52.

101 There are also Neo-Assyrian letter prayers, which are different from the Old Babylonian examples. They speak in the voice of the king and address a deity in formal language; see Lenzi, *Reading Akkadian Prayers and Hymns*, 54.

prayer genres, letter prayers use an epistolary form to express the petition in prose. They were composed for specific situations rather than for ritual use, so the texts reflect particular unrepeatable circumstances. They were delivered to the god at a temple and deposited as reminders to the deity of the petition sent by post and likely read to the deity by a priest. The present corpus of Old Babylonian letter prayers consists of six prayers, only one of which mentions weeping (*AbB* 6:135). The prose text is presented according to sense lines:[102]

4′ *i-na na-ri-ṭi-im na-di-[a-ku]*	In a swamp I lie,
5′ *[ù] i-na di-im-ma-tim ù bi-ki-tim*	and in wailing and weeping
6′ *[a-t]a-šu-uš*	I am distressed.
7′ *[...an-n]i-tum i-di-pa-am-ma*	This ... bore down on me
8′ *[i-na] a-la-ki-ia ṭup-pí a-na* ^d^*inanna be-e[l-ti-ia aš-pur]*	During my journey [I sent] my letter to Inanna my mistress.

The text has frequent gaps that make its interpretation difficult. The petitioner encounters problems on a journey and composes a prayer to be written down and delivered to the temple of Ishtar. The letter continues to ask that the letter may be read to the goddess and deposited in her temple. The letter is prose, but it reflects the poetic language known from prayers used in liturgy. The reference to lying in a swamp resembles imagery from the *dingiršadabbas*, where paralysis or immobilization are common images of distress and helplessness. The letter writer composes a prayer informed by past experience of liturgy and of Ishtar. The prayer reflects emotional coregulation, and weeping is part of that regulation. The letter reflects only the voice of the petitioner and involves no intercessor.

ROYAL PRAYERS

Royal prayers are not a well-defined genre of prayer. Many prayers of various kinds were developed for the king's use. Modern scholars tend to use the royal prayer category for occasional and miscellaneous prayers that do not fit into other categories. Lenzi limits his discussion to "the largest, most coherent group of texts," which are the prayer included in Neo-Babylonian building inscriptions.[103] Neo-Babylonian kings typically concluded their building inscriptions with prayers to a deity appropriate to the purpose. Neo-Babylonian kings ask for long life in exchange for their building work on behalf of the deity. The Royal Inscriptions of

---

102 *AbB* 6:135 includes weeping. The others do not: *AbB* 9:141; 12:99; 13:162; Fritz Rudolph Kraus, "Ein altbabylonischer Privatbrief an eine Gottheit," *RA* 65 (1971): 27–36 and Kraus, "Eine Neue Probe Akkadischer Literatur: Brief eines Bittstellers an eine Gottheit," *JAOS* 103 (1983): 205–9. See van der Toorn, *Family Religion*, 84 on this text and 130–47 on letter prayers generally.

103 Lenzi, *Reading Akkadian Prayers and Hymns*, 55.

Babylonia online (RIBo) Project lists the inscriptions of Neo-Babylonian kings, which often include prayers but never include weeping.[104] Because completing building activity is a happy occasion, the prayers that conclude building inscriptions do not include lament and weeping.

HYMNS

The boundary between prayers and hymns "is not hard and fast."[105] Both prayers and hymns address a benevolent suprahuman entity, but they differ in their general content and emotion. Prayers focus on petitions and seek to down-regulate negative emotions such as guilt and anxiety, but hymns focus on praise and up-regulate positive emotions such as joy and gratitude. Petitionary prayers often involve some praise, and hymns may include some petition. The discernment of a "hymn" category in Akkadian is further complicated by the lack of correspondence between ancient scribal classificatory rubrics and formal features of hymnic texts. Consequently, discussions of hymns tend to identify texts that have struck modern scholars as hymnic in nature. The corpus of hymns in Akkadian is relatively small, and the well-preserved examples even smaller. The present study employs the eighteen texts identified by Lenzi as well-preserved independent hymnic compositions as distinct from hymnic material embedded in other texts (e.g., *Ludlul Bēl Nēmeqi*).[106] This corpus could be doubled by adding additional texts identified as hymns by Benjamin Foster in *Before the Muses*, but this expansion would not result in any additional examples of weeping. The corpus could also be expanded by the inclusion of over one hundred prayers in the Sources of Early Akkadian Literature (SEAL).[107] The highly fragmentary nature of many of these texts points to a further advantage of the eighteen hymns identified by Lenzi: they are relatively complete. Only two texts of the eighteen include weeping, and both are edited by Lambert, who identifies them as "literary prayers," meaning that, unlike most prayer texts, they are "properly considered works of literature."[108] Subsequent scholars have not followed Lambert in distinguishing prayers on the basis of their perceived literary quality, but the six literary prayers he identifies do

---

[104] To browse the corpus, see the Open Richly Annotated Cuneiform Corpus (ORACC), University of Pennsylvania Museum of Archaeology and Anthropology, http://oracc.museum.upenn.edu/ribo/babylon7/corpus/.

[105] Lenzi, *Reading Akkadian Prayers and Hymns*, 9.

[106] For description of the eighteen hymns and bibliography, see Lenzi, *Reading Akkadian Prayers and Hymns*, 58–60.

[107] For this online text corpus, see "Sources of Early Akkadian Literature (SEAL): A Text Corpus of Babylonian and Assyrian Literary Texts from the Third and Second Millennia BCE," http://www.seal.uni-leipzig.de/.

[108] Lambert, "Three Literary Prayers," 47.

show heightened sophistication. Perhaps it is not coincidental that the two hymns that include weeping both occur within this smaller corpus of so-called literary prayers. Note, however, that weeping also appears in what Foster calls the Great Hymn to Ishtar but is elsewhere categorized as a *šuilla* and discussed above as Ishtar 2. As might be expected, weeping is rare in hymns given their focus on praise.

LITERARY PRAYER TO ISHTAR

The Literary Prayer to Ishtar praises the goddess but also includes lamentation by the petitioner, variously in the first and third person. Like other hymns and prayers, it appears to be a composite from various sources and is not easily categorized. Lambert decided that it is a prayer rather than a hymn, but Foster classifies it as a hymn.[109] The beginning of the prayer is lost or broken, but the surviving fragments indicate that it consisted of praise of Ishtar. The conclusion is also praise and addresses a group of women (using second-person feminine language), urging them to praise Ishtar. The hymn praises Ishtar in large measure for her willingness and power to save people in distress (e.g., lines 73–80). The speaker is in distress, suffering from illness, and confesses guilt (67–70). Ishtar's wrath may be in the background as the cause of the petitioner's misery, but the (broken) text nowhere identifies her as angry. A lament section includes multiple references to weeping, one of which is clear and elaborate, while the other two are brief or less clear. The first appears in a broken context among lines that lament the speaker's sickness in third-person language. Line 94 is broken, but the word for dove is clear, and the term for "moaning" can be reconstructed: *šu-um-meš x [(x) i]d*?-[*m*]*u*?-*ma x* […], "Like a dove he moaned." As noted above, moaning doves frequently appear in contexts of weeping, although the text here is too fragmentary to know whether typical weeping vocabulary occurs.

A clear and detailed reference to the petitioner's weeping appears shortly after, still in the third person:

144 *e-li-lu-šú ṣur-ru-pu x* […]	His songs are bitter…
145 *bu-ul-lul ina di-ma-ti i-bak-k*[*i ṣar-piš*]	covered in tears, he weeps [bitterly].
146 *làl-la-ru-šú dím-ta-šu i-ṣíp-*[*šu*]	His hired mourner multiplied his tears [for him],
147 *ana nu-bé-e-šú mar-ṣu-ti ip-ḫu-ra sa-la*[*t-su*]	for bitter mourning over him [his] family gathered.
148 *ur-ra ú-tak-ka-ak mu-šá i-na-aḫ-ḫi-*[*iš*]	By day he scratches himself, by night he sheds tears.
149 *ina ṣe-ri-šu it-ku-šu re-e-mu un-ni-*[*ni*]	From him pity (and) mercy have left,

109 Lambert, "Three Literary Prayers," 47 and Foster, *Before the Muses*, 606–10.

150 *ṣur-ru-up šu-us-suk a-ri-im ka-la-a-*[*šú*]	he is bitter, cast aside, overwhelmed completely.[110]

The fourfold description of the sufferer's weeping emphasizes his constant pain and the social support his tears have elicited. In addition to professional mourners who amplify his tears with their own, his family has also gathered to lament over him. Among fellow humans, his weeping has had the desired effect of gaining empathy and social support. This human reaction offers hope that Ishtar too may respond with help.

Weeping seems to appear also in line 166 of the prayer: *a-na šat-ti ni-ʾ-li-šu* [...], "For this reason, his tears...." The term *naʾālu* means "to flow" and likely refers to weeping here (cf. *Ludlul Bēl Nēmeqi* II 60).[111] The context is broken, but the speaker seems to ask Ishtar to be present with the sufferer, and the sufferer's tears are further motivation for her to help him. The weeping in this hymn is hard to categorize as protest or sad crying. The dove image suggests sad, quiet weeping, but the presence of hired mourners and grieving family members suggests more fear and anger characteristic of protest crying. The prayer combines first-person and third-person language about the petitioner, reflecting multiple voices engaged in the process of emotion regulation with Ishtar. The petitioner turns to Ishtar as a safe haven in a time of distress.

Literary Prayer to Marduk

The Literary Prayer to Marduk includes both praise and lament.[112] The rubric refers to it as an *unninnu*, a term with a range of meaning comparable to the English "prayer." The term is etymologically related to *enēnu*, "to pray, ask for mercy or forgiveness, to wail," but the noun *unninnu* was applied to all kinds of compositions, from supplications to praise.[113] Like *Ludlul Bēl Nēmeqi*, this prayer praises Marduk's saving power and attributes various illnesses to Marduk's anger.[114] It begins with the emotion regulatory language familiar from *eršaḫungas*:

1 *be-lum še-zu-zu li-nu -uḫ lib-bu-u*[*k*]	Lord, fierce one, let your heart be at rest,
2 *i tap-šaḫ kab-ta-tuk a-na* ì[R-*ka*]	may your liver become calm for your servant.

---

110 Translation modified from Lambert, "Three Literary Prayers," 52.

111 W. G. Lambert, *Babylonian Wisdom Literature* (Oxford: Oxford University Press, 1960; repr., Winona lake, IN: Eisenbrauns, 1996), 292.

112 Lambert, "Three Literary Prayers," 47–55 edits the text as "Prayer to Marduk No 1," while Takayoshi Oshima, *Babylonian Prayers to Marduk*, ORA 7 (Tübingen: Mohr Siebeck, 2011) 137-90 re-edits the text as "Prayer to Marduk no. 1."

113 Oshima, *Babylonian Prayers*, 138–39.

114 Oshima, *Babylonian Prayers*, 140.

3 dAMAR.UTU *še-zu-zu li-nu-uḫ lib-bu-uk*	Marduk, fierce one, let your heart be at rest,
4 *i tap-šaḫ kab-ta-tuk a-na* ÌR-*ka*	may your liver become calm for your servant [115]

The opening goes on to praise Marduk, especially for his kindness and mercy, and then transitions to speak about the petitioner in the third person. He languishes in illness, and the speaker asks Marduk to relent from this punishment (57–59), noting that there is no profit for Marduk in letting his servant die (66–70), and that everyone is guilty of something (104–10). After further description of his miserable sick state, the prayer turns to the sufferer's weeping:

129 *iḫ-ti-ṭam-ma mar-ṣa-tuš i-[ba]k-ki-ka*	He saw his difficulties and he is weeping to you.
130 *kab-ta-as-su na-an-gul-lat-ma uḫ-[ta]m-maṭ-ka*	His liver burns, he is ablaze for you.
131 *na-an-ḫu-uz di-im-ta ki-ma im-ba-ri ú-ša-a[z-ni]n*	Tears flow, like a drizzly rain he lets them fall.
132 *ut-taḫ-ḫas-ma ú-šab-ka-a la a-lit-t[iš]*	He sobs and gives free reign to his weeping like a barren woman.
133 *ki-i lal-la-ri qu-bé-e ú-šá-aṣ-rap*	Like a professional mourner he utters bitter cries,
134 *du-lup-šú i-qab-bi ina te-ni-ni*	he speaks of his lack of sleep in his prayer.

The description of the petitioner's tears explicitly indicates the desired goal of the weeping: to move Marduk to help. The suffix on *i-[ba]k-ki-ka* indicates that the weeping behavior has an intended audience; it is understood as a social behavior that seeks to engage in coregulation of emotion. The petitioner's emotional arousal (burning liver) and display of tears should motivate Marduk to action. Lambert takes the verb *ḫummuṭu* here in the sense of "make restless."[116] Takayoshi Oshima sees the verb as Gt-stem instead of D (as Lambert), and his translation ("he pines for you") tries to capture both the sense of "to rush" and "to be ablaze."[117] My translation emphasizes the second meaning, because language of heat describes emotional arousal in Akkadian literature, especially anger and grief. Here the sufferer burns with sorrow, and the suffix indicates Marduk as the audience and goal. The next line returns to weeping but focuses on tears.

Lambert thinks the root of *na-an-ḫu-uz* (131) must be *aḫāzu* and offers a literal translation in a note: "he is spread around with reference to tears." Oshima

115 Translation of this prayer modified from Oshima, *Babylonian Prayers*.

116 *CAD* 6:65 and Lambert, "Three Literary Prayers," 58 n. 130.

117 Oshima, *Babylonian Prayers*, 184–85.

understands it as a form of *naḫāsu*, which also appears in the next line, and notes the problem of distinguishing sibilants in the writing system.[118] *CAD* offers both possibilities.[119] Oshima's solution is appealing because it connects the term with a verb that has well-attested meaning related to weeping (i.e., "to sob, lament, wail"), whereas it is not easy to connect any of the many senses of *aḫāzu* to fit weeping contexts.

The Š stem of *bakû* likely has here the sense of "allow to weep." The ill man is likened to a professional mourner because of his bitter cries (*lallāru* designated of owls, crickets, etc). The Š stem of *ṣarāpu* II, "to make cries resound," intensifies the lamentations by indicating a loud noise, as might be expected from a professional mourner. He talks about his sleeplessness or restlessness (*dulpu*) in his lamentation (*tēnīnu*). The patient's lament is partially represented in the text of the prayer. In addition to the short "I am ill" quoted above, the voice of the patient appears in the first person shortly after the weeping passage (137–40), but this short speech is focused on confessing guilt and asking forgiveness. The line evidently refers to the private prayer of the patient separate from the ritual presented in the written text, which is itself described in the rubric as a "prayer" (*unnīnu*). Both *unnīnu* and *tēnīnu* derive from the verb *utnēnu*, "to pray," but the first retains the general meaning of the verb, while the second has a more specific connotation of "prayer of lament."

The appearance of weeping in the prayer employs terms for weeping, tears, and sobbing and emphasizes the sound of the weeper and the emotional arousal that motivates his tears. The reference to his lack of sleep suggests that he weeps at night. The weeping behavior is oriented toward Marduk, whose anger is understood to be the cause of the sufferer's misery. The sufferer rarely speaks, but the third-person narrator describes the patient's pain and amplifies his supplication.

Summary

Few hymns in the corpus mention weeping: two out of eighteen (11 percent). Weeping appears in the context of lament, or a recollection of former misery from which the deity has saved the person. These hymns have a thanksgiving message for which the memory of past suffering and tears is important to highlight the divine salvation. The laments within the prayers recollect previous emotion coregulation aimed at seeking relief from anxiety, while the present thanksgiving contexts reflect a process of regulating into a state of joy and gratitude. The

---

118 Oshima, *Babylonian Prayers*, 184, citing *GAG* §30.

119 *CAD* 1.1:183b notes that *dīmtu šuḫuzat* may derive from *naḫāsu* rather than *aḫāzu* based on a variant spelling *it-ḫu-sa*. *CAD* 11.1:132b–33a refers to the discussion under *aḫāzu* and wonders whether the expressions *nanḫuz dīmta* and *dīmtu nanḫuzat* might derive from *aḫāzu* after all since *naḫāsu* is not otherwise attested in the Š-stem.

combination of lament and praise shows the deity as an attachment figure to whom the person turns as a safe haven in time of stress and as a secure base in better times. Both have a literary quality that may partially explain why both of these prayers, but no other in the hymnic corpus, include weeping.

LANGUAGE OF WEEPING

The three terms most often used to indicate weeping in the Akkadian prayers are *bakû*, "to weep," *bikītu*, "weeping," and *dimtu*, "tear." Every example analyzed here includes one of these terms, and about half include two. The verb appears almost always in the durative because the weeping motif normally emphasizes the ongoing aspect of the petitioner's weeping (*Er* 1.7d; 1.14; 1.15; *Dš* 11.1; Literary Prayer to Ishtar; Literary Prayer to Marduk). In every case, the frequentive aspect of the weeping is further reinforced with additional vocabulary such as "daily" (*ūmīšam*, *Er* 1.6d, 1.7d), "night and day" (*mūša u urra*, Ishtar 2, Ishtar 10), "cannot stop" (*ul ikalla*, *Er* 1.7d). The recurrent emphasis on the continuity or frequency of weeping highlights the extreme helplessness of the petitioner. Such consistent crying suggests sincerity and perseverance; these are tears not of manipulation but of genuine need. The only case where weeping appears in the preterite involves a reference to past weeping before a human audience that proved unresponsive (*Er* 1.16). The Literary Prayer to Marduk includes two unusual verbal forms. First the durative *ibakkīka* includes a suffix. The suffix emphasizes that the weeping has a targeted audience, in this case Marduk. The petitioner does not merely weep, "he weeps to you." The same prayer also includes a preterite form of *bakû* in the Š-stem, meaning "to allow to weep." These unusual verb forms contribute to the elevated and literary quality of the prayer. The only other example of *bakû* in the preterite is a G-stem form in *Er* 1.16. The speaker refers to a past act of weeping that did not motivate anyone to offer him comfort, so the preterite refers to past weeping to a human audience rather than present weeping to a divine audience.

The above weeping vocabulary often appears with a range of other terms that do not denote weeping but describe associated activities. The term *naḫāsu* clearly describes an activity related to weeping because it occurs only in weeping contexts, but its precise meaning remains uncertain, perhaps "to sob, to lament, to wail." The most frequent term in a weeping context is "sighing" (*tānēḫu*), often paired with *bikītu* or *dimtu*, although it appears primarily in *eršaḫungas* (*Er* 1.2f; 1.6d; 1.7d; 1.14; 1.15b; also *Dš* 9; 11.5; Ishtar 2). The verb *naḫāsu*, "to sob, wail," appears in two examples (*Dš* 11.1, Literary Prayer to Marduk). The motif of weeping as sustenance appears once in connection with tears (*Er* 2.1d), but it also appears in weeping contexts specifically connected with sighing (*Dš* 9; 11.5). *Eršaḫungas* mention several bodily postures and actions in connection with weeping: bowing (*Er* 1.2f), kneeling (*Er* 1.6d), collapsing (*Er* 1.14), prostration (*Er* 1.15b), and crawling (*Er* 1.16). The terms *nubû*, "lament, wailing," and *qubû*, "lamentation," both of which involve voiced sounds, are also attested. The verb *damāmu*, "to moan, wail," occurs only with the image of the cooing dove (Ishtar 2; Ishtar 10; *Dš* 1.15b; *Dš* 11.1; Literary Prayer to Ishtar). The image suggests a mournful voiced sobbing and therefore the sad type of weeping. Apart from the dove, the only other animal image is a cow, which appears with the dove in *Er* 1.15b. There the petitioner "bellows" (*nagāgu*) or, in a variant, "shouts" (*šasû*) like a cow. All three *dingiršadabba*s include images of imprisonment or being stuck, which are also common to *dingiršadabba*s that do not involve weeping. The images involve being stuck in a thicket or quagmire or being like a bird with clipped wings. The weeping motif often appears with references to eyes that appear as full of tears, but one reference substitutes weeping (*bikītu*, *Er* 1.14) instead. Two examples make the deity the agent who fills the petitioner's eyes with tears or weeping (*Er* 1.2g; 1.14), emphasizing active divine anger. One reference to eyes specifies the iris of the eye (*Er* 1.2f), and one text mentions cheeks as wet with tears (*Er* 2.3).

DIVINE ANGER AND HUMAN TEARS

The Akkadian evidence shows a significant correlation between divine wrath and human tears. Akkadian literary texts and prayers attribute human suffering to divine anger.[120] Other texts show that the Mesopotamians admitted a range of explanations for illness. For example, some illnesses were understood as due to the season or other natural causes such as poison, although these could not be easily distinguished from supernatural causes.[121] An ancient Mesopotamian, like a modern Westerner, might perceive a snake bite as a natural event (snakes sometimes bite people) that has a supernatural cause (why did a snake bite *me*?). Analogously, ancient and modern people often employ multiple means in their quests for healing, turning both to medicine and religion, which were discreet but overlapping categories in Mesopotamia. The professions of the *āšipu*, "exorcist," and *asû*, "physician," were associated with separate corpora of literature: *āšipūtu*, "magic," and *asûtu*, "medicine." The first consists of lengthy incantations (marked with ÉN) and brief rituals or recipes, while the second involves short incantations and long recipes and a casuistic "if-then" format common to legal and omen texts.[122] These professions and their associated texts correspond to two approaches to healing.

---

[120] Karel van der Toorn, *Sin and Sanction in Israel and Mesopotamia: A Comparative Study* (Assen: Van Gorcum, 1985), 56–67.

[121] van der Toorn, *Sin and Sanction*, 67–69.

[122] Markham J. Geller, *Babylonian Medicine: Theory and Practice* (Malden, MA: Wiley-Blackwell, 2010), 161–67; Geller, "Incantations within Akkadian Medical Texts," in *The Babylonian World*, ed. Gwendolyn Leick (New York: Routledge, 2007), 389–99; and Hector Avalos, *Illness and Health Care in the Ancient Near East: The Role of the Temple in Greece, Mesopotamia, and Israel*, HSM 54 (Atlanta: GA: Society of Biblical Literature, 1995), 128–72.

One involved addressing the symptoms with medicines and incantations to enhance their effectiveness. The other involved discerning the divine sender of the disease so that a reconciliation between the patient and the deity could be accomplished.[123]

The deity in question might be a personal god or high god, and the rituals for reconciliation may have accordingly involved *dingiršadabba*s, *eršaḫunga*s, or *šuilla*s (or some combination of them).[124] Anger would be the presumed motive for the deity to inflict disease on a person, so these prayers address the problem of divine wrath. As we have seen, *eršaḫunga*s, *dingiršadabba*s, and *šuilla*s were all forms of prayer useful for calming divine wrath and restoring a person's circumstances. Human tears appear overwhelmingly in these types of prayers, especially *eršaḫunga*s. Weeping is entirely absent from the corpus of *namburbi*s, *ikribu*s, *tamītu*s, and royal prayers. Weeping appears infrequently in hymns (two of eighteen, or 11 percent), and divine anger appears to be in view in both cases. *Šuilla*s in general do not mention weeping frequently (three of forty-six, or 7 percent), but those *šuilla*s that mention divine wrath are much more likely to mention human weeping (three of ten, or 30 percent). *Dingiršadabba*s involve weeping in two of twelve prayers, or 17 percent. *Eršaḫunga*s make the most frequent mention of weeping, which appears only in the lament section. The corpus of twenty-nine *eršaḫunga*s includes eight with weeping, or 22 percent, but this percentage rises dramatically to 69 percent if one narrows the corpus to the eleven examples with fairly complete lament sections. Weeping is almost a standard element of an *eršaḫunga*. Throughout the corpus of prayers as a whole, divine anger correlates with human weeping. The emotion regulatory function of Akkadian prayers reflects internal working models of deities as attachment figures with whom petitioners can ease their anxieties by mollifying the anger of the deity.

[123] Mesopotamian medicine acknowledged potential sources of illness apart from deities, such as demons, ghosts, and witches, although even these evils seem to be due to lack of divine protection; see, e.g., Tzvi Abusch, "Witchcraft Literature in Mesopotamia," in *The Babylonian World*, ed. Gwendolyn Leick (New York: Routledge, 2007), 373–85 and Abusch, "Witchcraft and the Anger of the Personal God," in *Mesopotamian Magic: Textual, Historical, and Interpretive Perspectives*, ed. Tzvi Abusch and Karel van der Toorn, Ancient Magic and Divination 1 (Groningen: Styx, 1999), 83–121.

[124] Nils P. Heeßel, "The Hands of the Gods: Disease Names and Divine Anger," in *Disease in Babylonia*, ed. Irving Finkel and M. J. Geller, CM 36 (Leiden: Brill, 2006), 126–27 and van der Toorn, *Sin and Sanction*, 123.

3
Weeping in Hebrew Psalms

The genres or categories of psalms often have some basis in the emotions that motivate the prayers. Although many different genres have been proposed to analyze the psalms, some scholars argue that psalms can be divided into two major categories: praise and lament. Psalms in the praise category express joy and gratitude, and the person praying may use the psalm to elevate these emotions. By contrast, feelings of fear and anxiety may drive people to prayer, and prayers of lament help people to present their sorrows to God in the hope of finding relief. The relief may come in the form of prayers answered or the sense of being heard even if the negative situation does not change. Some scholars have seen this basic dichotomy between praise and lament through the several major and minor psalm types. Claus Westermann argues that there is no distinction between psalms of thanksgiving and psalms of praise, but that thanksgiving is a type of hymn. Consequently, "in the Psalter there are two dominant categories, the hymn (including the Psalm of thanks) and the lament."[1] Walter Brueggemann reintroduces the distinction between hymns and thanksgiving psalms to identify three thematic categories of psalms: "psalms of orientation," "psalms of disorientation," and "psalms of new orientation."[2] Psalms of orientation express "a happy settlement

---

[1] Claus Westermann, *Praise and Lament in the Psalms*, trans. Keith R. Krimm and Richard N. Soulen (Atlanta, GA: John Knox, 1981), 18; see also his 1977 preface (11). Similarly, Herman Gunkel, *An Introduction to the Psalms: The Genres of the Religious Lyrics of Israel*, Mercer Library of Biblical Studies; trans. James D. Nogalski (Macon, GA: Mercer University Press, 1998); trans. of *Einleitung in die Psalmen: Die Gattugen der religiösen Lyrik Israels* (Göttingen: Vandenhoeck & Ruprecht, 1933), 214. Craig C. Broyles, *The Conflict of Faith and Experience in the Psalms: A Form-Critical and Theological Study*, JSOTSup 52 (Sheffield: Sheffield Academic, 1989), 35–36 notes that "even a casual reading of the Psalms reveals that their basic form of speech may be described most generally as praise and lament, or praise and petition."

[2] Walter Brueggemann, *The Message of the Psalms: A Theological Commentary*, Augsburg Old Testament Studies (Minneapolis, MN: Augsburg, 1984).

of life's issues."[3] The form-critical category of hymn often expresses this confidence in God's benevolent rule and includes texts such as torah psalms and wisdom psalms. By contrast, psalms of disorientation overlap with the traditional category of individual and communal lament and represent moments of conflict, stress, anxiety, or catastrophe when God's benevolent rule appears in doubt. Psalms of new orientation roughly correspond to the categories of thanksgiving psalm or enthronement psalm that reflect on past suffering in contrast to present joy. Brueggemann's threefold typology offers insight into broad categories of prayer by relating several genres traditionally identified by form criticism to each other by focusing on the functions of the prayers more than their form.

Brueggemann's categories cohere with the present reading of psalms as emotional sharing and coregulation for two primary reasons: his typology connects well to research on grief, and his emphasis on process and transition fits into a model of emotion regulation. First, the three types of psalms that Brueggemann articulates correlate well with grief processes identified in empirical research on bereaved people.[4] In a "loss orientation," people experience hyper-activation of their attachment behaviors (e.g., weeping, seeking, yearning, ruminating). At other times, they defensively seek to suppress attachment through a "resotoration orientation" in order to distract themselves from grief and engage in other necessary tasks such as work, relationships, and self-care. Mourners and those who have suffered traumas may oscillate between these two processes for coping that correspond well to Brueggemann's disorientation and new orientation. His orientation theme would correspond to the relatively happy state that prevailed before the loss or trauma. He rightly notes that there is no return to the old orientation, but that one establishes a new stable orientation.[5] Grief and trauma change reality in permanent ways (our deceased loved ones remain gone), but the initial shock and period of intense grief often give way to a return to living without those who have died.

Second, Brueggemann emphasizes that these three types of psalms imply two transitions: one from orientation to disorientation and one from disorientation to new orientation. He structures his discussion to emphasize these transitions, which amount to emotion regulatory processes: "I have grouped the Psalms in this way to try to make a point that is decisive for pastoral experience: the lives of people and communities are never static. They are always on the move, and I have

---

[3] Brueggemann, *Message*, 25.

[4] David A. Bosworth, "Understanding Grief and Reading the Bible," in *Mixed Feelings and Vexed Passions: Exploring Emotions in Biblical Literature*, ed. F. Scott Spencer, RBS 90 (Atlanta, GA: SBL Press, 2017), 117–38.

[5] Brueggemann, *Message*, 123–24.

structured it, either into orientation or out of orientation."[6] This observation holds for emotions, which are frequently in flux. We are also constantly seeking to regulate this emotional flow, both consciously and unconsciously. Prayers of disorientation seek to reduce the emotional pain and turmoil described in the laments by motivating God to change the speaker's situation. Psalms of reorientation elevate positive emotions and help orient a person or community to a new period of security so they can focus on new experiences, relationships, and living life. Brueggemann's emphasis on transitions between psalm types draws attention to the emotional regulation that occurs both within and between prayer types.

The primary distinction between praise and lament, or between the elements of Brueggemann's threefold orientation, disorientation, and new orientation, offers helpful insight into the purposes of psalms and the emotions they involve. Efforts to categorize psalms together according to form or content have not been entirely satisfactory, although a workable scholarly consensus has emerged. Early form-critical work continues to shape how scholars classify psalms. Most researchers acknowledge the forms identified in Hermann Gunkel's foundational work. Within the broad type of praise, there are hymns and thanksgivings. Hymns have been further subdivided in various ways to include such categories as creation hymns, entrance liturgies, enthronement psalms, Zion psalms, and psalms of trust or confidence. Some include wisdom psalms, torah psalms, and royal psalms as variations on hymns. Hymns tend to praise God in descriptive terms, while thanksgiving psalms refer to specific events.[7] There are fewer subcategories within the lament psalms, which include only individual and communal laments. Many scholars also acknowledge historical psalms as a separate category. This list of psalm types can be bewildering, and a novice reader may be confused about how to label a psalm according to this form-critical scheme. Even experienced form critics sometimes characterize a psalm as "mixed," meaning it has characteristics of several genres and does not fit any existing category. In this wide array of psalm types, the basic division between lament and praise, or recognition of movements into disorientation or into orientation, facilitates reading a prayer for its emotional content and context. Form critics have responded to emotional content and context but have also created a potentially confusing plethora of psalm types based on detailed analysis of structure and language, especially within the category of praise. This close attention to the text is a strength of form criticism, and further subdivision of laments based on close analysis of psalms will be important in the present study. As we shall see, the recognition of "complaint psalms" within the

---

6 Brueggemann, *Message*, 125.

7 See the distinction between declarative and descriptive praise in Westermann, *Praise*, 31–34.

lament category by Craig C. Broyles will have implications for understanding the function and distribution of the motif of weeping in the Psalter.[8]

The present analysis of weeping in the book of Psalms will discuss similar psalms together based on the form-critical categories. The index of form-critical categorizations of psalms complied by Philip S. Johnson helpfully indicates how six scholars have classified every psalm.[9] I have relied on this appendix and other commentators to ensure that my genre classifications for all the psalms in the Psalter are not idiosyncratic. For the psalms discussed in detail (i.e., those involving weeping), some discussion of genre is included, especially when there is disagreement. The psalms that include the motif of weeping are primarily laments, as one would expect. The motif also appears in two thanksgiving psalms, an historical psalm, and a torah psalm. The present analysis will discuss these genres in that order. Then I will review the language used in the weeping motif in psalms. The relationship between divine anger and human tears merits a section of its own.

INDIVIDUAL LAMENTS

There are forty-two psalms that scholars generally agree to categorize as individual laments, which makes them the largest class of psalms.[10] These prayers are characterized by first-person singular language in which the speaker petitions God for deliverance from suffering, which is typically described in vivid but general terms, sometimes mentioning illness or enemies. These prayers may involve shifts in speakers and changes in tone, which sometimes overlap. The changes in tone have been noted since the beginning of form criticism of the Psalms and have become part of the standard structure of the individual lament genre. An individual lament might consist of the following parts, typically in this sequence: address or invocation, complaint, petition, concluding thanks and praise. Some laments include expression of trust in God between the complaint and petition.

---

8 Broyles, *Conflict*.

9 The index appears as appendix 1 in Philip S. Johnson and David G. Firth, eds., *Interpreting the Psalms: Issues and Approaches* (Downers Grove, IL: IVP Academic, 2005), 295–300. The six scholars are: Gunkel, *Introduction*; Leopold Sabourin, *The Psalms: Their Origin and Meaning* (Staten Island, NY: Alba House, 1974); Klaus Seybold, *Die Psalmen*, HAT 1/15 (Tübingen: Mohr Siebeck, 1996); John Day, *Psalms*, OTG (Sheffield: JSOT, 1990); William H. Bellinger, *Psalms: Reading and Studying the Book of Psalms* (Peabody, MA: Hendrickson, 1990); Susan E. Gillingham, *The Poems and Psalms of the Hebrew Bible* (Oxford: Oxford University Press, 1990); and Ernest C. Lucas, *The Psalms and Wisdom Literature*, vol. 3 of *Exploring the Old Testament* (London: SPCK, 2003).

10 These individual laments are: 3; 4; 5; 6*; 7; 9/10; 12; 13; 17; 22; 25; 26; 28; 31; 35; 36; 38; 39*; 42/43*; 51; 54; 55; 56*; 57; 59; 61; 63; 64; 69*; 70; 71; 86; 88; 102*; 109; 120; 130; 138; 140; 141; 142; 143. The asterisk indicates those that mention weeping. Pss 9–10 are understood as one prayer, as are Pss 42–43.

The expression of trust and concluding thanks and praise are moods distinct from the lament and petition. The concluding vow and thanksgiving have received the most attention. Scholars have largely accepted that a movement from lament to praise is characteristic of individual lament psalms. The concluding praise has sometimes obscured interest in the lament, and the movement from lament to praise has itself been the subject of considerable discussion. One solution has posited a liturgical context in which the lamenting speaker receives a divine oracle promising salvation, and the conclusion to the psalm represents the speaker's reaction to the unquoted oracle.[11] Others have looked to internal psychological dynamics rather than external events to explain the shift in mood.[12] The discussion of the inner voice in chapter 1 suggests that there is no hard and fast distinction between voices heard in the social environment and voices within the individual mind. Since the inner voice is dialogic (i.e., it is many voices) and derives from the social environment, the internal psychological explanation and the external liturgical explanation are not mutually exclusive. Carleen Mandolfo has discerned the dialogic nature of the psalms and identified multiple speakers in several psalms. She recognizes that these speakers may reflect social and liturgical realities lost to us but overlooks the dialogic nature of the self. Even if all the speakers are internal, they originate from the social world. Mandolfo postulates based on the biblical textual evidence "that in ancient Israel there was a more or less institutionalized culture of protest, even protest against God."[13] The existence of such sanctioned protest within the social world of Israel would also manifest in the internal voices of individual Israelites, including the authors of the Psalms and their subsequent audiences. She further concludes that, "in the case of lament psalms, access is granted through generic means to transform a disordered situation to one of harmony, a goal that, even on the individual level, is for the ultimate benefit of the entire society. This situation pertains whether we are speaking of congregational or family ritual."[14] I would add private (even silent) prayer to her observations about communal prayer and note that private prayer develops from the modeling of public prayer, as the inner voice develops from the voices heard in the

---

[11] Joachim Begrich, "Das priesterliche Heilsorakel," *ZAW* 52 (1934): 81–92. Similarly, Artur Weiser, *The Psalms*, trans. H. Hartwell, OTL (London: SCM, 1962), 80, 149–52.

[12] Friedrich Heiler, *Prayer: A Study in the History and Psychology of Religion*, ed. and trans. Samuel McComb (London: Oxford University Press, 1932).

[13] Carleen Mandolfo, *God in the Dock: Dialogic Tension in the Psalms of Lament*, JSOTSup 357 (Sheffield: Sheffield Academic; New York: Bloomsbury T&T Clark, 2002) 189. Dorothea Erbele-Küster, *Lesen als Akt des Betens: Ein Rezeptionsästhetik der Psalmen*, WMANT 87 (Hamburg: Neukirchener Verlag, 2001), 111–12 identifies the switching between first and third person as one means by which the text draws the reader into the "I" of the psalms.

[14] Mandolfo, *God*, 194.

environment.[15] Mandolfo correctly sees emotion regulation taking place in these dialogues, although she focuses on the external circumstances that create the dysregulation (e.g., injustice). She also rightly notes that if one person experiences dysregulation, then the whole community is dysregulated. The community therefore provides opportunities for people to transition toward what Brueggemann has termed "new orientation."

Frederico Villanueva's work on mood changes in the psalms advances prior discussion of the sudden shifts from lament to praise by carefully showing that there are multiple patterns of mood changes in many psalms, including movements from praise to lament and multiple shifts between praise and lament. The patterns are significantly more complex than form critics have realized. The conventional wisdom that lament leads to praise has overemphasized praise and relegated lament to a mere preliminary to praise. The dialogic reading of Psalms proposed by Mandolfo and developed by Villanueva and others helps explain why form critics have sometimes had difficulty categorizing psalms into the various forms they developed. Sometimes the confessions of trust, vows, and thanksgivings may be so extensive that scholars cannot agree whether the prayer is a lament or a thanksgiving psalm in which past pain is remembered for the purpose of present praise. Psalms 3 and 4 both provide good examples. Psalm 3 begins with lament and moves quickly to praise. The theme of lament returns briefly in verse 8 before concluding with confidence.[16] The lament that opens the psalm provides sufficient reason for many scholars to identify Ps 3 as a psalm of lament.[17] The change of tone toward praise and confidence provides sufficient reason for others to classify it as a psalm of confidence.[18] Psalm 4 also provides a complex mix of lament and praise that leads to diverse evaluations. The opening plea recalls a past favor, then enters into further lament ("how long?") interspersed with a confident voice of

---

[15] Rolf A. Jacobson and Karl N. Jacobson, *Invitation to the Psalms: A Reader's Guide for Discovery and Engagement* (Grand Rapids, MI: Baker Academic, 2013), 112 note the duality of the psalms generally: "Are the psalms written for individual use, or for the congregation as a whole? As with many such questions, the answer depends in large measure on whom one asks, because the answer is yes." Howard Neil Wallace, *Words to God, Word from God: The Psalms in the Prayer and Preaching of the Church* (Hampshire: Ashgate, 2005) develops the idea of psalms and prayer as dialogue and conversation but without drawing on Bakhtin. He likewise sees similarities between public and private prayer.

[16] Federico G. Villanueva, *The "Uncertainty of a Hearing": A Study of the Sudden Change of Mood in the Psalms of Lament*, VTSup121 (Leiden: Brill, 2008), 52–57 chronicles the attempts of scholars to make sense of v. 8a with their conviction that a shift to praise cannot go back to lament because it does not fit the form of the individual lament. Villanueva thinks the dominant tone of Psalm 3 is trust and confidence.

[17] E.g., Gunkel, *Introduction*, 121 and Bellinger, *Psalms*, 19.

[18] E.g., Sabourin, *Psalms*, 90.

wisdom addressing a plurality of humans (note the masculine plural imperative in v. 4a, 5–6).[19] Some have identified Ps 4 as a psalm of lament.[20] Others have called it a psalm of confidence.[21]

Because the present study examines prayer as emotion regulation, the mood changes in psalms may be expected. People often oscillate between methods of emotion regulation, and emotional experiences can be exceptionally complicated and contradictory. We may indulge in lament and dwell on our suffering, then distract ourselves from the pain with hope of a better future grounded in memories of a happier past. In response to distress, we may feel mixed emotions that are not easily disentangled into a linear progression. The widely accepted cultic explanation for the concluding praise to psalms of lament may have merit, and the psalms may only partially imply a lost liturgical context. But even if we imagine a salvation oracle, we are still well within the realm of psychological coregulation of emotion between a human and a deity with some involvement from a wider human community. If we prefer not to postulate lost sections of text, then such oracles are not strictly required to understand the concluding praise. LeAnn Snow Flesher has argued for a rhetorical reading of the psalms so that the concluding praise is less a reflection of a mood change in the speaker and more a strategy for moving God.[22] Her argument has merit and rightly challenges assumptions that have undergirded prior scholarship, but she too easily separates the emotion of the speaker and the emotion of the deity. Her guiding questions asks: "Are the laments evidence of attempts to change the heart of God, or are they evidence of a shift in mood on the part of the psalmist?"[23] These are not mutually exclusive possibilities. Indeed, because humans coregulate emotions, changing the heart of the deity and the heart of the speaker are intimately related. The anger of the deity creates fear in the petitioner, who then seeks to mollify divine wrath in an effort to assuage his

---

[19] Mandolfo, *God*, 30–35.

[20] Day, *Psalms*, 4 and Bellinger, *Psalms*, 23.

[21] Gunkel, *Introduction*, 121; Gillingham, *Poems*, 225; and Jean-Luc Vesco, *Le psautier de David traduit et commenté*, LD 210–11, 2 vols. (Paris: Cerf, 2006) 1:111–12.

[22] LeAnn Snow Flesher, "Rapid Change of Mood: Oracles of Salvation, Certainty of a Hearing, or Rhetorical Play?," in *"My Words Are Lovely": Studies in the Rhetoric of the Psalms*, ed. Robert L. Foster and David M. Howard Jr., LHBOTS 467 (New York: T&T Clark, 2008), 33–45. Like Flesher, others have undertaken rhetorical readings of lament psalms grounded in the observation by Gunkel, *Introduction*, 169 that "the goal of the complaint song is *to obtain something from YHWH*." See also Broyles, *Conflict*, esp. 14, 29–34.

[23] Flesher, "Rapid Change," 35. Similarly, she concludes: "If the laments are understood as dialogical prayers intended to change the heart of the petitioner, then perhaps the move from petition to oracle to confidence can be interpreted as a sudden change of mood. But, if the laments are understood as petitionary prayers that seek to move the heart of God, then another logical interpretation arises" (44)

own anxiety. The change of mood may then be read, as Flesher proposes, as a rhetorical device designed to move the deity, but it may still reflect or create an emotional shift in the speaker. This emotional shift need not be understood as a simplistic movement from lament to trust over the course of a single prayer. As James L. Mays notes, "we do not begin at one end and come out the other."[24]

Furthermore, the text of a prayer should be understood not as a simple transcript of the inner voice that captures emotional changes in real time but as a rhetorical construct that reflects experience, or at least a rhetorical representation of an experience. (Consider all the times people have prayed Ps 6 without crying.)[25] As people share emotional experiences, their listeners become emotional and responsive to their needs, so emotion is rhetorically powerful.[26] Lament and praise mingle in human experience and therefore also in the psalmic reflection of that experience. Since our emotions are in flux, we live most of life in transition toward disorientation or new orientation. As Westermann observes, the fact that in the Psalter

> there is no, or almost no, such thing as "mere" lament and petition, shows conclusively the polarity between praise and petition in the Psalms. The cry to God is here never one-dimensional, without tension. It is always somewhere in the middle between petition and praise. By nature it cannot be *mere* petition or lament, but is always underway from petition to praise.[27]

Westermann's observation does not mean that concluding praises in the Psalms overwhelm or displace lament; it means that the combination of praise and lament reflect a dynamic of human emotional processing. Even in moments of deep misery we often find some hope, and the expression of lament is an expression of the hope that someone is listening.

Psalm 6

Psalm 6 is the first psalm in the Psalter to include weeping and also provides the most elaborate reference to weeping in the Psalter. It is one of two psalms that employ the motif in two verses, and it uses both בכה and דמעה to speak about weeping (the other is Ps 126). The change of mood from lament to praise has led some commentators to wonder what event must be imagined to explain the shift

---

[24] James L. Mays, "Psalm 13," *Int* 34 (1980): 282.

[25] Davida H. Charney, *Persuading God: Rhetorical Studies of First-Person Psalms* (Sheffield: Sheffield Phoenix, 2016), 1–8 and Herbert Levine, *Sing unto God a New Song: A Contemporary Reading of the Psalms* (Bloomington: Indiana University Press, 1995), 146.

[26] See discussion of social sharing of emotion on pages 11–15.

[27] Westermann, *Praise*, 75.

or theorize that the psalm was originally two psalms.[28] Others rightly argue that Ps 6 shows evidence of unity with repetitions of בהל (vv. 3, 4, 11) and שׁוב (vv. 5, 11).[29] The recurrence of weeping in both sections is more compelling evidence for the connection between them.[30] Although the vocabulary is not common, the motif of weeping appears first as an expression of the speaker's suffering, then as a sound that God has heard and responded to. This use of the motif reflects the understanding of weeping as powerful emotional sharing involved in the coregulation of emotion. Specifically, the weeping of the psalmist calms the anger of YHWH and therefore the frustration of the psalmist. The beginning of the prayer announces God's anger as the primary reason for the prayer in the first two imperative statements:

יהוה אל־באפך תוכיחני	2 YHWH, do not discipline me in your anger
ואל־בחמתך תיסרני	nor chasten me in your wrath

As a result of divine anger, the speaker suffers physically and emotionally. The speaker describes his plight in emotionally evocative terms: he is languishing (אמלל, v. 3), his bones are troubled (נבהלו, v. 3), and his life is very troubled (ונפשי נבהלו מאד, v. 4). Interestingly, the psalmist describes his own emotional state with a term used for anger in v. 8: כעס. Some translate this term as "grief," but Deena Grant argues persuasively that it "relates to anger" and "underscores the pain and sadness that underlie anger."[31] The term in v. 8 might be rendered as "frustration" or "vexation." The speaker responds to divine anger with some anger of his own. The LXX renders both God's אף (v. 2) and the psalmist's כעס as θύμος, establishing a clear and strong parallel between the emotional states of the deity and the

---

28 Weiser, *Psalms*, 130 posits that the last three verses were recited at a later stage in the cult, after the petitioner experienced relief. Hans Schmidt, *Die Psalmen*, HAT 15 (Tübingen: J. C. B. Mohr, 1934), 11 thinks they come from an entirely different song.

29 Villanueva, "*Uncertainty*," 63–64 and Pierre Auffret, "Il a entendu, Yhwh: Étude structurelle du Psaume 6," *ETR* 82 (2007): 595–602. Richard J. Clifford, *Psalms 1–72*, AOTC (Nashville, TN: Abingdon, 2002), 60 notes that the two halves of the psalm (vv. 1–5, 6–10) both consist of thirty-nine words.

30 Fredrik Lindström, *Suffering and Sin: Interpretation of Illness in the Individual Complaint Psalms*, ConBOT 37 (Stockholm: Almqvist & Wiksell, 1994), 133 gives some further details connecting the parts of the poem but deletes v. 2 because it appears to contradict his thesis that individual laments do not assume a connection between sin and suffering. He then devotes more than half his discussion of the psalm to arguing unpersuasively that v. 2 does not really contradict his argument.

31 Deena Grant, *Divine Anger in the Hebrew Bible*, CBQMS 52 (Washington, DC: Catholic Biblical Association of America, 2014), 32.

one praying.[32] The connection as presented in the LXX may be too strong, as the psalmist's anger appears to be directed into weeping and a prayer for mercy rather than an outright attack of the kind evidently imagined as emanating from God. Both terms used to describe divine wrath appear frequently and, when describing divine anger, almost always together. Both terms also draw on a conceptual metaphor of anger as heat, as אף almost always appears with חרה, "to be hot," and חמה may derive from the root חמם, "to be hot."[33] The contexts of both terms emphasize the destructiveness of divine anger as it impacts its target.[34] Both terms denote an anger that is motivated by some wrongdoing, sin, or offense, but the speaker of Ps 6 never indicates what may have motivated YHWH's anger. Instead, he dwells on the consequences of that anger.

The seven imperative petitions that open the psalm pertain to the desire for relationship and social support from the deity: do not rebuke me, do not discipline me, be gracious to me, heal me, turn back, rescue my life, heal me.[35] Three of the imperatives are followed by motive clauses. The first two focus on the psalmist's need, and the last on the merciful nature of God and God's presumed need for praise, which the dead cannot give (cf. Ps 88:12–13). The second motive clause includes the question "how long?" This string of imperatives and motive clauses culminates in the motif of weeping in verses 7–8:

יגעתי באנחתי	7 I am exhausted from my sighing
אשחה בכל־לילה מטתי	Every night I flood my bed
בדמעתי ערשי אמסה	I soak my couch with my tears
עששה מכעס עיני	8 My eyes grow dim because of my grief
עתקה בכל־צוררי	They are worn out because of all my foes

[32] Augustine, *Expositions of the Psalms*, trans. Maria Boulding, 6 vols. (Hyde Park, NY: New City, 2000–2006), 1:109 notes that the Greek text may refer to the psalmist's own anger or his experience of the anger of God. The Hebrew idiom is not so ambiguous, but it indicates the speaker's emotional state.

[33] Grant, *Divine Anger*, 27–28. See also Ellen van Wolde, "Sentiments as Culturally Constructed Emotions: Anger and Love in the Hebrew Bible," *BibInt* 16 (2008): 1–24; as well as H. Julia Eksner, "Indexing Anger and Aggression: From Language Ideologies to Linguistic Affect," and Cristina Soriano, "Emotion and Conceptual Metaphor," both in *Methods of Exploring Emotions*, ed. Helena Flam and Jochen Kleres (London: Routledge, 2015), 193–205 and 206–214, respectively.

[34] Grant, *Divine Anger*, 22–30.

[35] Antonius Kuckhoff, *Psalm 6 und die Bitten im Psalter: Ein paradigmatisches Bitt- und Klagegebet im Horizont des Gesamtpsalters*, BBB 160 (Göttingen: Bonn University Press, 2011) provides an excellent analysis of the psalm and the parallels with imperatives in the Psalter but does not provide a similar contextual analysis of the weeping motif.

The term אשחה means “to cause to swim.” The psalmist claims that his tears are so copious that they float his bed. Some commentators have reacted negatively to this hyperbolic claim.[36] Perhaps motivated by a similar distaste for the image, Wolfram von Soden suggested that the term has the meaning “to flood, overflow.”[37] He identifies שחה as an Aramaic loanword, and this proposal has been widely accepted.[38] Oswald Loretz notes that von Soden’s interpretation corresponds with an Ugaritic parallel in *KTU* 1.14 i.28–30:[39]

tntkn . udmʿth	his tears are poured forth
km . ṯqlm . arṣh	like shekels on the ground
km ḫmšt . mṭth	like five-weight shekels on the couch

Kirta moistens his bed with tears. The psalmist uses stronger imagery that exaggerates the volume of tears, but the image of weeping on a bed or couch is common to both texts. Like the speaker in Ps 6, Kirta weeps at night and finds divine help.[40] Kirta falls asleep on his tear-soaked bed and receives a vision from El telling him how to get an heir. The speaker in Ps 6 expresses confidence in divine assistance in verses 9–11 but provides no explanation for this change of tone. Nighttime is elsewhere identified as a time for weeping (Ps 42:4; Lam 1:2; 2:18) and prayer generally (Pss 16:7; 17:3; 42:9; 77:7–10; 88:1–2; 92:3; 119:55, 62; 134:1). Psalm 30:6 identifies night as a time for weeping and morning as a time for rejoicing, and the theme of salvation in the morning appears in several texts (Pss 5:4; 46:6; 88:14; 90:14).[41] Although night and day may contrast like sorrow and joy, some texts combine night and day to emphasize the continuity and duration of suffering and weeping (Ps 42:4; Lam 2:18).

Both von Soden’s interpretation and the traditional understanding share a common image of copious tears soaking the bed or making it float. This image of

---

[36] John Goldingay, *Psalms*, BCOTWP, 3 vols. (Grand Rapids, MI: Baker Academic, 2006–8), 1:138.

[37] Wolfram von Soden, “Ist im Alten Testament schon vom Schwimmen die Rede?,” *ZAH* 4 (1991): 165–70.

[38] Kuckhoff, *Psalm 6*, 33, 80 and Oswald Loretz, “Psalm 6: Klagelied enes Einzeln: Totenklage im Keret-Epos und Weinen in Ps 6,7b–8 und Ps 55,4,” in *Psalmstudien: Kolometrie, Strophik und Theologie ausgewählter Psalmen* (Berlin: de Gruyter, 2002) 75–102, esp. 84.

[39] Loretz, “Psalm 6,” 84.

[40] Loretz, “Psalm 6,” 86.

[41] Joseph Ziegler, “Dir Hilfe Gottes ‘am Morgen,’” in *Alttestamentliche Studien: Friedrich Nötscher zum 60. Geburtstag Gewidmet* (Bonn: Hanstein, 1950), 281–88; J. W. McKay, “Psalms of Vigil,” *ZAW* 91 (1979): 231–47; and Bernd Janowski, *Rettungsgewissheit und Epiphanie des Heils: Das Motiv der Hilfe Gottes “am Morgen” im Alten Orient und im Alten Testament*, WMANT 59 (Neikirchen-Vluyn: Neukirchener Verlag, 1989).

flooding tears connects the psalmist's tears to the wider motif of flooding water representing chaos and destruction.[42] In several psalms, the speaker uses the image of flooding water to represent his precarious position and desperate need for help (e.g., Pss 18:5; 42:8; 69:2–3; 88:8). Only Ps 6 establishes a connection between these dangerous flooding waters and the speaker's own tears. Psalms 42 and 102 mention tears and the chaotic waters, but they are not connected as in Ps 6. In Ps 6, the rhetoric of weeping as a signal of distress and motive for divine help is combined with the motif of flooding water to heighten the appeal for help by combining two separate images: the weeping suppliant and the petitioner encompassed by water. This striking image of the weeper drowning in his own tears paints a vivid picture of emotional pain, anxiety, and need for rescue.

After the speaker articulates this detailed description of his weeping, the next line builds on this motif but changes mood and address in v. 9. Instead of speaking to God seeking help, the psalmist speaks about God to the evil doers. The change in emotion from anxiety to confidence represents an example of the famous change of mood in individual laments. The emotional shift is explained by God's response to the speaker's tears:

סורו ממני כל־פעלי און	9 Depart form me all you evildoers
כי שמע יהוה קול בכיי	For YHWH has heard the sound of my weeping
שמע יהוה תחנתי	10 YHWH has heard my supplication
יהוה תפלתי יקח	YHWH has received my prayer

The continuity of the weeping motif across the petition and confidence sections of Ps 6 strongly suggests that, in the suppliant's view, his weeping plays a key role in his salvation. To hear the sound of weeping, like hearing supplication and receiving prayer, means to respond with empathy and help. In 2 Kgs 20:5 (// Isa 38:5), God responds to Hezekiah's tearful prayer: "I have heard your prayer, I have seen your tears. Now I am healing you." Weeping is a powerful plea for pity and help, and the speaker of Ps 6 verbalizes his weeping to motivate God to heed his petition, then identifies his weeping as the key to God's favorable response. The text may reflect the sad type of crying, although it is not clear. More importantly, the psalm presents weeping as an effective means of softening God's wrath and gaining divine mercy. It presents night as a time for weeping. It speaks in one voice throughout, but the audience includes both God and an audience of "evildoers." The prayer is motivated by illness, and the speaker coregulates with God to alleviate his own anxiety and God's related wrath. The ending expresses the desired

---

[42] Kuckhoff, *Psalm 6*, 140.

change of emotion, which correlates with a rebuke to the (previously unmentioned) evildoers because God has heard the sufferer's prayer.

PSALM 39

Psalm 39 reflects emotion regulation in explicit terms. The speaker describes trying to be silent in the presence of the wicked but becoming increasingly overwrought such that silence becomes impossible, and the speaker then shares his frustrations with God in prayer.[43] The prayer consists of four parts: verses 2–4, 5–7, 8–12, and 13–14. The first and third parts develop the theme of silence, and the second and fourth the theme of the transience of human life.[44] The silence of the psalmist is part of a coping process that ends when he finally articulates the prayer. The silence and inactivity of God suggests divine collaboration in a situation perceived as unjust that motivates the psalmist's petition.[45] The poem opens with quoted inner speech. The opening "I said" appears to be inner speech because there is no external addressee, and the content of the inner speech focuses on the need to stay silent. The speaker draws on an inner voice in an attempt to regulate emotion and behavior. This inward dialogue ultimately fails, and the speaker addresses God in a speech that appears to be uttered aloud ("with my tongue"), although this speech may be understood as an internal discourse directed at God as distinct from the previous speech to the self. The key point is that the emotional turmoil overwhelms the individual's resources such that the speaker turns to God for help and support.

The speaker describes his emotional arousal in vivid terms in verses 3–4. Keeping silent does not work.[46] His distress (כאב) grows worse, his heart becomes hot (חם־לבי), and he says, "As I mused, the fire burned." The outpouring of speech reads like a well-considered meditation on the brevity of human life (vv. 5–6).[47]

---

[43] Psalm 73 provides a similar first-person narrative of effortful emotional regulation.

[44] Clifford, *Psalms 1–72*, 197–98 and Pierre Auffret, "'Car toi, tu as agi': Etude structurelle du Psaume 39," *Bijdr* 51 (1990): 118–38.

[45] Eleuterio Ramón Ruiz, "El silencio en el primero libro del Salterio (Salmos 1–41): Primera parte," *RevistB* 67 (2005): 31–83, esp. 75–80. See also Ruiz, "El silencio en el primero libro del Salterio (Salmos 1–41): Segunda parte," *RevistB* 67 (2005): 163–78. He builds on the prior work of Silvio José Báez, *Tiempo de callar y tiempo de hablar: El silencio en la Biblia Hebrea* (Rome: Teresianum, 2000), esp. 135–41. Báez sees the silence of the psalmist as ineffective in vv. 2–4 but resigned in v. 10.

[46] The preposition מן here is a privative marker of what is missing; see *IBHS* 11.2.II.e.2. The psalmist's silence does no good.

[47] The petition in v. 5 to know the brevity of life (see also Ps 90:12) is normally understood as an attempt to find equanimity in the face of suffering by reflecting on the shortness of life and therefore pain. Richard J. Clifford, "What Does the Psalmist Ask For in Psalms

The poem then briefly introduces another voice that also accentuates the brevity of human life (v. 7).[48] This voice resembles the wisdom tradition, making a general observation about human existence that stands outside the first- and second-person language of the surrounding verses. The voice is integrated in other ways. The first two lines begin with אך, like the last line of the speaker in verse 6. The content of the expressions also fits the speaker's theme of the brevity of human life. This voice affirms the speaker's perspective. The image of accumulating wealth without knowing who will profit appears in wisdom contexts (e.g., Eccl 2:18–23) and connects with the reference to moths in verse 12. This shift in voice shows the dialogic nature of the prayer, whether understood as a private prayer by one person or a public liturgy with several speakers. Following this interjection, the psalmist's speech to God resumes with a new emphasis: instead of dwelling on the shortness of life, the prayer now turns to petition. The petitions focus on seeking relief from suffering brought by God as punishment for sin and culminate in a reference to weeping:

הסר מעלי נגעך	11 Remove from me your blow.
מתגרת ידך אני כליתי	From the strength[49] of your hand I am exhausted.
בתוכחות על־עון יסרת איש	12 With rebukes for sin you discipline man,
ותמס כעש המודו	you consume like a moth what is dear to him.[50]
אך הבל כל־אדם סלה	Surely every man is a breath! Selah
שמעה־תפלתי יהוה	13 Hear my prayer, YHWH
ושועתי האזינה	and to my cry give ear!
אל־דמעתי אל־תחרש	At my tears, do not be silent,
כי גר אנכי עמך	for a sojourner I am with you,
תושב ככל־אבותי	an alien like all my ancestors.

39:5 and 90:12?," *JBL* 119 (2000): 59–66 has proposed instead that the speaker wants to know the limits of the period of divine wrath.

48 Mandolfo, *God* does not discuss Ps 39, but this interjection resembles the kind of wisdom voice she discerns in other laments.

49 The meaning of this hapax is uncertain. LXX and P may be reading מגבורת, "strength" or interpreting the MT term in this sense. In construct with "hand," the expression continues the image of violent physical contact from the previous line.

50 A few manuscripts read חמדו, "his beauty," perhaps meaning the beautiful things he owns rather than his personal beauty. The MT reading refers to what a person treasures or desires, which must here be materials made of fibers that moths can consume. LXX reads "you melt like a spider web their soul."

השע ממני ואבליגה	[14] Look away from me[51] so that I may revive
בתרם אלך ואינני	before I depart and am not.

The speaker identifies God as the cause of his suffering and therefore also as the source of hope for relief. The prayer does not employ any of the vocabulary for anger, but it does use terms associated with the consequences of divine wrath. Rebukes (תוכחות) and discipline (יסר) are often motivated by anger as in Ps 6:2. The prayer assumes that God's anger at sin leads to punishment (Ps 39:12) in a context complaining of suffering at God's hand (v. 11). God's discipline for sin focuses on hitting people where it hurts. Like a moth, God targets what one loves (המודו). There are two ways that moths may torment a householder: consuming grains or fabrics. Different species specialize in each. Biblical references to moths identify clothing as the target of damage, but never food (Job 13:28; Isa 50:9; 51:8; Jas 5:2). The moth species *tineola bassellieila*, native to western Asia, avoids light and dwells in dark places like closets. It lays its eggs in the folds and corners of fabrics where its larvae hatch and feed on natural fibers. As with most moth species, the moths do not actually feed at all but only mate and lay eggs. They prefer fabric that is dirty or stained with sweat, which provides minerals for the larvae. They can survive on an extraordinary range of fibers as well as feathers and grains. Once established, they are difficult to eradicate, especially without modern technologies.[52] Biblical texts therefore rightly associate moths with destruction and decay (Job 4:19; Hos 5:12; Matt 6:19–20; Luke 12:23). Most Israelite clothing was made from wool that was spun and woven by hand and was much more expensive than clothing in the modern era of mechanized mass production. Clothing ranks with gold and silver jewelry as a significant source of wealth (Exod 3:22; 12:35). As a result, moth damage could be much more ruinous for an ancient Israelite than for most modern people who can replace damaged clothing relatively inexpensively.

---

[51] The MT השע is a rare term that refers to "sealing, smearing" eyes to make a person blind (Isa 6:10; 29:9). The sense of the *hiphil* here appears to be "shut (your eyes) to me" or as often rendered "look away from me." The second translation closely resembles the expression שעה מעלי in Job 14:6, from the verb שעה, "to gaze." Some emend השע in Ps 39:14 to שעה to resemble Job 14:6. In either case, the sense of Ps 39:14 closely resembles that of Job 14:6.

[52] D. Stuart, "Moth," *ISBE* 3:426. Modern people can use various chemical repellents (e.g., mothballs) or seal stored clothes in airtight containers. Ancient Israelites, like others around the world, may have used such plants as wormwood or rosemary to prevent moth infestations in fabrics; see Renata Sõukand, Raivo Kalle, and Ingvar Svanberg, "Uninvited Guests: Traditional Insect Repellents in Estonia Used against the Clothes Moth *Tineola bisselliella*, Human Flea *Pulex irritans*, and Bedbug *Cimex lectularius*," *Journal of Insect Science* 10 (2010): 1–18.

The text of Ps 39 does not present moth damage as divine punishment, but it does understand moth damage to expensive fabrics as analogous to divine damage inflicted on people. This damage afflicts "what he loves," which might refer to a person's health, wealth, or close relationships. This lament concludes with a brief interjection that reprises the theme of the brevity of human life, a reflection related to the image of the decay caused by the moth.

The speaker asks God three times to pay attention to the petition for relief. The first two occur often in the Psalms: "listen" (שמעה, v. 13) and "give ear" (האזינה, v. 13). The third involves weeping and a negative plea: "do not hold your peace at my tears" (אל דמעתי אל־תחרש, v. 13). The verb provides yet another connection to the theme of silence in the psalm (vv. 2–3, 10), but now the focus is on the silence of God rather than the psalmist. Even the reference to weeping is silent: the speaker refers to tears rather than to the noise of sobbing (cf. Ps 6:9). The speaker then provides a reason why God should respond that returns to the theme of the brevity of human life. The shortness of human life should remind an immortal deity to have pity on human creatures.

The conclusion to the prayer provides a striking contrast to the pleas for divine attention that immediately precede it. The speaker's final petition is that God may "look away from me" (v. 14). Divine neglect should allow some brief joy before the speaker dies. This conclusion, reminiscent of Job 7:19 and 14:6, represents a change of mood quite different from the joy and praise that have drawn so much attention in other psalms. The type of crying is difficult to discern with the passing reference to tears. The motif of silence suggests sad crying, but the cry (שועתי, v. 13) may reflect protest. The motive for the prayer involves the speaker's unspecified suffering, and the text alludes to the speaker's need to coregulate with God after failing to regulate alone. The prayer includes both the voice of the speaker and a third-person wisdom voice, and it identifies the self as having multiple parts or aspects ("my heart burned within me"). As a result of the weeping and prayer, the petitioner expects relief in the form of divine neglect. God's attentiveness to the petitioner has been a source of pain, so the solution is not God's kindness so much as God's indifference. The text arguably resembles the prayer of an avoidantly attached person[53] who seeks independence rather than interdependence and has an internal working model of God as unhelpful or sabotaging. The speaker expects not that God can become kind and supportive but that God might be persuaded to go away, thereby removing the source of trouble.

[53] See pages 6–7.

PSALM 42–43

Scholars generally agree that Pss 42 and 43 are one psalm as indicated by the refrain that appears in 42:6, 12; 43:5, 10b. The lack of a superscription to Ps 43 also supports this conclusion.[54] The refrain reflects the dialogic nature of the self:

מה־תשתוחחי נפשי	6 Why are you cast down, my self,
ומה־תהמי עלי	and why are you disquieted within me?
הוחילי לאלהים כי עוד אודנו	Hope in God, for I shall again praise him
ישועת פני ואלהי	my help and 7 my God[55]

The speaker addresses his **נפש** like a separate person. If one wonders who speaks and who listens in self-talk, the answer in the Psalms appears to be that the "I" (**אנכי**) speaks and the "self" (**נפש**) listens. The **נפש** is evidently capable of speaking but is never quoted: "Bless, O YHWH, my **נפש**" (Ps 103:2). The direct address to the **נפש** in the refrain of Ps 42–43 coheres with the **נפש** in the remainder of the prayer. It is the **נפש** that longs and thirsts for God and is "cast down." The psalmist "pours out" his **נפש**, an image that appears to connect to weeping, or at least petition. Hannah also pours out her **נפש** to YHWH in 1 Sam 1:15 (cf. Job 30:16; Lam 2:12). The water image in Ps 42 reflects the pleasant familiar stream in a desert in the first stanza (42:2) and intensifies into the waters of chaos in the second stanza (42:8).[56] Tears contribute to the wider water imagery:

כאיל תערג על־אפיקי־מים	2 As a deer longs for streams of water
כן נפשי תערג אליך אלהים	so my life longs for you, God.
צמאה נפשי לאלהים לאל חי	3 My life thirsts for God, the living God
מתי אבוא ואראה פני אלהים	When will I come and see the face of God?
היתה־לי דמעתי לחם יומם ולילה	4 My tears have been my bread day and night
באמר אלי כל־היום איה אלהיך	As they ask me every day "Where is your God?"

---

[54] Gerald H. Wilson, "The Use of 'Untitled' Psalms in the Psalter," *ZAW* 97 (1985): 404–13, esp. 407–8.

[55] The quoted text follows the MT of the refrain as given in 42:12 and 45:5. Small errors appear to have crept into its first appearance in the poem, errors that should be harmonized with its subsequent repetitions.

[56] Luis Alonzo Schökel, "The Poetic Structure of Psalm 42–43," *JSOT* 1 (1976): 4–11, esp. 7–8 and Alonzo Schökel and Cecilia Carniti, *Salmos*, Nueva Biblia Española, 2 vols. (Villatuerta: Editorial Verbo Divino, 1992–1993), 1:616–17.

This expression ties weeping to the crisis of separation from God and may imply, as in Ps 102, that the psalmist is fasting as a means of petitioning God. But the parallel in Ps 102:10 suggests that the tears may accompany food. The line refers to weeping as something the psalmist does day and night, stressing the quantity of tears and the continuity or frequency of weeping. Tears as food rather than water heightens the contrast between what the psalmist needs (he needs God like he needs food and water), and what he gets (tears are a poor substitute for food).[57] The reference to tears as sustenance occurs in immediate juxtaposition to the question asked by an indefinite "they" (identified as enemies when the question is repeated in v. 11): "Where is your God?" The speaker focuses throughout on his social isolation, his separation from God, and his hope for future restoration of a happier past (described in vv. 5–6). The poem continues in Ps 43, but this third stanza does not return to the motif of tears, although the theme of isolation continues. The hopeful conclusion to the threefold refrain indicates that the speaker maintains hope of divine response to his tears.

The first two stanzas include water imagery beyond the one reference to tears. The speaker "pours out" his נפש in 42:5, suggesting that his life or self is liquid (cf. 1 Sam 1:15). Like the first stanza, the second opens with water imagery, but now the waters are the destructive and threatening waters of chaos rather than the life-giving waters desired in the first stanza. These destructive waters are not identified with the speaker's tears as in Ps 6, but, like the tears, they indicate the seriousness of the psalmist's distress and need for divine deliverance. The mention of tears vividly depicts the speaker's isolation and desire for relationship with God. The weeping may reflect protest or sad crying in an effort to reestablish relationship. The urgency of the deer's need for water may reflect the urgency of protest, and the water imagery generally heightens the sense of anxiety that drives the weeping.

The prayer responds to the threat of separation from God as an attachment figure, and the weeping is a strategy to regain proximity to God. The weeping is not described in enough detail to determine whether the sad or angry type of crying is in view, although the overall tone of the poem may suggest a sad and plaintive weeping. The weeping is depicted as constant, specifically including the nighttime. The language indicates a dialogic view of the self and explicitly quotes inner speech. The speaker hopes for reunion with God that will correlate with liberation for enemies and turns to God as an attachment figure with whom to coregulate emotions.

---

[57] Wong Fook Kong, "Use of Overarching Metaphors in Psalms 91 and 42/43," *Sino-Christian Studies* 9 (2010): 7–27, esp. 19–20 and Adele Berlin, "On Reading Biblical Poetry: The Role of Metaphor," in *Congress Volume: Cambridge 1995*, ed. J. A. Emerton, VTSup 66 (Leiden: Brill, 1997), 25–36, esp. 31.

PSALM 56

Scholars concur that Ps 56 is an individual lament even though expressions of confidence and praise exceed the petitions and lament. This praise appears as part of the typical form of the individual lament, which includes petition and complaint (vv. 2–3, 6–8), statements of trust (vv. 4–5, 9–12), and promise of praise (vv. 13–14). In his study of mood changes in the Psalms, Villanueva identifies Ps 56 as showing a shift from lament (vv. 2–10a) to praise (vv. 10b–14), which overlooks the intrusion of praise in vv. 4–5.[58] Thus Ps 56 shows a pattern of lament–praise–lament–praise and therefore shares the same pattern with Pss 31, 59, and 71. These shifts of mood do not coincide with any change of voice, as the language uses first person throughout. The psalmist speaks of his נפש in the sense of his "life" (vv. 7, 14) rather than as an aspect of his self that he speaks to or about. The reference to weeping appears not in an expected expression of lament but in the context of a statement of trust. The speaker complains about the assaults of enemies but expresses confidence in God's protection expressed in the refrain "In God I trust, I do not fear. What can flesh do to me?" (vv. 5, 11). Weeping is mentioned in a way that expresses the psalmist's distress in the context of his trust in God in v. 9:

נדי ספרתה אתה	My wanderings you have noted.[59]
שימה דמעתי בנאדך	Are my tears not stored in your flask?[60]
הלא בספרתך	Are they not in your book?

The container for collecting the tears is a skin flask commonly used to carry liquids when traveling (Josh 9:4, 12–13; 1 Sam 16:20), which fits the sense of נד as "wandering" rather than "tossing."[61] The term also establishes paranomasia between "my wandering" (נדי) and "your flask" (נאדך). There is also wordplay between "you have noted" (ספרתה) and "your book" (ספ־תך). The dual images of the bottle and book indicate the psalmist's confidence that God has observed his suffering. Although the idea that God has a book appears elsewhere (Exod 32:32; Mal 3:16; Job 19:23), the gathering of tears in a flask occurs only here. There is no evidence that ancient Israelites collected tears in containers. Small glass bottles are found in

---

58 Villanueva, *"Uncertainty,"* 49. He does not discuss Ps 56 in detail, but he does include it in his chart of mood changes.

59 Following the imperatives in v. 8, Goldingay, *Psalms*, 2:187 takes the perfect verb as a precative: "May you yourself have recorded my lamenting."

60 The LXX reads "you put my tears before you," which captures the meaning of collecting tears in a flask.

61 Carey Ellen Walsh, *The Fruit of the Vine: Viticulture in Ancient Israel*, HSM 60 (Winona Lake, IN: Eisenbrauns, 2000), 216–17.

tombs dating to Roman times throughout the Mediterranean basin that were formerly believed to be lacrymatories in which mourners collected their tears to deposit in the grave. Scholars now think they are unguentaria that contained perfumes or ointments.[62] The language of Ps 56 probably does not reflect any Israelite custom of collecting tears but expresses God's concern for the speaker.[63] Or, rather, the speaker expresses his confidence that God has seen his tears (cf. 2 Kgs 20:5) and heard his weeping (cf. Ps 39:13).

The psalm seems to reflect sad crying rather than protest crying. Although the motive (overcoming separation) is shared with Ps 42, the imagery is less urgent and the prayer reflects more trust. The striking image of the flask reflects confidence rather than anxiety. This confidence indicates an expectation of salvation from the environmental adversity (enemies) that motivates the prayer. The speaker seeks to down-regulate anxieties related to the enemies who oppress him and up-regulate a sense of safety and confidence. God is the emotion regulation partner and source of a sense of security.

Psalm 69

Commentators concur that Ps 69 in an individual lament. It reminds many of Jeremiah because it appears to represent the situation of someone who suffers persecution as a consequence of loyalty to YHWH and involves references to sinking in waters that recall Jeremiah in the cistern (Jer 38). The reference to rebuilding the cities of Judah (v. 36) implies a postexilic context. The independent pronouns at the start of several verses alternate between second person (אתה, vv. 6, 20) and first person (אני, vv. 14, 30). These independent pronouns mark five divisions of the prayer (vv. 2–5, 6–13, 14–19, 20–29, 30–37). The third and fourth sections repeat words and motifs from the first two sections in the same sequence, implying a deeper break at verse 14. Both halves of the lament begin with references to God's saving (הושיעני, v. 2; ישעך, v. 14) the psalmist from sinking in the deep (טבעתי, v. 3; אטבעה, v. 15), deep waters (מעמקי־מים, vv. 3, 15), and flood (שבלת, vv. 3, 16). Both include lament about enemies (איבי, vv. 5, 19) and "those who hate me" (משנאי, vv. 5, 15) and refer to God's knowledge (ידעתי, vv. 6, 20) of the

[62] Virginia R. Anderson-Stojanovic, "The Chronology and Function of Ceramic Unguentaria," *AJA* 91 (1987): 105–22; Andrea M. Berlin, "Archeological Sources of the History of Palestine. Between Large Forces: Palestine in the Hellenistic Period," *BA* 60 (1997): 32–33; Karen B. Stern, "Keeping the Dead in Their Place: Mortuary Practices and Jewish Cultural Identity in Roman North Africa," in *Cultural Identity on the Ancient Mediterranean*, ed. Erich S. Gruen (Los Angeles, CA: Getty Research Institute, 2011), 317.

[63] Alonzo Schökel and Carniti, *Salmos*, 1:767–68. Clifford, *Psalms 1–72*, 267 calls this "one of the most memorable images in the Psalter" and likens it to the practice of shepherds keeping track of their lambs by keeping pebbles in a bag.

speaker's shame (בוש, vv. 7, 20), dishonor (כלם, vv. 7, 20), and reproach (חרפה, vv. 8, 21). The prayer maintains a second person address throughout the lament but shifts to speaking of God in the third person in the third verse of the concluding praise (v. 32). This shift suggests a change of addressee rather than change in speaker. The admission of guilt in the opening of the second section has caused problems for commentators who think there should be no such admission. Some identify verse 6 as a later insertion.[64] Others interpret the verse as a protestation of innocence.[65] The verse appears to acknowledge some wrongdoing, but nothing so serious as to merit the suffering the speaker experiences.[66] Similarly, Job acknowledges that he may have sinned, but his suffering is massively disproportionate (Job 7:20–21). Lamentations 1:14 and 22 acknowledge Zion's "rebellions" (פשע), but the fuller context vigorously denies that these sins merit the punishment inflicted. Psalm 69, like Job and Lamentations, focuses on human suffering as a challenge to divine justice, but this argument does not require pretensions of perfect innocence.

As often in the Psalms, the speaker's sufferings are not precisely clear. The psalmist here likens his situation to one flailing in deep waters. The opening verses do not refer to weeping, but crying out with reference to dim eyes and overwhelming water seems so suggestive of crying that some translations render קרא as "crying" (RSV, NRSV) rather than "crying out" (NABRE). The speaker mentions weeping in the next section in a different context. The second section (vv. 6–13) opens with a petition but makes an intercessory rather than direct appeal. The speaker asks that others who hope in God "not be brought to shame through me" (v. 7). The speaker elaborates on the theme of shame, which is central to the prayer, and claims to have suffered shame and consequent social alienation "for your sake" (vv. 7–8). The psalm continues in this vein:

כי קנאת ביתך אכלתני וחרפות חורפיך נפלו עלי	10 For zeal for your house consumes me and the insults of those who insult fall on me

64 Lindström, *Suffering*, 341–43.

65 Clifford, *Psalms 1–72*, 322–23 connects the statement to the immediately following verse to argue that the speaker claims innocence in v. 6, and that others will be discouraged if they see the speaker suffer for his righteousness. Goldingay, *Psalms*, 2:341–42 connects the statement to the immediately preceding verse and reads v. 6 as a logical expression of the stupidity of sin given God's omniscience.

66 Craig C. Broyles, *Psalms*, NICOT (Peabody, MA: Hendrickson, 1999), 287 acknowledges that v. 6 includes a confession of guilt but notes that it "is not developed beyond the next verse, and thus does not appear to be a key issue in the psalm."

ואבכה בצום נפשי	11 I weep,[67] my life is in fasting
ותהי לחרפון לי	and it becomes an insult to me.
ואתנה לבושי שק	12 I changed my clothing for sackcloth
ואהי להם למשל	and I became I byword to them
ישיחו בי ישבי שער	13 they talk about me, who sit in the gate
ונגינות שותי שכר	drinking songs drunkards (sing about me).

The details remain vague, but the speaker claims to be loyal to God at a time when most people are not. The zeal for God's house (temple) manifests as fasting and weeping, which are here public displays of grief.[68] By these actions, the psalmist demonstrates passionate concern about something seriously wrong in society or perhaps specifically the temple, but others do not share this consternation. Indeed, others may (correctly) see that the psalmist criticizes their own behavior and therefore they turn against him. He is alienated from his own family (kin, mother's children, v. 9) and the community as a whole. The respected leaders of the community and the lowly despised members of the city mentioned in verse 13 constitute a merism for the whole society. Since the petitioner suffers for the sake of God, the strong implication is that God should do something to save his situation. As the speaker continues to endure humiliation, others who love God may similarly suffer or abandon God.

The weeping appears in an unusual context in this psalm. The weeping does *not* occur as directed primarily at God in the midst of distress as his "calling out" does in verse 4. As described in verse 11, the speaker weeps and fasts as a display of grief in which others do not share. Indeed, these others respond to the speaker's grief with anger and humiliate him. His reference to his weeping, then, is not a present crying directed toward God as in Pss 6, 39, 42–43, or 56 but a recollection of past habitual behavior that is not a direct part of the present prayer. One may imagine that the psalmist has been previously fasting and weeping while asking God to repair whatever problems caused this zealous person to seek divine intervention. This public act, however, made his suffering worse, because his community did not share in his perspective and, rather than joining him, decided

67 The NRSV deletes weeping from this passage by following LXX συνέκαμψα, "I bent," perhaps reflecting a vorlage with ואדכה or ואענה. Denise Dumbkowski Hopkins, *Psalms Books 2–3*, Wisdom Commentary 21 (Collegeville, MN: Liturgical Press, 2016), 199–207 follows the NRSV and locates weeping in v. 3 but not in v. 11. Erhard S. Gerstenberger, "Psalm 69: Complaint and Confession," *Covenant Quarterly* 55 (1987): 3–19, esp. 5 similarly characterizes v. 3 as "a sordid description of crying and pleading to God." Leslie C. Allen, "The Value of Rhetorical Criticism in Psalm 69," *JBL* 105 (1986): 577–98, esp. 594 identifies several parallels between Pss 69 and 102 that argue in favor of reading the MT (because 102:10 refers to weeping), although he inexplicably proposes a *piel* pointing.

68 See Ps 35:13–14, where the psalmist fasts for sick people who then turn on him.

to mock him.[69] The social consequences of his public grief intensify his misery and motivate his present prayer. The original issue involving the temple fades into the background as the psalm focuses on the present (but related) problem of social alienation and shame. This focus becomes clear in the imprecations in Ps 69:19–29. This background to the psalmist's weeping demonstrates a negative reaction to tears. As noted previously, tears may elicit empathy or anger. The psalmists generally assume that God will respond with empathy to their tears, but this psalmist describes the anger his tears provoke from his community, even his own family. The type of crying (sad or protest) is hard to discern from the minimal indications, but the unexpectedly negative social response comes through clearly. The prayer is motivated by social conflict within the speaker's environment. God appears in the prayer as an emotion regulation partner and source of salvation. There is no voice other than the petitioner's in the text.

Psalm 102

Even though it blends individual and communal language, commentators agree that Ps 102 is an individual lament, perhaps because the unusual superscription points clearly in this direction: תפלה לעני כי־יעטף ולפני יהוה ישפך שיחו, "A prayer of an afflicted one, when he is faint and pours out his complaint before YHWH." This superscription reads like an ancient Hebrew way of saying "individual lament." The term "prayer" in the superscription reappears in the prayer itself in verses 2 and 18 (twice). The prayer has three main parts: an individual lament (vv. 2–12), a communal praise (vv. 13–23) and concluding complaint (vv. 24–29). Some commentators have been puzzled by the combination of individual and communal concerns, but the two are central to the prayer and to the consolation that the psalmist expresses in the end.[70] The first section includes weeping and frequent references to the brevity and fragility of human life.[71] The prayer then

---

69 Saul M. Olyan, *Biblical Mourning: Ritual and Social Dimensions* (Oxford: Oxford University Press, 2004), 88 notes that the person likely had a reasonable expectation that he would be comforted by those who would join him in his separation from others and self-abasement out of solidarity with him and out of agreement with his perspective.

70 Frank-Lothar Hossfeld and Erich Zenger, *Psalms 3: A Commentary on Psalms 101–150*, Hermeneia, trans. Linda M. Maloney (Minneapolis, MN: Augsburg Fortress, 2011), 20 note that "the contrast between the individual and collective is especially obvious"; similarly, see Erhard S. Gerstenberger, *Psalms*, FOTL 14–15, 2 vols. (Grand Rapids, MI: Eerdmans, 1988–2001), 2:211. Andrew Witt, "Hearing Psalm 102 in the Context of the Psalter," *VT* 62 (2012): 582–606 resurrects an older argument that the speaker in Ps 102 is a Davidic king.

71 Amy Cotrill, "The Traumatized 'I' in Psalm 102: A Feminist Biblical Theology of Suffering," in *After Exegesis: Feminist Biblical Theology: Essays in Honor of Carol A. Newsom*, ed. Patricia K. Tull and Jacqueline E. Lapsley (Waco, TX: Baylor University Press, 2015),

shifts into praise that contrasts God's eternity with human frailty and shifts language to the enduring community rather than the short-lived individual. The prayer finally returns the individual's complaint, but the speaker finds comfort in the eternity of God and future generations of the community. The conclusion thereby draws together the lament and praise from the earlier sections.

The first section of the psalm paints a picture of the psalmist's misery:

יהוה שמעה תפלתי	2 Hear my prayer, YHWH
ושועתי אליך תבוא	let my cry come to you!
אל־תסתר פניך ממני	3 Do not hide your face from me
ביום צר לי	in the day of my distress!
הטה־אלי אזנך	Incline your ear to me
ביום אקרא מהר ענני	answer me quickly in the day I call!
כי־כלו בעשן ימי	4 For my days pass away like smoke,
ועצמותי כמו־קר נחרו	and my bones burn like a furnace.
הוכה־כעשב ויבש לבי	5 My heart is smitten like grass and dried out.
כי־שכחתי מאכל לחמי	I forget to eat my food.
מקול אנחתי	6 Because of the sound of my groaning,
דבקה עצמי לבשרי	my bones cling to my flesh
דמיתי לקאת מדבר	7 I am like a desert pelican.
הייתי ככוס חרבות	like an owl among the ruins.
שקדתי ואהיה	8 I lie awake.
כצפור בודד על־גג	I am like a lone bird on the roof.
כל־היום חרפוני אויבי	9 All day my enemies taunt me,
מהוללי בי נשבעו	and those who deride me curse me.
כי־אפר כלחם אכלתי	10 I eat ashes like food,
ושקוי בבכי מסכתי	and mingle my drink with weeping.
מפני־זעמך וקצפך	11 Because of your wrath and anger
כי נשאתני ותשליכני	you have picked me up and thrown me away.
ימי כצל נטוי	12 My days are like an evening shadow,
ואני כעשב איבש	I wither away like grass.

The speaker elaborates on his suffering, which, as is typical in psalms, is vague. The elaborate lament in verses 4–12 makes no unambiguous mention of illness, but it does express a keen sense of the fragility of human life consistent with illness

---

171–86, esp. 182–83 reads this seeming relinquishment of agency as a survival strategy of a traumatized person. The psalmist does not raise the question of theodicy but does acknowledge divine agency in human suffering. Sometimes those who suffer need the world to make sense again and may find solace in divine control and agency.

or other serious threat.[72] The description of misery continues from verse 4 to verse 10 of poetry before identifying the cause as divine anger in verse 11. In the immediate context, God's anger explains why the psalmist weeps. The expression "I mingle my drink with weeping" likely focuses on the frequency or regularity of weeping rather than tears as literal drink. It also implies a copious quantity of tears. The reference to ashes with food and the earlier (seemingly contradictory) statement, "I forget to eat my food," seem to indicate that the speaker is fasting. Fasting occurs in context of supplication (e.g., 2 Sam 12:16; Isa 58:3; Jer 14:12), sometimes with weeping (Judg 20:26; Ps 69:11). The psalmist may be fasting, although his meager food may be a consequence of illness rather than a petitionary strategy.[73] Like fasting and weeping, the mention of ashes evokes supplication in the face of disaster.[74]

The motif of weeping in verse 10 flows from earlier mentions of petition and directly into divine wrath as the ultimate cause of the speaker's suffering. The psalmist speaks of mixing drink with "weeping" (בכי) rather than the expected liquid "tears" (דמעה as in Pss 42:4; 80:6). Tears by themselves can be silent, but "weeping" implies voiced sobbing (cf. Ps 6:9). The speaker may have chosen this term over the more obvious "tears" in order to connect his weeping with previous references to audible petitions. The plea for attention repeats "prayer" (v. 2) from the superscription and adds "cry" (שועתי, v. 2) and "call" (אקרא, v. 2) as things that God should hear (אזנך, v. 3). The speaker later refers specifically to "the sound of my groaning" (מקול אנחתי, v. 6), which initiates a series of references to audible petitions that culminate in "weeping" (בכי, v. 10). These references focus on birds. The calls of the birds seem doleful, and the psalmist colors these sounds with images of loneliness: the owl is in a ruin, and the sparrow is alone. Some birds' songs seem mournful, and the dove is especially famous for its mournful call (Isa 38:14; 59:11; Ezek 7:16). Psalm 102 does not mention doves, however, but uses the general term for bird (צפור) and two terms of uncertain meaning. The term כוס may refer to the tawny owl (*athenae noctua*), and קאת to the white pelican (*pelicanus onocrotalus*).[75] In Ps 102, the isolation of the calling birds underscores their sorrowful

---

[72] Klaus Seybold, *Das Gebet des Kranken im Alten Testament*, BWANT 99 (Stuttgart: Kohlhammer, 1973), 169 identifies Ps 102 as a probable psalm of illness, but not as certainly so as Pss 38, 41, and 88. His other probable illness psalms are 30, 39, 69, and 103. He adds a third rank of possible illness psalms: 6, 13, 32, 35, 51, 71, 73, 91.

[73] Seybold, *Das Gebet*, esp. 138–42.

[74] Hossfeld and Zenger, *Psalms 3*, 23–24.

[75] On birds in the Bible, see Oded Borowski, *Every Living Thing: Daily Use of Animals in Ancient Israel* (Walnut Creek, CA: AltaMira, 1998), 149–54; Tova L. Forti, *"Like a Lone Bird on a Roof": Animal Imagery and the Structure of the Psalms*, CSHB 10 (University Park, PA: Eisenbrauns, 2018), 75–76. To hear the call of any owl species, see Deane Lewis, "The Owl

tone.[76] In the context of this isolation of lonesome birds in desolate places, the psalmist then mentions mixing his drink with tears and accuses God as the cause of his suffering (v. 11: "because of your furious wrath, you lifted me up only to cast me down") and again likens himself to withering grass (vv. 12; cf. v. 5). The wider context of the prayer contrasts the fleeting lifetime of the speaker with the eternal existence of God and begs God to extend the life of the psalmist (v. 25) and the community (v. 29, cf. 19).[77] The mention of weeping heightens the speaker's depiction of his misery and isolation and therefore hopefully God's motivation to extend his life (v. 23).

The speaker understands YHWH's "wrath" and "anger" as the sources of his present suffering (מפני־זעמך וקצפך, v. 11) and deploys several strategies in prayer to address the root of his misery. Both these terms for anger appear in contexts that emphasize the consequences of anger and its destructive power.[78] In Ps 102, the consequences are first described in terms of the speaker's misery, then divine anger finally identified as the cause. God is then the subject of verbs of attack on the petitioner ("you have picked me up and thrown me away," v. 11). The psalmist identifies his audible supplication in several ways at the start of the prayer, then heightens these with poetic images of lone birds calling mournfully at night, and ultimately culminates these images in his own weeping, deploying a novel twist on a poetic expression known from Pss 40:4 and 80:6 that keeps the focus on his voiced supplication. His frequent reference to the brevity of his own life serves further to elicit empathy from the eternal deity, whom he praises as one who hears the prayer of the destitute (v. 18) and the groans of the prisoners (v. 21). By seeking to ameliorate the anger of YHWH, the psalmist also seeks to mitigate his own anxiety and suffering. His prayer makes explicit reference to itself and the sounds of groaning and sobbing that accompany it. By sharing these emotions with an angry deity, divine anger may be mollified, and the situation of the petitioner improved. In the context of the emotional coregulation, weeping offers a potentially potent demonstration of helplessness that may assuage anger. The text reflects sad weeping with its bird imagery and mournful sense of frailty and isolation. Night appears as a time for weeping given the complaint "I lie awake" sandwiched between the bird metaphors.

Pages," http://www.owlpages.com/sounds.php. To hear the call of a lone white pelican, see multiple recordings at https://www.xeno-canto.org/species/Pelecanus-onocrotalus.

[76] Forti, "Like a Lone Bird," 76–78.

[77] Alonzo Schökel and Carniti, *Salmos*, 2:1274–75 identify the two intertwined themes of time/eternity and individual/community as thematic to the prayer.

[78] Grant, *Divine Anger*, 32–34, 36–37.

SUMMARY

Of the forty-two individual laments in the Psalter,[79] five involve weeping (12 percent). God is the audience of the weeping except in Ps 69, which recollects human reactions to the petitioner's weeping. In contrast to the negative human reaction to tears in Ps 69, the other prayers expect a positive and helpful response from God, with Ps 6 most explicitly connecting weeping to God's reaction. Most of the individual laments involving weeping also assume that God is angry and that tears may mollify divine wrath. Psalm 56 is the only real exception because God is not the audience for tears in Ps 69. Psalm 56 reflects a confident tone and view of God as supportive in contrast to the other prayers that envision an angry God. Psalm 42–43 evinces a dialogic view of the self by quoting the inner voice, and Ps 39 by incorporating multiple voices in the prayer. All the laments view God as an emotion regulation partner, and prayer as a means of coping with illness (Pss 6, 102), separation from an attachment figure (Ps 42–43), or environmental situations causing fear and distress (Pss 39, 56, 69).

COMMUNAL LAMENTS

The communal petitions resemble the individual laments with a few differences. First, the language is first-person plural rather than singular. Second, the recollections of God's past acts that serve as a basis for future hope refer to historical traditions (e.g., the exodus) rather than the personal experiences or confessions of trust characteristic of prayers of individuals. Third, concluding vows of praise and thanksgiving are often shortened or eliminated, and therefore do not stand out as typical elements as they do in most individual laments. As a result, the perceived change of mood that has motivated so much scholarship on individual laments is not prominent in communal laments. The typical form of a communal lament consists of six parts: address and introductory petition, lament, confession of trust, petition, vow of praise, and thanksgiving.

PSALM 80

Psalm 80 is a communal lament in time of military defeat. The language is sufficiently vague that the psalm could be applied to multiple national catastrophes, although it seems especially evocative of the fall of Israel (the Northern Kingdom) as seen from a Judahite perspective, which may explain the LXX's addition to the superscription "concerning the Assyrians." It refers to Joseph, Ephraim, and Manasseh as needing help, but it also mentions the ark (v. 1) and the Davidic king

---

[79] See page 92 n. 10 above.

(vv. 18–19), references that suggest a Judahite perspective.[80] The four refrains in verses 4, 8, 15, and 20 structure the prayer into four parts. The first opens the prayer with a petition for help, and the second provides a brief description of present suffering, including weeping. The latter two sections are longer and deploy the metaphor of Israel as a vine planted by God that God should save from those attacking it.

The opening line identifies God as "the shepherd of Israel." The opening request for help does not yet indicate the scope of the problem, which is initially described in verses 5–8:

יהוה אלהים צבאות	5 YHWH God of Hosts,
עד־מתי עשנת	how long will you be angry
בתפלת עמך	at the prayers of your people?
האכלתם לחם דמעה	6 You have fed them the bread of tears
ותשקמו בדמעות שליש	and made them drink tears in great measure
תשימנו מדון לשכנינו	7 You have made us the strife of our neighbors
ואיבינו ילעגו־למו	and our enemies laugh among themselves.
אלהים צבאות השיבנו	8 God of Hosts, restore us!
והאר פניך ונושעה	Let your face shine that we may be saved.

The language in these lines vividly depicts the anger of God and directly accuses God of causing the suffering of the people in contrast to the expected behavior of a shepherd to his flock (Ps 23). The term עשן is not generally regarded as an anger term because it means "to exude smoke" and only here refers to anger within the metaphorical scheme of anger as heat.[81] God exudes smoke "at the prayers of your people" (v. 5). The second-person possessive suffix emphasizes the speaker's sense of betrayal that YHWH would cause such pain to YHWH's own people. The normal means of assuaging divine anger through prayer has thus itself become a provocation. God's anger is so intense that pleas and tears intensify the anger rather than cooling it. The sense of God's implacable wrath may explain the heightened accusation in this prayer. The motif of tears as sustenance contributes directly to the accusation against God in verse 6. As the subject of *hiphil* verbs, God is portrayed as actively forcing the people to consume their tears rather than depicting the people as the subject of *qal* verbs as in Pss 40:4 and 102:9. This shift

---

80 Richard J. Clifford, *Psalms 73–150*, AOTC (Nashville, TN: Abingdon, 2002), 53 notes that some in the north (Hos 3:5) shared the view that Israel was one people under Davidic rule located with the temple in Jerusalem. He also argues that vv. 18–19 refer to a Davidic king, not Israel as a whole (cf. Ezek 19:10–14).

81 van Wolde, "Sentiments"; Eksner, "Indexing,"; and Soriano, "Emotion."

heightens God's responsibility for the calamity, which is a dominant theme in the remainder of the poem. The repetition of both singular and plural forms of דמעה is emphatic.[82] Elsewhere tears appear as an expression of emotion that might assuage divine wrath, but if God is feeding the people their own tears, what hope can they have of mollifying God's anger? This direct accusation may serve to grab God's attention and focus it on the extreme suffering of the people as part of the larger strategy to calm divine wrath by contrasting the suffering of Israel with God's role in creating and protecting the nation.

The image of God planting Israel like a vine and then handing it over to enemies accuses God of betraying Israel while also drawing attention to God's past care and concern for Israel, which makes God's cruelty more shocking. The poem shifts between third- and first-person language, and the LXX and Vulgate read the first person: "you have fed us bread of tears and made us drink tears in great measure." Most translators and commentators prefer the MT.

The directness of the accusation embedded in the motif of weeping coheres with the subsequent use of the vineyard image that dominates the remainder of the prayer. The shepherd of verse 2 is reimagined as a gardener who takes a vine from Egypt and plants it in a newly cleared land, in language that recollects the exodus and conquest. The development of the vine image becomes an extended metaphor that constitutes the remembrance of past favors that normally appears in a communal lament. The metaphor of Israel as a vine or vineyard appears elsewhere (Isa 5:1–7; Jer 2:21; 12:10; Hos 10:1). God first establishes the vine and then inexplicably attacks it and makes it vulnerable to the ravages of humans and animals. God's anger is never explained in reference to sin or disobedience within this prayer, so God's actions appear as a shocking act of betrayal. Indeed, the use of "turn" (שוב) in the refrain suggests divine wrongdoing. In the refrains, the *hiphil* stems ask God to "restore us," which may mean from exile (1 Kgs 8:34; Jer 27:22), but the refrain in verse 15 employs the *qal* in the middle of the extended vine metaphor. This refrain asks God to "turn," implying that God is the one who needs to repent, not the people.[83] This turning should be followed up with looking, seeing, and visiting the vine (הבט משמים וראה ופקד גפן זאת, v. 15).

The tears as sustenance motif shows both consistency and variation in its three occurrences (Pss 42:4; 80:6; 102:10). In all cases, the tears are copious and frequent and could be interpreted as indicating both the sorrow of the weeper and the lack of food due to fasting, illness, or famine. But Ps 102:10, where tears mix with food or drink, suggests that the image should not be read too literally as fasting or famine. Those who are said to consume their tears may have access to adequate food but show little interest in eating. The image may also suggest that

---

[82] Alonzo Schökel and Carniti, *Salmos*, 2:1062.

[83] Hopkins, *Psalms*, 294 and Broyles, *Psalms*, 331.

weeping is as habitual as eating (i.e., weeping coincides with eating). The significant commonality in this weeping motif is the sense of abandonment and isolation from God and neighbors. The individual laments indicate a high degree of social isolation in addition to distance from God. Psalm 80 focuses on the isolation of the whole community from God but does not point to factions within the nation. Rather, the nation as a whole suffers at the hands of national enemies and experiences God's absence in contrast to God's former help. Speakers employ the motif of tears as sustenance because it indicates their incessant weeping and therefore their desperate need for attachment and relationship. The intensity of the speaker's anger suggests protest weeping more than sad crying.

The angry protest weeping in Ps 80 reacts to the anger of God, questions the justice of this wrath, and presents its consequence in ways calculated to soften anger and elicit empathy. The text shows the community as a whole seeking to regulate out of a miserable state by regulating God out of anger. The prayer is motivated by environmental events causing extreme fear and suffering.

Psalm 126

Psalm 126 is generally considered a communal lament even though it includes clear expressions of joy. Commentators generally imagine a setting in the near future when exiles will begin to return to Israel, but many will remain abroad.[84] This time calls for both rejoicing that the exile is over and lamenting that the restoration is not yet complete because many remain absent and Judah is not independent. The first half of the prayer (vv. 2–3) focuses exclusively on the extraordinary good news of restoration, but the second half (vv. 4–6) asks that the restoration be completed. The second half resumes language from the opening line, but with two "crucial modifications": it modifies the past reference of YHWH's return to a future petition for YHWH's return, and it locates this return as "to us" rather than the more specific "to Zion":[85]

שׁובה יהוה את־שׁביתנו	4 Return to us again, YHWH[86]
כאפיקים בנגב	like the streams in the Negev.

[84] This reading assumes that the opening line is in the past tense ("when YHWH restored") rather than present ("when YHWH restores"); see Clifford, *Psalms 73–150*, 235.

[85] Zenger, "Psalm 126," in Hossfeld and Zenger, *Psalms 3*, 377.

[86] Zenger notes that this line, literally translated, might read "Return again YHWH in a returning with regard to us." The ancient versions understand שבית (here and in v. 1) as derived from שבה, "to be in prison" and therefore translate "Turn back Zion's imprisonment," a reading that suits a postexilic context. The *qere* may reflect a similar Masoretic understanding. Zenger, *Psalms* 3, 375 follows Willi-Plein in reading סבות, 'return' with some manuscripts, which is then an internal accusative.

הזרעים בדמעת	5 May those who sow in tears
ברנה יקצרו	reap with shouts of joy.
הלוך ילך ובכה	6 He that goes forth weeping,
נשא משך־הזרע	bearing the seed for sowing,
בא־יבוא ברנה	shall come home with shouts of joy,
נשא אלמתיו	bringing his sheaves with him.

The streams of the Negev refer to wadis, which flow with water in the winter but dry up in the summer. This cyclic return of water enabled agriculture to continue and allowed people to live in the Negev. The image imagines God's return to the people like the life-giving return of water to the Negev. This return is broadly predictable (the waters eventually come) but also surprising and sudden. The wadis begin to flow with water that seems to come out of nowhere, as the rains that produce them originate far away. One may see dramatic footage of the first waters returning to the Negev in modern Israel.[87] This striking return of water becomes an appropriate image for God's return. The prayer continues with images of agriculture that the water makes possible. As the first image contrasts the cyclical change of drought and flood, the remainder twice contrasts the cycle of sowing and reaping and links them to sorrow and joy, respectively. Importantly, the image begins with sorrow and ends with joy, drawing on agricultural life to represent sorrow as a temporary period that gives way to joy. There is nothing intrinsically sorrowful about sowing seed, but it is an uncertain endeavor. For any number of reasons, the crop may fail. Harvest, however, is intrinsically joyful because it represents the fulfillment of hopes held from the time of sowing. The prayer draws on seasonal change to offer hope that the petition for God's return will be realized, that present sorrow will dissolve in future joy. The opening of the prayer grounds this hope in the recent past, recalling the extreme joy of the initial end of exile as a basis for optimism in petitioning God to complete the great work that has begun. The brief reference does not enable one to distinguish whether sad or protest crying is more in view. The prayer seeks the return of God, whose absence is indicated by unspecified problems. God appears as an attachment figure, and the prayer strives to maintain proximity to God. Weeping emerges not as a direct strategy for gaining God's nearness but as an image for a hoped for conversion of misery to joy. There is no indication of divine anger or other explanation for God's absence.

---

87 Chris Kitching, "An Old Testament Wonder! Dramatic Moment the River Zin is Reborn as Flash Flood Sweeps across Arid Landscape in Israel's Negev Desert," *Daily Mail*, 1/16/2016, http://www.dailymail.co.uk/news/article-2913486/Zin-River-reborn-flash-flood-sweeps-arid-landscape-Israel-s-Negev-Desert.html.

PSALM 137

Commentators agree that Ps 137 is a communal lament and that it can be dated early in the exile. As Richard J. Clifford writes, "Psalm 137 has the distinction of having one of the most beloved opening lines and the most horrifying closing line of any psalm."[88] Its famous opening involves weeping, and its infamous closing line baby killing. The intervening verses connect these two motifs. The people (first-person plural language) weep when they recollect Jerusalem in exile as their captors torment them (vv. 1–4). The speaker (now first-person singular) promises never to forget Jerusalem (5–6). The last part (vv. 7–9) returns to plural language and asks God to remember what the enemies did to Jerusalem and to repay them in kind. The psalm is shaped by the contrast between Jerusalem and Babylon and the need to remember Jerusalem.[89]

Grief may be the paradigmatic motive for tears, and grief hinges on memory. The psalm expresses how the collective people and an individual speaker vividly remember Jerusalem and suffer from the recollection of its brutal destruction and their forced exile from it. The misery of their situation is a source of amusement to their captors who demand to hear one of the "songs of Zion." Several psalms identified by modern scholars as psalms of Zion may provide insight into what songs these captors have in mind. Most scholars count Pss 46, 48, 76, 84, and 122 among these psalms. These prayers resemble hymns or thanksgiving psalms and recollect the splendor of Jerusalem, as well as YHWH's protection of the city and the Davidic dynasty. In the wake of the catastrophe of Babylonian conquest, these songs are too painful to perform, especially for an audience of enemies responsible for the destruction of the city. The prayer quickly unpacks this context and thereby explains why the people are weeping in the first verse:

על נהרות בבל	[1] By the canals of Babylon,
שם ישבנו גם־בכינו	there we sat down and wept
בזכרנו את־ציון	when we remembered Zion.
על־ערבים בחוכה	[2] On the willows there
תלינו כנרותינו	we hung up our harps,
כי שם שאלונו	[3] for there they required of us,
שובינו דברי־שיר	our captors, words of songs,
ותוללינו שמחה	our tormentors for joy,
שירו לנו משיר ציון	"Sing for us one of the songs of Zion!"

The initial prepositional phrase "by the canals of Babylon" already indicates a cause for weeping to anyone who knows why the people would be in Babylon at

---

[88] Clifford, *Psalms 73–150*, 275.

[89] Pierre Auffret, "Essai sur la structure littéraire du psaum 137," *ZAW* 92 (1980): 346–77.

all. The line specifies that the people "sat" by the canals. The verb here refers to the posture of sitting rather than the new reality of dwelling in Babylon.[90] Sitting and weeping are sometimes associated, and both (independently or together) represent mourning. For example, Hagar sits while she weeps for her dying child (Gen 21:16), the Israelites sit and weep following their initial defeat (Judg 20:26), David evidently sits while weeping for Absalom (2 Sam 19:1–2, note "get up" in vv. 8–9), Zion sits and weeps (Lam 1:1–2) and the LXX version of Lamentations opens with Jeremiah sitting and weeping before beginning his lament. Similarly, Job's friends weep and join him sitting (Job 2:12–13). Sitting therefore emerges as an appropriate posture for one weeping due to grief and mourning.

The weeping reflects grief, trauma, and powerlessness. The weepers recollect Jerusalem and the lives they formerly enjoyed in contrast to their present forced migration to a foreign land under the control of "tormentors," who are likely the overseers who drove them into exile.[91] This loss of home and status, grief for these losses, and the anger at those who imposed these traumas explains both the weeping that initiates the prayer and the vengeance that characterizes its conclusion.[92] The poem recollects weeping in Babylon, named at the start and end of the poem (vv. 1, 8), but otherwise simply "there" (שם, vv. 1, 2) and "foreign soil" (אדמה נכרי, v. 4). The audience of the weeping may be threefold. The people can see one another's tears, which can also be seen by the Babylonian captors. These tears are then verbally recalled to YHWH in prayer. This poem does not explicitly address God here (it does in v. 7), but its location in the Psalter suggests its use as a prayer and therefore YHWH as an intended audience of the tears. The communal weeping enhances the bond among the weepers as they visibly share an emotional reaction to a common traumatic experience. Their captors might be moved to show some compassion to the exiles as a result of their tears. Finally, YHWH might deliver them from their distress and accomplish the vengeance against Babylon that they desire. Although divine wrath may be understood as a reason for the exile in some texts, the prayer does not depict God as angry. The concern appears less to assuage anger than to respond to the problem of separation from

---

[90] John Aun, "Psalm 137: Complex Communal Laments," *JBL* 127 (2008): 279.

[91] Alfred Guillaume, "The Meaning of תולל in Psalm 137:3," *JBL* 75 (1956): 143–44.

[92] The conclusion of the psalm has elicited far more scholarship than the beginning. See Matthew Ramage, "Christian Discernment of Divine Revelation: Benedict XVI and the International Theological Commission on the Dark Passages of the Old Testament," *ScrTh* 47 (2015): 71–83; William H. Bellinger, "Psalm 137: Memory and Poetry," *HBT* 27 (2005): 5–20; Christopher B. Hays, "How Shall We Sing?: Psalm 137 in Historical and Canonical Context," *HBT* 27 (2005): 35–55; and George Savran, "'How Can We Sing a Song of the Lord?': The Strategy of Lament in Psalm 137," *ZAW* 112 (2000): 43–58.

God and home. If God returns, then the hoped-for result is the devastation of Babylon, because attachment figures protect those in their care.

Summary

Scholars generally that sixteen psalms are communal laments.[93] Three of these include weeping (19 percent). Only Ps 80 assumes that God is angry and that human tears might assuage this anger. The reasons for divine absence in Pss 126 and 130 are not stated, although tears may have the effect of restoring relationship with God by signaling helplessness and need. In all cases, a sense of divine absence motivates the prayer. Psalm 80 elaborates on the causes of this absence (divine anger) and its consequences (human suffering). The (collective) speaker of the prayers seeks to regulate the emotion with God in ways analogous to the individual laments: reduce divine wrath and/or human misery and anxiety.

Thanksgiving Psalms

Thanksgiving psalms are individual rather than communal prayers that form the counterpoint to individual laments in that they express the praise promised by the lament in the event of salvation. Thanksgiving psalms normally consist of the following elements: proclamation of praise, account of suffering and salvation, renewed vow of praise, and hymnic praise. The thanksgiving prayers include praise of God for specific acts of deliverance. Westermann calls this praise "declarative praise," distinct from "descriptive praise" characteristic of hymns that praise God for God's attributes rather than specific acts.[94] Thanksgiving prayers focus more on specific acts of God that motivate gratitude and declarative praise but conclude with more descriptive or hymnic praise.

Psalm 30

Scholars categorize Ps 30 as an individual thanksgiving. The superscription and liturgical use, however, suggest that this individual prayer has long been used for communal purposes.[95] It has several connections with Ps 29, including the themes of glory and strength.[96] The superscription reads: מזמור שיר־חנכת הבית לדוד, "A

---

93 The communal laments are: 20; 44; 66; 67; 74; 79; 80*; 83; 85; 94; 108; 115; 123; 126*; 129; 137*. An asterisk marks those that mention weeping.

94 Westermann, Praise, 31–34.

95 Gunkel, *Introduction*, 9 cites Ps 30:1 to demonstrate that the use of a poem proves nothing about its origin. Sigmund Mowinckel, *Psalm Studies*, trans. Mark E. Biddle, HBS 2, 2 vols. (Atlanta, GA: SBL Press, 2014), 1:166 says that it "was originally an individual psalm that had nothing to do with the Feast of the Dedication of the temple." The individual former sufferer was interpreted in the Maccabean period as the people liberated by Judas (168).

96 Vesco, *Le psautier*, 2:288.

psalm. A song of dedication of the temple. For David." The individual language of the prayer might suggest that הבית is a house (Deut 20:5) rather than the temple, but the definite article suggests the temple. Midrash Tehillim links Ps 30 with the initial dedication of Solomon's temple (1 Kgs 8:63), the initial dedication of the Second Temple (Ezra 6:16–17), and the rededication following the desecration of Antiochus Epiphanes (1 Macc 4:52–59). The last of these gave rise to the festival of dedication (Hanukkah), in which Ps 30 has long been used (*Soferim* 42a). The expression "for David" helps connect the individual voice of the prayer with its corporate use.

Psalm 30 has been used as a textbook example of a thanksgiving psalm.[97] It includes the proclamation of praise (v. 2a), introductory summary (v. 2), report of deliverance (vv. 4, 7–12), renewed vow of praise (v. 13), and hymnic praise (vv. 5–6). The most explicit reference to weeping appears in the invitation to others to join in praise of God. This invitation is a common element in thanksgiving psalms (e.g., Ps 34:4) and a means by which God's reputation is enhanced, as is often promised in petitions (e.g., Ps 22:26, 32):

זמרו ליהוה חסידיו	5 Sing to YHWH his faithful ones
והודו לזכר קדשו	give thanks to his holy memory
כי רגע באפו	6 for his anger is but for a moment
חיים ברצונו	his favor a lifetime
בערב ילין בכי	weeping stays for the night
ולבקר רנה	but in the morning, joy

The psalmist speaks from experience of suffering and redemption. The suffering involves the threat of enemies and illness at a time when the speaker felt secure and immune from danger. The subsequent catastrophe is understood as following from the absence of God due to divine anger (אף). Seen in retrospect, the speaker's suffering has turned to joy, and past weeping provides an occasion to thank rather than accuse or petition God. The overall life of the psalmist suggest that divine anger is brief and favor long-lived, which reflects a generally comfortable life into which sorrow was a momentary exception. The prayer associates weeping with nighttime for a couple reasons. First, people generally weep more in the evening than during the day. Second, night often symbolizes fear, anxiety, and suffering. Both literal and figurative considerations associate tears with darkness. Furthermore, the night/day alternation provides an opportunity to reinforce the belief that suffering is temporary and ends in joy. The expression that weeping "stays

97 Broyles, *Psalms*, 19; Goldingay, *Psalms*, 1:55–56, 424; and Jacobson and Jacobson, *Invitation*, 56–58.

for the night" (ילין) personifies weeping as a traveler and overnight guest.[98] The morning joy will not collapse when the sun sets, for the traveler has moved on.

The language of verse 6 explicitly mentions weeping (בכי), but several other lines describe the speaker's behavior in ways that elucidate this crying and its function. The psalmist shouts for help (שועתי, v. 3), calls out (אקרא, v. 9), makes supplication (אתחנן, v. 9), and asks God to hear (שמע, v. 11). This context indicates that the term בכי in v. 6 refers primarily to the sound of voiced sobs, not quiet tears. The other expressions also clarify the purpose of the psalmist's crying: to elicit help (עזר, v. 11) and healing (ותרפאני, v. 3). The psalmist notes specifically that this supplication worked, and that God intervened. As his weeping turned to joy, so his mourning turned to dancing, and God removed his sackcloth and girded him with gladness (שמחה, v. 12). The thanksgiving psalm focuses on the effectiveness of the petitioner's lament and crying, as well as God's attention to his cry for help.

The observation that thanksgiving prayers form the counterpart to individual laments appears in the relationship between Ps 30 and Ps 6. One might understand Ps 30 as the fulfillment of the promise of praise offered in Ps 6. The two prayers share references to weeping at night (6:7; 30:6), healing (6:3; 30:3), God's anger (6:2; 30:6), God's remembrance (6:6; 30:4), and the lack of praise by the dead as an incentive to save the psalmist (6:6; 30:10). Taken together, these motifs tie Pss 6 and 30 together more tightly to one another than to any other psalm. The type of weeping is hard to discern in the brief mention of weeping, but the contrast of night and day is made clear. Like Ps 6, Ps 30 connects divine anger and human weeping and identifies night as a time for weeping. The type of weeping in Ps 30 is hard to classify due to lack of descriptive detail. The text indicates that the self is dialogic, referring to the נפש as separable from the first-person speaker (v. 4), and it quotes inner speech (v. 7). The prayer presents God as an attachment figure whose absence provokes distress (v. 8), and it seeks to recollect and experience gratitude to God motivated by the contrast between present joy and past pain. The prayer also addresses a wider human audience in order to draw them into this joy (v. 5) and offer instruction (vv. 6–7) about God using a voice that may be the same speaker of a separate voice similar to the wisdom voice in some laments.

---

98 Sigrid Eder, *Identifikationspotenziale in den Psalmen: Emotionen, Metaphern und Textdynamik in der Psalmen 30, 64, 90 und 147*, BBB 183 (Göttingen: Vandenhoeck & Ruprecht, 2018), 121–22.

PSALM 116

Scholars generally agree that Ps 116 is an individual thanksgiving psalm.[99] In the LXX, the psalm ends at verse 9, and verses 10–19 are a separate psalm. The term "hallelujah" appears at the end of 116:19 in MT but at the beginning of the new LXX Ps 117:1 (MT 116:10). Modern commentators agree that the MT represents the original text and that the LXX divided the psalm inappropriately, likely responding to the shift back to recollection in verse 10 and the need to have 150 total psalms. The prayer expresses desire to serve God in gratitude for God's attentiveness and mercy. The text involves several verbal repetitions, but they do not seem to structure the prayer as refrains, and commentators cannot agree about how the poem is structured.[100]

The psalmist begins by explaining his love for God as grounded in God's attentiveness:

אהבתי כי ישמע יהוה	1 I love YHWH because he has heard
את־קולי תחנוני	my voice and my supplications
כי־הטה אזנו לי	2 because he inclined his ear to me
ובימי אקרא	in my days I will call on him

The opening emphasizes God hearing the psalmist's noise. His supplications are clearly spoken aloud (קולי). The expression "call on YHWH" appears frequently in the prayer as both a past action (v. 4) and a future promise (vv. 13, 17). In the past case, the speaker provides a direct quote of the content of the call: "I beg YHWH, save my life" (v. 4). This plea for help comes from a speaker near death (v. 3), although the precise nature of his suffering is unclear. Immediately after the direct quote from the speaker's past prayer, the prayer shifts to first-person plural, then recalls weeping:

חנון יהוה וצדיק	5 Gracious is YHWH and righteous.
ואלהינו מתחם	Our God is merciful.
שמר פתאים יהוה	6 YHWH preserves the simple.
דלותי ולי יהושיע	When I was brought low, he saved me
שובי נפשי למנוחיכי	7 Return, my life, to your rest,
כי־יהוה גמל עליכי	for YHWH has dealt well with you.
כי חלצת נפשי ממות	8 For you have delivered my life from death,

99 Gunkel, *Introduction*, 2 notes that, due to uncertainty about the Hebrew verb tenses, some read Ps 116 as a complaint about present suffering rather than a thanksgiving for deliverance.

100 Clifford, *Psalms 73–150*, 199 and Willem S. Prinsloo, "Psalm 116: Disconnected Text or Symmetrical Whole?," *Bib* 74 (1993): 71–84.

את־עיני מן־דמעה	my eyes from tears,
את־רגלי מדחי	my feet from stumbling.
אתהלך לפני יהוה	9 I walk before YHWH
בארצות החיים	in the land of the living.

The first few lines resemble a wisdom voice sometimes evident in Psalms.[101] The thanksgiving prayer as a whole is directed toward a human audience, beginning with speech about God in the third person. The direct address to YHWH in verse 4 recalls a past experience with YHWH that the speaker now shares with other humans. The wisdom voice in verses 5–6a marks a transition in tone and voice, but the content remains the same. The wisdom voice states general beliefs about YHWH shared by the community that are reinforced by the personal experience of the psalmist. The voice of the psalmist appears again, addressing "my life" (נפשי) as if it were another person. One might read this as the present self addressing the future self about the past self in an effort to reaffirm that safety has been reached, reliving the emotional calming of recent salvation, and reducing anxieties about a potential repeat of pain.[102] This internal dialogue is made external to the divine and human audiences and will continue in the second half of the prayer. But first the speaker finally addresses YHWH directly in the second person and talks about his "self" in the third person (v. 8). In the LXX, the text maintains third person throughout, which may reflect confusion or discomfort with the change of address.[103] The first of three lines sharing the verb חלץ (*piel*, "to deliver") refers to deliverance from death as described previously in verses 3–4. The next two lines expand on what this salvation meant: relief from tears and distress. The image of delivering the eyes from tears is a unique way of referring to relief from crying. It makes the eyes themselves the objects of God's care, like the feet in the next line delivered from stumbling. The verse associates tears with the proximity to death and the distress this creates but does so specifically in the context of God's merciful response.

The remainder of the prayer focuses on the psalmist's gratitude rather than the previous deliverance. Luis Alonzo Schökel and Cecilia Carniti state, "more than Ps 30, Ps 116 impresses us with the intensity of its emotion… The one praying turns into himself in order to observe and describe his emotions, he unfolds

---

[101] Mandolfo, *God* focuses on individual laments, but the dialogism of Psalms is not limited to this genre.

[102] See pages 15–20.

[103] Michael L. Barré, "Psalm 116: Its Structure and Its Enigmas," *JBL* 109 (1990): 78 prefers the smoothness of the third person and suggests that second person of MT may have been influenced by Ps 56:14.

internally for a mental dialogue with himself."[104] Interestingly, they single out the two psalms of thanksgiving that include weeping as the two most emotionally intense. Both psalms also reflect explicit internal dialogue (30:7; 116:7). In Ps 116, the speaker twice quotes his own past inner speech, asks himself a question about what he will do for YHWH (v. 12), and answers his own question (vv. 13–14). Next, a wisdom voice reaffirms God's attentiveness. The speaker shifts again into second-person address to God (vv. 16–17, also in LXX), and concludes with third-person talk about God as he affirms that he will perform his vows of thanksgiving (v. 18–19). These changes of voice and address around a coherent and common theme reflect the inner dialogue of the speaker's self, which is here made public so that a wider audience of listeners can participate in the joy and gratitude of the psalmist. The speaker relives the emotional memory of suffering and redemption, crediting God's attentiveness to cries for help and tears of distress for his restoration to health and happiness. By sharing the experience in public prayer, he shares his gratitude with a wider audience and reaffirms for them their image of God as merciful and concerned for humans in distress. The prayer thereby evokes memories in others of their own salvation and consequent gratitude and provides hope of help to those in agony. The brief retrospective reference to weeping does not allow one to determine whether the weeping was of the sad or protesting type. The dialogic self and inner voice come through clearly and both as involved in coregulation of emotion with the deity and a human audience.

Summary

Most scholars concur that at least fifteen palms are thanksgiving prayers.[105] Two of them (11 percent) include weeping. Both mention weeping only briefly in the context of past suffering, but the focus is on present comfort. Both prayers quote inner speech, manifest a dialogic self, and engage in coregulation of emotion with both God and a human audience.

OTHER PRAYERS

Scholars generally recognize several genres of psalm beyond the laments and thanksgiving psalms. Hymns may represent the most important of these genres, but none of the psalms recognized as hymns include weeping. This lack of tears may be expected, because hymns celebrate the many positive attributes of God and generally do not include recollections of previous suffering as thanksgiving

---

[104] Alonzo Schökel and Carniti, *Salmos*, 2:1414: "Más que el Sal 30, el 116 nos impressiona por la intensidad de su sentiment.… El orante se vuelve sobre si para observar y describir sus sentimientos, se desdobla internamente para un diálogo mental consigo."

[105] The thanksgiving prayers are: 18; 21; 30*; 32; 34; 40; 41; 65; 66; 75; 92; 107; 116*; 118; 124. An asterisk marks those psalms that mention weeping.

psalms do. Scholars have recognized several other types of psalms, consisting of a handful of examples. These minor categories include psalms of confidence, royal psalms, wisdom psalms, torah psalms, and historical psalms. Some psalms defy form-critical categories and may be labelled as "mixed" or classified in different ways by different scholars. Of these minor psalm types, most might not be expected to involve weeping. Psalms of confidence express a sense of security in divine protection, while wisdom and torah psalms are hymnlike in their celebration of God. The so-called royal psalms encompass various emotions, and some could include weeping but do not (e.g., Ps 18). Two psalms in these minor categories do include weeping: one historical psalm (Ps 78) and one torah psalm (Ps 119).

Psalm 78

Scholars most commonly characterize Ps 78 as an historical psalm. It narrates the history of Israel from the exodus from Egypt to the elevation of David as king. The psalm never addresses God directly. In the introduction (vv. 1–8), the speaker uses first- and second-person language to refer to Israel ("my people" and "your ear," v. 1; "our ancestors," v. 5). The opening states the purpose of the psalm:

וישימו באלהים כסלם	7 to put their trust in God
ולא ישכחו מעללי־אל	and not forget the works of God
ומצותיו ינצרו	and keep his commandments
ולא יהיו כאבותם	8 and not be like their ancestors,
דור סורר ומרה	a stubborn and rebellious generation,
דור לא־הצין לבו	a generation whose heart was not steadfast
ולא־נאמנה את־אל רוחו	and whose spirit was not faithful to God.

The poet speaks from concern for the formation of future generations. The remainder of the poem narrates God's history with earlier generations of Israelites, referring to both God and the ancestors in the third person. This history is told twice (vv. 9–19 and 40–72). Both narrations contrast God's wondrous grace to the people and their ungrateful refusal to keep his commandments. The history ends optimistically, with God's choice of Zion and David suggesting a future better than the past. The mention of weeping appears in the second of the two narrations, in a section focused on the disobedience of Israelites after their settlement in the land. It explains God's wrath at the idols and high places and God's consequent rejection of Israel and abandonment of Shiloh. The catastrophe described might be imagined during the military defeat at the hands of the Philistines or a later period, such as the Assyrian destruction of the Northern Kingdom:

ויסגר לחרב עמו	62 He gave his people up to the sword
ובנחלתו התעבר	and vented his wrath on his heritage.

בחוריו אכלה־אש	63 Fire consumed their young men,
ובתולתיו לא הוללו	and their young women had no wedding songs.
כהניו בחרב נפלו	64 Their priests fell by the sword,
ואלמנתיו לא תבכינה	and their widows did not weep.

The reference to weeping is the last in the list of miseries, and the poem transitions to God awakening, routing enemies, and establishing David as king (vv. 65–72). The pairing of young men and priests with their respective female counterparts draws attention to the totality of military defeat and its different consequences for men and women. As Erich Zenger notes: "While men die by fire and sword, the women survive and endure a fate reserved for women."[106] The young women will not marry because the men are dead, so they sing no wedding song (cf. Jer 7:34; 16:9). The married women become widows but do not weep or mourn for their late husbands. Their lack of weeping is not explained. Zenger says they are "forbidden to sing laments after the death of their husbands (cf. Job 27:15b and Ezek 24:15–24), which means they cannot mourn for them as piety and custom require."[107] The present verse, however, makes no reference to any divine prohibition against weeping. The inhibition may rather derive from the occupying enemy soldiers who may punish displays of mourning as a protest to their victory and conquest. Weeping and mourning can be acts of rebellion and resistance. In this context, tears may be more likely to generate anger than empathy from those in power who regard the weeping over their victims as a rejection of their rule. The widows of the priests, therefore, may stifle their tears to hide them from the enemy soldiers. The image of women suffering in the wake of the deaths of men closes this description of Israel's suffering as the death of the firstborn closes the description of the punishments on Egypt.

Psalm 78 seeks to enliven a sense of gratitude for God's repeated salvation of Israel in spite of the people's several defections. It paints a negative image of the audience's ancestors and a positive portrait of God. It frequently refers to divine anger at past generations with a variety of terms (אף, vv. 1, 8, 10, 21, 31, 38, 49, 50; עבר, vv. 21, 49, 59, 62; זעם, v. 49; כעס, v. 58). By participating in this divine wrath and the speaker's wonder at God's ongoing commitment to Israel, the audience feels an emotional connection to God and a desire to be faithful to God's commands. The poem does not present the anger of God as a present reality for the audience, so weeping does not appear as a strategy for mitigating wrath. The

---

106 Zenger, "Psalm 78," in Frank-Lothar Hossfeld and Erich Zenger. *Psalms 2: A Commentary on Psalms 51–100*, Hermeneia, trans. Linda M. Maloney (Minneapolis, MN: Augsburg Fortress, 2005), 299.

107 Zenger, "Psalm 78," in Hossfeld and Zenger, *Psalms 2*, 299.

mention of weeping in the psalm is not the weeping of the speaker or audience but the lack of weeping by women from a past and disobedient generation whose negative example was punished. Weeping therefore has no close connection to the way the speaker seeks to shape the emotions of the audience. This historical psalm develops and reinforces a sense of community among the people through their common ancestry, shared history, and collective relationship with God. The historical narrative serves to inform the internal representations that the hearers have of God, of themselves, and of the relationship between them. God's wrath is to be feared but may be avoided through obedience motivated by gratitude.

Psalm 119

The genre of Ps 119 has been much discussed because it is so confusing. It is an exceptionally long prayer, an acrostic poem with eight verses per stanza, each verse starting with each letter of the alphabet through all twenty-two letters for a total of 176 verses. Most scholars agree that each verse consists of two poetic lines, for a total of 352 lines. There is no discernible thematic structure within the acrostic shaping of the prayer, but a clear focus on authoritative divine teaching appears in the fact that almost every stanza employs eight different terms related to this theme. Within this thematic focus and acrostic structure, the prayer "moves randomly between statement of trust, protest, confession, and plea."[108] For this reason, Gunkel identified it as a "mixed" psalm. Scholars have since classified it as either a wisdom psalm or a torah psalm, depending on whether they regard the emphasis on authoritative teaching to be related to the wisdom tradition or the law of Moses. Most likely, the poet intends no distinction between these two (cf. Sir 24). Those who call it a wisdom psalm do not acknowledge torah psalm as a category, but classify Ps 119 with other wisdom psalms (e.g., Pss 1, 37, 49, 73, 127, 128).[109] Those who acknowledge torah psalm as a category invariably include Ps 119 in this category, and sometimes Pss 1 and 19.[110] Although ninety of the verses in Ps 119 (over half) consist of individual lament, it does not seem possible simply to classify this unusual psalm with the other individual laments.[111] The clearest mention of weeping occurs at the end of the פ stanza in a context of individual lament reminiscent of Ps 69:

---

[108] Goldingay, *Psalms*, 3:373.

[109] Bellinger, *Psalms*, 23 and Gillingham, *Poems*, 228.

[110] Day, *Psalms*, 56 acknowledges Ps 119 as a torah psalm and hymn.

[111] *Pace* Clifford, *Psalms 73–150*, 209–10, whose verse count I cite here. He correctly notes that this proportion of petition is consistent with the proportions in Pss 3 and 5, but this observation obfuscates the extent to which Ps 119 stands apart from all other psalms, even in its placement between the Hallel (Pss 113–18) and the Songs of Ascents (Pss 120–34).

פלאות עדותיך	129 Wonderful are your testimonies,
על־כן נצרתם נפשי	therefore my life keeps them.
פתח דבריך יאיר	130 The opening of your words gives light,
מבין פתיים	it gives understanding to the simple.
פי־פערתי ואשאפה	131 With open mouth I pant
כי למצותיך יאבתי	because I desire your commandments.
פנה־אלי וחנני	132 Turn to me and be gracious to me
כמשפט לאהבי שמך	as is customary for those who love your name.
פעמי הכן באמרתך	133 Make my steps firm according to your promise
ואל־תשלט־בי כל־און	and let no iniquity gain dominion over me.
פדני מעשק אדם	134 Redeem me from human oppression
ואשמרה פקודיך	so that I may keep your precepts.
פניך האר בעבדך	135 Let your face shine upon your servant
ולמדני את־חקיך	and teach me your statutes.
פלגי־מים ירדו עיני	136 Streams of water my eyes shed
על לא־שמרו תורתך	because they do not keep your law.

The reference to weeping employs a Hebrew idiom in which the term עין, "eye," is the subject of the verb ירד, "to go down" to indicate crying. In the Psalter, this idiom appears only in Ps 119:136, and in some manuscripts in 119:28. Psalm 119:136 refers to people who do not abide by God's law. The existence of this disobedience is cause for grief. It is not clear whether "they" are doing anything to persecute the speaker, but the situation is reminiscent of Ps 69 in which the speaker's zeal for YHWH merits scorn from people rather than praise. Indeed, a few verses into the next stanza, the speaker says, "My zeal destroys me because my foes forget your words" (Ps 119:139). The appearance of weeping shows the depth of the speaker's commitment to divine law. If he weeps when others disobey, then disobedience cannot be an option for him.

The potential appearance of weeping in Ps 119:28 is difficult to evaluate. Most scholars and translators follow the MT:

דלפה נפשי מתוגה	My life drips for sorrow;
קימני כדברך	strengthen me according to your word

The image of the נפש dripping is unusual but not impossible (cf. Job 30:16). A few manuscripts read עין instead of נפש, which brings the expression closer to the familiar weeping idiom: "My eye weeps for sorrow." Elsewhere, the idiom includes the liquid that would "drip" from the eye and omits reference to the immediate cause of weeping. This variant would leave the tears as understood and insert an emotion term (תוגה) to explain the motivation for weeping. The only parallel is Job 16:20b: אל־אלוה דלפה עיני, "to God my eye weeps." It is difficult to discern whether a scribe substituted עין for נפש or the other way around because both expressions are unusual.

LANGUAGE OF WEEPING

The most important weeping terms in Hebrew derive from the roots בכה and דמע. The verb בכה appears most frequently, and the noun בכי relatively rarely. The term דמעה appears almost exclusively in poetry (but cf. 2 Kgs 20:5; Ezek 24:16 [> LXX]; Eccl 4:1). The denominative verb occurs three times (Jer 13:17; Isa 15:9; Sir 12:16). Within the Psalter, דמעה occurs eight times (Pss 6:7; 39:13; 42:4; 56:9; 80:6 [twice]; 116:8; 126:5), בכה four times (Pss 69:11; 78:64; 126:6; 137:1), and בכי three times (Pss 6:9; 30:6; 102:10). Hebrew also has a poetic idiom for weeping that may occur without either of the common roots for weeping: "my eyes flow with water." The idiom admits of flexibility, as various terms can be substituted for each element. The eye may be represented by עין or פלפל. The term for "eye" is then made the subject of a verb that may describe flowing liquid. Although ירד is the most common verb (Ps 119:136; Jer 9:17; 13:17; 14:17; Lam 1:16; 3:48), several other verbs also occur: נזל ("to trickle," Jer 9:17), נגר ("to flow," Lam 3:24), דלף ("to drip," Job 16:20; Ps 119:28 [variant]). The expression may specify that the eyes go down "with tears" (דמעה, Jer 9:17; 13:17; 14:17), or the term מים may occur with the meaning of "tears" (Jer 9:17; Ps 119:136; Lam 1:16; 3:48). The poetic idiom may thus be employed in such a way that none of the typical weeping vocabulary appears (e.g., Ps 119:126).

The Psalms include several terms for crying out to God—especially קרא, "call," and זעק, "cry out"—that resemble weeping as behaviors that can elicit compassion and help. Although one may weep while "crying out," these terms do not specifically identify the behavior as weeping and therefore have not been included in the present study. A different study, however, might examine various other means by which prayers seek to elicit God's help through acoustic and other signals. Weeping behavior in the psalms is also associated with תחנה, "groaning," אנחה, "supplication," תפלה, "prayer," שועה, "cry," and קול, "sound." These terms, together with verbs of vocalizing prayer, suggest the potential for a wider study of ways in which people seek divine attention.

Several images cluster around mentions of weeping in the Psalms. The vivid image of tears or weeping as sustenance appears three times. The precise literal meaning is unclear. It may mean that the speaker weeps as frequently as eating or drinking, whether the weeper fasts or not. Each example of the motif is tailored to its context. In Pss 40:4 and 102:10, it captures the sorrow of the isolated speaker, connecting to water imagery in Ps 42 and lonely bird images in Ps 102. In Ps 80:6, God actively feeds tears to the people, contributing to the prayer's larger theme of

God's responsibility for the people's pain. Divine wrath also explains the speaker's misery in Ps 102, but the motif of weeping shies away from the direct accusation that is explicit in Ps 80. Often, psalms present night as a time for weeping. Sometimes night is paired with day to express the continuity of weeping (Ps 42–43), while other times night alone is emphasized as a time for crying (Pss 6, 102, 130). The sound of weeping appears in view in some cases, and the doleful sounds of certain birds provide an analogy to human sobbing (Ps 102). To the extent that the texts allow a categorization of weeping references into types of weeping, most seem to reflect sad crying, although the urgent anger or panic of protest weeping may appear in Ps 42. Outside lament contexts, the motif is less developed and the type of crying hard to determine.

DIVINE ANGER AND HUMAN TEARS

Weeping appears most often in psalms in which the speaker is concerned about suffering from the consequences of divine anger. Broyles originally distinguished "psalms of plea" and "psalms of complaint" within the widely recognized category of "psalms of lament." Psalms of lament may be individual or communal and include three traditionally recognized types of laments: I-laments complain about the speaker's miserable situation and suffering, "enemy-laments" focus on how others create misery for the speaker, and God-laments identify God as at least partly responsible for the speaker's affliction and therefore like an enemy. Broyles rightly argues that the God lament is not just a third kind of lament but evinces a significantly different relationship with God. In psalms of plea involving I- and enemy-lament, the psalmist approaches God as benevolent, but in psalms of complaint involving God-lament, the speaker approaches God as "indifferent or hostile."[112] These psalms also express especially intense and prolonged suffering compared to psalms of plea.[113] Ingvar Fløysvik further develops Broyles's observations about psalms of complaint and elaborates on divine anger as the root problem in the psalms of complaint: "In these Psalms we note that the wrath of God is not only a problem insofar as it deprives people of health, social security, or national independence. God's wrath is a problem because it deprives people of God himself and of life with him. The heart of the distress in the complaint psalms is, therefore, the wrath of God."[114] These complaint psalms disproportionately involve the motif of weeping. Broyles identifies the following individual and communal lament as complaint psalms:

---

[112] Broyles, *Conflict*, 53.

[113] Broyles, *Conflict*, 83–109.

114 Ingvar Fløysvik, *When God Becomes My Enemy: The Theology of the Complaint Psalms* (St. Louis, MO: Concordia Academic, 1997) 142 and Broyles, *Conflict*, 61–67.

Individual: 6, 13, 22, 35, 39, 42–43, 88, 102
Communal: 9–10, 44, 60, 74, 77, 79, 80, 85, 90, 108

Of these eighteen psalms, five involve weeping (6, 39, 42–43, 80, 102), or 28 percent. By contrast, only 7 percent of the 148 psalms refer to the speaker weeping in the presence of God (in addition to the above: 30, 56, 116, 119, 137). Note that the speaker in Ps 69 recalls his weeping before an unsympathetic human audience but does not speak of weeping before the divine audience. Of the seven lament psalms that include the speaker weeping (6, 39, 42–43, 56, 80, 102, 137), five are complaint psalms, or 71 percent. Stated another way, between eighteen complaint psalms and seven lament psalms including weeping, five psalms belong to both categories. The correlation between weeping speakers and complaint psalms may be due in part to the concern about divine anger that Fløysvik places at the heart of the complaint psalms. He argues that divine anger informs all the complaint psalms but acknowledges that only ten of the eighteen complaint psalms include vocabulary directly identifying God's wrath (6, 39, 60, 74, 79, 80, 85, 88, 90, 102).[115] This narrower range of psalms yields an even higher percentage of weeping psalms: 40 percent. The only complaint psalm involving weeping without explicit mention of divine wrath is 42–43. These data collectively indicate a significant relationship or correlation between divine anger and the tears of the psalmist.

The cause of God's wrath in the complaint psalms is usually obscure. In Pss 6, 39, 79, and 90, the speaker identifies sin as the cause of God's anger, but the problem is less the past sin and more the ongoing and unrelenting anger of God. In Ps 6, for example, the speaker acknowledges deserving God's wrath, but "his problem is not sin as such but that God deals with him in his wrath rather than being gracious according to his steadfast love."[116] Similarly, the speaker in Ps 39 has confessed sin already, yet God will not let go of anger. In most of the complaint psalms, however, divine wrath seems inexplicable. "It is not always described as morally motivated, nor is it necessarily considered comprehensible."[117] The speaker of Ps 44, for example, emphatically insists on his innocence. The complaint psalms disproportionately involve weeping because they disproportionately involve divine anger. Weeping appears in some of these psalms as a strategy for mollifying divine anger and therefore the suffering of the petitioner.

---

[115] Fløysvik, *When God Becomes*, 144–46. On divine anger, see Grant, *Divine Anger*; Bruce Edward Baloian, *Anger in the Old Testament*, American University Studies 7/99 (New York: Peter Lang, 1992); and van Wolde, "Sentiments."

[116] Fløysvik, *When God Becomes*, 152.

[117] Broyles, *Conflict*, 66.

4
Comparative Perspectives

The scientific research on weeping and emotion regulation offers insight into prayer, including ancient prayer texts. It is possible to discern in the texts of prayers language about weeping and its role in wider coregulation of emotion between the human speaker of the prayer and the divine audience. The Akkadian and Hebrew corpora of prayer share some deep similarities that may be partly explained by their common roots in the human attachment system. Both corpora show evidence that tears can assuage anger and that people coregulate their emotions with deities in prayer. They also draw on animal imagery to illustrate weeping, refer to tears as sustenance, and reflect the reality that people weep more at night. This conclusion will describe these similarities and differences and ask why weeping is not more widely distributed in both corpora.

The most striking similarity between the two prayer corpora consists of the high correlation between divine wrath and human weeping. The research on weeping has uncovered interesting evidence of the complex interaction between tears and anger. Weeping can either mollify or elicit anger, depending on factors such as the quality of the relationship between weeper and audience, the context of the crying episode, and the cultural rules about weeping. Under some circumstances, weeping may be an effective strategy for mollifying anger and reconstructing relationship, so one might expect weeping to occur in prayer contexts where divine anger is in view. As the sophisticated literary example from Jane Austen shows,[1] weeping can have complex interactions with anger. Fanny's tears check Sir Thomas's anger but do not convince him to change his goals. The analogy of this episode suggests that, in prayer, tears may be understood by petitioners to check divine wrath, but further persuasion is needed to reconcile the divine-human relationship (e.g., rhetorical persuasion, ritual offerings).

Both *eršaḫungas* and *dingiršadabbas* are genres of prayer developed for the purpose of calming the anger of a deity. The *šuillas* that share this purpose also show a high proportion of weeping (weeping only appears in *šuillas* mentioning divine

---

[1] See pages 29–31.

wrath). The Hebrew prayer corpus also shows a significant correlation between divine anger and human tears. The present study of weeping in Hebrew prayers adds further evidence that Craig C. Broyles has rightly identified a distinct psalmic genre in the complaint psalm. Complaint psalms resemble *eršaḫunga*s and *dingiršadabba*s as prayers oriented toward addressing divine wrath. This category of psalms focuses on the "God-lament" and imagines YHWH as angry rather than benevolent. While weeping appears in 7 percent of all psalms, 28 percent of complaint psalms include weeping. Of the seven individual laments that include weeping, five of them are complaint psalms (72 percent). The correlation between divine anger and human tears fits known findings about anger and weeping, reinforces Broyles's identification of the complaint psalm genre, and invites further comparison among *dingiršadabba*s, *eršaḫunga*s, and complaint psalms (and potentially a subset of "complaint *šuilla*s" that explicitly respond to divine anger). A wider comparison of Sumerian and Akkadian texts and attention to categorizing prayers by likely date of composition may contribute a diachronic dimension to the development of the weeping motif over time. The specific motif of tears as sustenance appears to be a Sumerian invention carried over into Akkadian and thereby more widely into the Semitic world and Hebrew prayer.

The difference between *eršaḫunga*s and *dingiršadabba*s merits consideration. One might predict that weeping would be more common in prayers to personal gods compared to high gods due to the intimacy of relationships with personal gods. The evidence, however, shows more weeping in *eršaḫunga*s. Weeping is a powerful nonverbal form of communication, and the eloquence of this physiological response to helplessness may appear more necessary when addressing distant high gods than close personal gods. Personal gods might be believed to be more inclined to forgive based on the closeness of the relationship, whereas a high god might be deemed less inclined to relinquish anger. Alternatively, the difference between *eršaḫunga*s and *dingiršadabba*s may be due to change over time. *Eršaḫunga*s are Sumerian prayers with Akkadian translations that manifest a high frequency of weeping. *Dingiršadabba*s may be divided into three corpora: Sumerian prayers, Sumerian prayers with Akkadian translations, and Akkadian prayers. As noted above,[2] weeping is frequent in the Sumerian *dingiršadabba*s and becomes increasingly less frequent in the bilingual and Akkadian texts. This evidence suggests that weeping may have been common in Sumerian prayers and may have become less common as Akkadian texts displaced Sumerian. The different frequency of weeping in *eršaḫunga*s and *dingiršadabba*s may therefore be a function of culture and language rather than the deity addressed.

---

[2] See pages 75–76.

The motif of weeping participates in the wider emotion regulatory function of prayer. Although present in all examples, some texts make this coregulation of emotion between petitioner and deity especially obvious. Ishtar 2, for example, refers to the liver and heart of both the deity and the petitioner, as the prayer seeks to regulate the emotions of both relationship partners. In this example, as in most others, the anxious petitioner seeks to calm his own heart and liver, which are both afflicted with "tears and sighs," by deploying his suffering and sorrow to calm the heart and liver of Ishtar, who is angry with him. The text of the prayer establishes parallels between these emotion organs in the petitioner and the goddess because the relationship partners depend on one another to down-regulate their negative arousal and restore a formerly tranquil relationship. Similarly, Ps 6 identifies weeping as the key that explains the mood change between verses 8 and 9. YHWH's anger at the start of the psalm melts before the petitioner's tears and supplications, and the speaker's expressions of misery give way to optimism and confidence. The content of the Akkadian and Hebrew prayers indicates that the deity is a relationship partner with whom the petitioner can coregulate emotion through sharing emotional experience.

The prayers also reflect the dialogic nature of the human self and the inner voice. People often use their socially derived inner voices to regulate themselves and may turn to prayer in an effort to enlist the deity's help with emotion regulation. Evidence of the dialogic inner voices appears in some psalms in which the speaker either quotes his past inner speech in the present moment (Pss 30:7, 10–11; 39:2; 42:10; 116:4, 10–11) or speaks about or to an aspect of his self (נפש, Pss 42:2–3, 5, 6–7, 12; 43:5; 116:7). Sometimes a different voice interjects in the prayer (Ps 39:7, 12; maybe 30:5–6; 116:5), and this may be one of the speaker's own voices or evidence of a liturgical performance, because public and private prayer are mutually reinforcing. Some Akkadian prayers include the voices of both a petitioner and an intercessor who speaks about the petitioner (e.g., *Eršaḫunga* 1.15b). Unlike Hebrew prayer, the Akkadian texts do not explicitly quote or refer to the inner voice. Akkadian prayers are more likely than Hebrew ones to combine an intercessory voice with the voice of the supplicant. Although some Hebrew prayers include a voice of a third person, this typically comes through as a wisdom voice expressing general truths rather than an allied intercessory voice speaking about the petitioner as in many Akkadian prayers and Lam 1. This difference between Akkadian and Hebrew prayer may reflect diverse understandings of the self and/or different contexts for the use of the prayers. Many of the Akkadian texts are known to be part of rituals performed by experts on behalf of clients, which invites the distinction between these two voices. The original context of the psalms remains obscure although some evidence cultic use. Both the Akkadian and Hebrew prayers reflect human attempts to regulate emotions with deities, and the beliefs about these divinities can be partially ascertained through the text of the prayers. For example, in all cases, the petitioner believes that the deity will respond to tears with empathy rather than anger, even though both are possible in relations with humans. In both Ps 69 and *Er* 1.16, the petitioners recall human failures to respond to tears with sympathy and support, yet still expect that the deities addressed will be more helpful. The motif of weeping therefore reflects the wider coregulation of emotion in the prayers.

In the Literary Prayer to Marduk, the language explicitly identifies Marduk as the intended target of the petitioner's tears with an object suffix (*ibakkīka*, "he is weeping to you"). The idea that weeping has an audience is common to every example of the motif, but this unusual linguistic expression makes this point especially clear. It also reflects the social reality of weeping as a behavior that evolved in humans because of its socially derived survival advantages. This linguistic expression of weeping as having an intended audience is rare, but it appears here within the corpus, and further examples may be found beyond the corpus. The Dialogue between a Man and His God[3] begins by narrating that "a young man is weeping to his god like a friend." The preposition *ana* identifies the personal god as an intentional target of weeping. The young man does not merely weep and happen to be seen by the personal god but seeks out the deity in order to weep. The infinitive of purpose in line 5 clarifies the man "has drawn near in order to weep" (*ba-ka-i-iš iq-ra-a*[*b*...]). In Hebrew also, the weeping may have an intended audience. YHWH spares Josiah from seeing the disaster that will befall Judah because "you wept before me" (לפני, 2 Kgs 22:19). These small linguistic nuances reflect the reality that weeping is a social behavior.

Even though weeping is social, people often weep alone. In the prayer texts, the speakers never understand themselves to be alone; they are speaking to a deity. They often refer to their weeping as something that is continuous, not merely switched on for the purpose of a brief prayer, and they sometimes refer specifically to night as a time for weeping. These references to nighttime weeping cohere with survey data on modern people who weep at night more than during the day. The fact that the pattern on evening weeping also holds with infants and other mammalian species suggests that it may be rooted in biology (e.g., related to the circadian rhythm) and not only the tendency of people to be alone or with trusted intimates in the evening hours.

In both Akkadian and Hebrew, authors draw on animal imagery to describe human weeping in prayer. Birds are common to both traditions. Akkadian examples make frequent reference to doves. Male doves make a cooing sound that may continue for hours, including the nighttime. This persistent "moaning" (*damāmu*, as Akkadian texts describe it) sounds doleful to human ears and would have been

---

[3] See pages 67–68.

a familiar sound because doves happily roost in human structures and have long been kept in dovecotes in the Near East since ancient times. Doves always appear in the Akkadian prayers as "moaning" "night and day" (Ishtar 2, Ishtar 10, *Er* 1.15b., *Dš* 11.1, Literary Prayer to Ishtar). The dove motif is thus fairly standard and reflects the behavior of the bird. Hebrew texts also refer to bird calls as sorrowful sounds but do not specifically mention the dove in this context. The Hebrew term for "dove" appears in the superscription of Ps 56, but it has no connection to the weeping in that psalm. Outside the corpus, after YHWH heals Hezekiah due in part to his weeping (Isa 38:5), Hezekiah speaks a prayer of thanksgiving that, in Isa 38:14, reads: "Like a swallow or crane I clamor, I moan like a dove (אהגה כיונה)." Psalm 102 refers to birds generally and owls and pelicans in particular but makes no reference to doves. These birds are characterized as lonely, which suggests the sadness of the sound. Birds are the only animal image in Hebrew examples, but the Akkadian corpus evidences one example of a mammal. In addition to a moaning dove, *Er* 1.15b also compares the petitioner to a cow: "to his own god like a cow he bellows." This bovine reference resonates with attachment theory which has relied on both human and animal studies (especially birds and mammals). Human weeping is a social behavior intended to elicit social help, and the analogous behavior in most mammals involved audible cries to establish reunion with conspecifics. Cows bellow in order to locate the herd or a missing calf. Although the Mesopotamians had no developed theory of attachment behaviors, they correctly saw the parallel between a human weeping to a deity in supplication and a cow bellowing. Outside the corpus, the Dialogue between a Man and His God has a similarly striking image. It describes the weeping and petitioning man as braying "like the weaned foal of a donkey," something young donkeys do to locate their mothers as part of their attachment behavior. Hebrew references to weeping never mention mammalian imagery. Bovine attachments do appear salient in 1 Sam 6, where the ark returns to Israel on a cart pulled by two milk cows who ignore their own calves to deliver the ark "lowing as they went" (1 Sam 6:12), indicating the divine power that overcomes strength of the cows' natural instinct. Mammalian images involve attachments similar to human parent-child relationships. The references to moaning doves may have inspired similar ideas of lonesome doves calling sorrowfully.

The motif of tears as sustenance appears in both Akkadian and Hebrew prayers (*Er* 2.1d; Pss 40:4; 80:6; 102:10). The poetic image appears to emphasize the continuity and frequency of the person's weeping, although it may also imply fasting as a further behavior intended to elicit divine care. The image likely reflects a common cultural inheritance rather than a coincidence or image grounded in attachment theory. Indeed, it appears to have been a Sumerian poetic motif borrowed into Akkadian literature and therefore into a wider Near Eastern context that includes biblical Hebrew prayers. The specific manifestations of the motif are tailored to the purposes of the prayer; the language is not fixed or stereotyped but permits flexibility. For example, the poet may present the deity as feeding the people tears in order to highlight divine anger and aggression (Ps 80). The motif is so specific (not common to European poetic traditions, for example) that this shared language indicates a common cultural matrix.

Both Akkadian and Hebrew prayers employ the motif of tears in ways consistent with weeping as a means of coregulating emotion and involve several specific similarities and differences in, for example, their use of animal imagery. There are also major differences between the two corpora. In both corpora, the task of differentiating prayer genres is notoriously complex, and native categories are not entirely clear. It does seem evident, however, that the specific cultural contexts for the prayers were likely very different. The Mesopotamian tradition developed two entire prayer categories specific to rituals for appeasing the heart of an angry deity (*eršaḫunga*s and *dingiršadabba*s). Although the complaint psalms have a similar function, there is no comparable evidence that the Israelites consciously developed a genre of prayer or a liturgical rite for the same express purpose of mollifying divine wrath. The native classifications of Akkadian prayers (insofar as we can discern them) and the modern scholarly classifications of psalm genres do not allow an easy mapping between them that would enable scholars to compare like with like. The present study has attempted to bypass this problem by examining both corpora of prayer for a specific motif and observing its distribution within the respective genre classification developed within the respective scholarly discussions rather than limiting the study to preselected and allegedly comparable Hebrew and Akkadian genres. By analyzing each corpus separately and comparing the results later, it is possible to notice that both corpora deploy the motif of tears primarily in reference to divine anger in the context of laments/petitions. These observations can offer insight without needing to claim similarity of genre. It also points to a potential similarity of genre between complaint psalms and *eršaḫunga*s and *dingiršadabba*s, with the caveat that the complaint psalm does not appear to be a native Hebrew genre like the two Akkadian prayer types are native Mesopotamian genres.

A further difference between Hebrew and Akkadian examples of weeping in prayer may be worth noting. The Akkadian examples involve a wide variety of linguistic means by which the motif may be realized. The Hebrew examples, by contrast, show a comparatively narrow range of expression. This difference does not seem to reflect the smaller scope of the Hebrew corpus because, even within narrow genre limitations (e.g., *eršaḫunga*s), the Mesopotamian variety stands out in comparison to Hebrew. The Hebrew expressions appear to be more constrained or limited for reasons that cannot be discerned.

A final question that both corpora raise is hard to answer with certainty: why is weeping so rare? If weeping is such a powerful nonverbal expression of helplessness that can elicit empathy, then why do speakers not deploy the weeping motif as a standard feature of petitions? Most individual laments in the book of Psalms do not refer to weeping, which is also absent from most *šuilla*s and *dingiršadabba*s. Two considerations may help make sense of the distribution and frequency of the weeping motif. First, poets may have avoided overusing the motif lest it lose its power by frequent application. Deities, like humans, might become desensitized to tears if they see them too frequently. Second, as described above, weeping does appear relatively frequently when divine anger is in view, notably in Hebrew complaint psalms and Mesopotamian *eršaḫunga*s. In short, where weeping appears, divine anger may be involved. This evidence suggests that weeping may have been regarded as a desirable means for mollifying divine anger but not an appropriate means of general petition. Recall that, within human relationships, weeping may elicit either empathy or anger. As a means of seeking help, weeping is a risky strategy. But what if the other person is already angry? In this case, there may be relatively little to lose by deploying weeping as a powerful signal of helplessness and surrender. It may or may not work, but evidence indicates that weeping can assuage anger in some cases, and the downside risk may be minimal where it fails. In the context of the prayers, when the petitioner is already suffering the effects of divine wrath, an angry deity might be placated by weeping and, if not, then nothing changes. Outside the context of divine wrath, weeping appears to be a riskier strategy, as it might incite divine anger if it is perceived as a manipulation. This logic may help explain why weeping is rare in psalmic laments outside the complaint psalms and most common in *eršaḫunga*s, some *dingiršadabba*s, and only *šuilla*s that refer to the deity as angry.

Works Cited

Abusch, Tzvi. "Witchcraft and the Anger of the Personal God." Pages 83–121 in *Mesopotamian Magic: Textual, Historical, and Interpretive Perspectives*. Edited by Tzvi Abusch and Karel van der Toorn. Ancient Magic and Divination 1. Groningen: Styx, 1999.

———. "Witchcraft Literature in Mesopotamia." Pages 373–85 in *The Babylonian World*. Edited by Gwendolyn Leick. New York: Routledge, 2007.

Ainsworth, Mary Salter, Mary C. Blehar, Everett Waters, and Sally N. Wall. *Patterns of Attachment: A Psychological Study of the Strange Situation*. Mahwah, NJ: Lawrence Erlbaum, 1978. Repr., New York: Routledge, 2015.

Allen, Leslie C. "The Value of Rhetorical Criticism in Psalm 69." *JBL* 105 (1986): 577–98.

Alonzo Schökel, Luis. "The Poetic Structure of Psalm 42–43." *JSOT* 1 (1976): 4–11.

Alonzo Schökel, Luis, and Cecilia Carniti. *Salmos* Nueva Biblia Española. 2 vols. Villatuerta: Editorial Verbo Divino, 1992–1993.

Anderson-Stojanovic, Virginia R. "The Chronology and Function of Ceramic Unguentaria." *AJA* 91 (1987): 105–22.

Archer, Margaret S. *Making Our Way through the World*. Cambridge: Cambridge University Press, 2007.

———. *The Reflexive Imperative in Late Modernity*. Cambridge: Cambridge University Press, 2012.

———. *Structure, Agency, and the Internal Conversation*. Cambridge: Cambridge University Press, 2003.

Auffret, Pierre. "'Car toi, tu as agi': Etude structurelle du Psaume 39." *Bijdr* 51 (1990): 118–38.

———. "Essai sur la structure littéraire du psaum 137." *ZAW* 92 (1980): 346–77.

———. "Il a entendu, Yhwh: Étude structurelle du Psaume 6." *ETR* 82 (2007): 595–602.

Augustine. *Expositions of the Psalms*. Translated by Maria Boulding. 6 vols. Hyde Park, NY: New City, 2000–2006.

Aun, John. "Psalm 137: Complex Communal Laments." *JBL* 127 (2008): 267–89.

Austen, Jane. *Mansfield Park*. Edited by R. W. Chapman. 3rd ed. Oxford: Oxford University Press, 1934.

Avalos, Hector. *Illness and Health Care in the Ancient Near East: The Role of the Temple in Greece, Mesopotamia, and Israel*. HSM 54. Atlanta: GA: Society of Biblical Literature, 1995.

Báez, Silvio José. *Tiempo de caller y tiempo de hablar: El silencio en la Biblia Hebrea*. Rome: Teresianum, 2000.

Bakermans-Kraneburg, Marian J., and Marinus H. van Ijzendoorn. "The First 10,000 Adult Attachment Interviews: Distribution of Adult Attachment Representations in Clinical and Non-Clinical Groups." *Attachment and Human Development* 11 (2009): 223–63.

Bakhtin, Mikhail. *The Dialogic Imagination: Four Essays*. Translated by C. Emerson and M. Holquist. Austin: University of Texas Press, 1981.

———. *Problems of Dostoyevsky's Poetics*. Edited and translated by Cheryl Emerson. Minneapolis: University of Minnesota Press, 1984.

Baloian, Bruce Edward. *Anger in the Old Testament*. American University Studies 7/99. New York: Peter Lang, 1992.

Barré, Michael L. "Psalm 116: Its Structure and Its Enigmas." *JBL* 109 (1990): 61–79.

Baylin, Jonathan, and Daniel Hughes. *The Neurobiology of Attachment-Focused Therapy: Enhancing Connection and Trust in the Treatment of Children and Adolescents*. Norton Series on Interpersonal Neurobiology. New York: Norton, 2014.

Beebe, Beatrice, and Frank M. Lachmann. *The Origins of Attachment: Infant Research and Adult Treatment*. Relational Perspective Book Series. New York: Routledge, 2014.

Begrich, Joachim. "Das priesterliche Heilsorakel." *ZAW* 52 (1934): 81–92.

Bellelli, G., G. Leoni, and A. Curci. "Emocion y memoria collectiva: El recuerdo acontecimientos públicos." *Psicología Política* 18 (1999): 101–24.

Bellinger, William H. "Psalm 137: Memory and Poetry." *HBT* 27 (2005): 5–20.

———. *Psalms: Reading and Studying the Book of Psalms*. Peabody, MA: Hendrickson, 1990.

Beristain, Carlos Martín, Darío Páez, and José Luis González. "Ritual, Social Sharing, Silence, and Collective Memory Claims in the Case of the Guatemalan Genocide." *Psicothema* 12 (2000): 117–30.

Beristain, Carlos Martín, José Luis González, and Darío Páez. "Memoria collectiva y genocido político en Guatemale: Antecedentes y efectos de los procesos de la memoria colectiva." *Psicología Política* 18 (1999): 77–99.

Berlin, Adele. "On Reading Biblical Poetry: The Role of Metaphor." Pages 25–36 in *Congress Volume: Cambridge 1995*. Edited by J. A. Emerton. VTSup 66. Leiden: Brill, 1997.

Berlin, Andrea M. "Archeological Sources of the History of Palestine. Between Large Forces: Palestine in the Hellenistic Period." *BA* 60 (1997): 2–51.

Blechman, Andrew D. *Pigeons: The Fascinating Saga of the World's Most Revered and Reviled Bird*. St. Lucia: University of Queensland Press, 2006.

Boer, Roland, ed. *Bakhtin and Genre Theory in Biblical Studies*. Atlanta, GA: Society of Biblical Literature, 2007.

Bollingmo, Guri C., Ellen O. Wessel, Dag Erik Eilertsen, and Svein Magnussen. "Credibility of the Emotional Witness: A Study of Ratings by Police Investigators." *Psychology, Crime, and Law* 14 (2008): 29–40.

Borowski, Oded. *Every Living Thing: Daily Use of Animals in Ancient Israel*. Walnut Creek, CA: AltaMira, 1998.

Bosworth, David A. "Ancient Prayers and the Psychology of Religion: Deities as Attachment Figures." *JBL* 134 (2015): 681–700.

———. "Daughter Zion and Weeping in Lamentations 1–2." *JSOT* 28 (2013): 217–37.

———. *Infant Weeping in Akkadian, Hebrew, and Greek Literature*. CHSB 8. Winona Lake, IN: Eisenbrauns, 2016.

———. "The Tears of God in the Book of Jeremiah." *Bib* 94 (2013): 24–46.

———. "Understanding Grief and Reading the Bible." Pages 117–38 in *Mixed Feelings and Vexed Passions: Exploring Emotions in Biblical Literature*. Edited by F. Scott Spencer. RBS 90. Atlanta, GA: SBL Press, 2016.

———. "Weeping in Recognition Scenes in Genesis and the *Odyssey*." *CBQ* 77 (2015): 613–33.

———. "Weeping in the Psalms." *VT* 62 (2013): 36–46.

Bottéro, Jean. *Religion in Ancient Mesopotamia*. Translated by Teresa Lavender Fagan. Chicago, IL: University of Chicago Press, 2001.

Bowlby, John. *Attachment*. 2nd. ed. New York: Basic, 1982

———. *Loss: Sadness and Depression*. New York: Basic, 1980.

———. *Separation: Anxiety and Anger*. New York: Basic, 1973.

Broyles, Craig C. *The Conflict of Faith and Experience in the Psalms: A Form-Critical and Theological Study*. JSOTSup 52. Sheffield: Sheffield Academic, 1989.

———. *Psalms*. NIBCOT. Peabody, MA: Hendrickson, 1999.

Brueggemann, Walter. *The Message of the Psalms: A Theological Commentary*. AOTS. Minneapolis, MN: Augsburg, 1984.

Burton, Tara Isabella. "In Defense of Fanny Price." *Paris Review*, 7/10/2014, http://www.theparisreview.org/blog/2014/07/10/in-defense-of-fanny-price/.

Byrne, Paula. "Mansfield Park Shows the Dark Side of Jane Austen." *Telegraph*, 7/26/14, http://www.telegraph.co.uk/culture/books/10987048/Mansfield-Park-shows-the-dark-side-of-Jane-Austen.html.

Calhoun, Lawrence G., Arnie Cann, James W. Selby, David Magee. "Victim Emotional Response: Effects on Social Reaction to Victims of Rape." *British Journal of Social Psychology* 20 (1981): 17–21.

Cassidy, Jude, and Philip R. Shaver, eds. *Handbook of Attachment: Theory, Research, and Clinical Applications*. 3rd ed. New York: Guilford, 2016.

Charney, Davida H. *Persuading God: Rhetorical Studies of First-Person Psalms*. Sheffield: Sheffield Phoenix, 2016.

Clark, Margaret S., and Eli J. Finkel. "Does Expressing Emotion Promote Well-Being? It Depends on Relationship Context." Pages 105–26 in *The Social Life of Emotions*. Edited by Larissa Tiedens and Colin Wayne Leach. Cambridge: Cambridge University Press, 2004.

Clifford, Richard J. *Psalms 1–72*. AOTC. Nashville, TN: Abingdon, 2002.

———. *Psalms 73–150*. AOTC. Nashville, TN: Abingdon, 2002.

———. "What Does the Psalmist Ask For in Psalms 39:5 and 90:12?" *JBL* 119 (2000): 59–66.

Cornell Lab of Ornithology. "All About Birds." https://www.allaboutbirds.org/

Correia, Isabel, Jorge Vala, and Patrícia Aguiar. "Victim's Innocence, Social Categorization, and the Threat to the Belief in a Just World." *Journal of Experimental Social Psychology* 43 (2007): 31–38.

Correia, Isabel, Hélder Alves, Robbie Sutton, Miguel Ramos, Maria Gouveia-Pereira, and Jorge Vala. "When do People Derogate or Psychologically Distance themselves from Victims? Belief in a Just World and Ingroup Identification." *Personality and Individual Differences* 53 (2012): 747–52.

Cotrill, Amy. "The Traumatized 'I' in Psalm 102: A Feminist Biblical Theology of Suffering." Pages 171–86 in *After Exegesis: Feminist Biblical Theology. Essays in Honor of Carol A. Newsom*. Edited by Patricia K. Tull and Jacqueline E. Lapsley. Waco, TX: Baylor University Press, 2015.

Curci, Antonietta, and Bernard Rimé. "The Temporal Evolution of the Social Sharing of Emotions and Its Consequences on Emotional Recovery: A Longitudinal Study." *Emotion* 12 (2012): 1404–14.

Day, John. *Psalms*. OTG. Sheffield: JSOT, 1990.

Duprez, Christelle. "Motives for the Social Sharing of an Emotional Experience." *Journal of Social and Personal Relationships* 36 (2014): 1–31.

Ebeling, Erich. *Die akkadische Gebetsserie "Handerhebung"*. Berlin: Akademie-Verlag, 1953.

Ebersole, Gary L. "The Function of Ritual Weeping Revisited: Affective Expression and Moral Discourse." *HR* 39 (2000) 211–46.

Eder, Sigrid. *Identifikationspotenziale in den Psalmen: Emotionen, Metaphern und Textdynamik in der Psalmen 30, 64, 90 und 147*. BBB 183. Göttingen: Vandenhoeck & Ruprecht, 2018.

Edlund, John E., Brad J. Sagarin, and Brian S. Johnson. "Reciprocity and the Belief in a Just World." *Personality and Individual Differences* 43 (2007): 589–96.

Eksner, H. Julia. "Indexing Anger and Aggression: From Language Ideologies to Linguistic Affect." Pages 193–205 in *Methods of Exploring Emotions*. Edited by Helena Flam and Jochen Kleres. London: Routledge, 2015.

Erbele-Küster, Dorothea. *Lesen als Akt des Betens: Ein Rezeptionsästhetik der Psalmen*. WMANT 87. Hamburg: Neukirchener Verlag, 2001.

Farber, Walter. *Schlaf, Kindchen, Schlaf! Mesopotamische Baby-Beschwörungen und -Rituale*, MC 2. Winona Lake, IN: Eisenbrauns, 1989.

Fernyhough, Charles. *The Voices Within: The History and Science of How We Talk to Ourselves*. New York: Basic, 2016.

Fischer, Agneta H., and Antont S. R. Manstead. "The Relation between Gender and Emotions in Different Cultures." Pages 71–94 in *Gender and Emotion: Social Psychological Perspectives*. Edited by Agneta Fischer. Cambridge: Cambridge University Press, 2000.

Flesher, LeAnn Snow. "Rapid Change of Mood: Oracles of Salvation, Certainty of a Hearing, or Rhetorical Play?" Pages 3–45 in *"My Words Are Lovely": Studies in the Rhetoric of the Psalms*. Edited by Robert L. Foster and David M. Howard, Jr. LHBOTS 467. New York: T&T Clark, 2008.

Fløysvik, Ingvar. *When God Becomes My Enemy: The Theology of the Complaint Psalms*. St. Louis, MO: Concordia Academic, 1997.

Fonagy, Peter, György Gergely, Elliot Jurist, and Mary Target. *Affect Regulation, Mentalization, and the Development of the Self*. New York: Other, 2002.

Forti, Tova L. *"Like a Lone Bird on a Roof": Animal Imagery and the Structure of the Psalms*. CSHB 10. University Park, PA: Eisenbrauns, 2018.

Foster, Benjamin R. *Before the Muses: An Anthology of Akkadian Literature*. 3rd ed. Bethesda, MD: CDL, 2005.

Frechette, Christopher. "Destroying the Internalized Perpetrator: A Healing of the Violent Language against Enemies in the Psalms." Pages 71–84 in *Trauma and Traumatization in Individual and Collective Dimensions: Insights from Biblical Studies and Beyond*. Edited by Eve-Marie Becker, Jan Dochhorn, and Else K. Holt. Göttingen: Vandenhoeck & Ruprecht, 2014.

———. *Mesopotamian Ritual-Prayers (Šuillas): A Case Study Investigating Idiom, Rubric, Form, and Function*. AOAT 379. Münster: Ugarit-Verlag, 2012.

Furnham, Adrian. "Belief in a Just World: Research Progress over the Past Decade." *Personality and Individual Differences* 34 (2003): 795–819.

Geller, Markham J. *Babylonian Medicine: Theory and Practice*. Malden, MA: Wiley-Blackwell, 2010.

———. *Evil Demons: Canonical* Utukkū Lemnūtu *Incantations*. SAACT 5. Helsinki: Neo-Assyrian Text Corpus Project, 2007.

———. "Incantations within Akkadian Medical Texts." Pages 389–99 in *The Babylonian*

World. Edited by Gwendolyn Leick. New York: Routledge, 2007.

Geller, Markham J., and Christian Bauer. "CT 58, No. 70: A Middle Babylonian Eršahunga." *BSOAS* 55 (1992): 528–32.

Gerstenberger, Erhard S. "Psalm 69: Complaint and Confession." *Covenant Quarterly* 55 (1987): 3–19.

———. *Psalms*. FOTL 14–15. 2 vols. Grand Rapids, MI: Eerdmans, 1988–2001.

Gillath, Omri, Gery C. Karantzas, and R. Chris Fraley. *Adult Attachment: A Concise Introduction to Theory and Research*. London: Elsevier, 2016.

Gillingham, Susan E. *The Poems and Psalms of the Hebrew Bible*. Oxford: Oxford University Press, 1990.

Goldingay, John. *Psalms*. BCOTWP. 3 vols. Grand Rapids, MI: Baker Academic, 2006–8.

Grant, Deena. *Divine Anger in the Hebrew Bible*. CBQMS 52. Washington, DC: Catholic Biblical Association of America, 2014.

Green, Barbara. *Mikhail Bakhtin and Biblical Scholarship: An Introduction*. SemeiaSt 38 Atlanta, GA: Society of Biblical Literature, 2000.

Grossmann, Karin. "Weinen, ein Bildungsverhalten." *Psychotherapeut* 54 (2009): 77–89.

Guillaume, Alfred. "The Meaning of תולל in Psalm 137:3." *JBL* 75 (1956): 143–44.

Gunkel, Hermann, completed by Joachim Begrich. *An Introduction to the Psalms: The Genres of the Religious Lyric of Israel*. Translated by James D. Nogalski. Mercer Library of Biblical Studies. Macon, GA: Mercer University Press, 1998. Translation of Gunkel, *Einleitung in die Psalmen: Die Gattugen der religiösen Lyrik Israels*. Göttingen: Vandenhoeck & Ruprecht, 1933.

Hackett, Louisa, Andrew Day, and Philip Mohr. "Expectancy Violation and Perceptions of Rape Victim Credibility." *Legal and Criminological Psychology* 13 (2008): 323–34.

Hart, Susan. *The Impact of Attachment*. New York: Norton, 2011.

Hasson, Oren. "Emotional Tears as Biological Signals." *Evolutionary Psychology* 7 (2009): 363–70.

Hays, Christopher B. "How Shall We Sing? Psalm 137 in Historical and Canonical Context." *HBT* 27 (2005): 35–55.

Heeßel, Nils P. "The Hands of the Gods: Disease Names and Divine Anger." Pages 120–30 in *Disease in Babylonia*. Edited by Irving Finkel and M. J. Geller. CM 36. Leiden: Brill, 2006.

Heiler, Friedrich. *Prayer: A Study in the History and Psychology of Religion*. Edited and translated by Samuel McComb. London: Oxford University Press, 1932.

Hendricks, Michelle C. P., Judith K. Nelson, Randolph R. Cornelius, and Ad J. J. M. Vingerhoets. "Why Crying Improves Our Well-Being: An Attachment-Theory Perspective on the Function of Adult Crying." Pages 87–96 in *Emotion Regulation: Conceptual and Clinical Issues*. Edited by Ad Vingerhoets, Ivan Nyklíček, and Johan Denollet. New York: Springer, 2008.

Hermann, Judith. *Trauma and Recovery*. New York: Basic, 1992.

Herranz, J. K., and N. Basabe. "Identidad nacional, ideología política y memoria colectiva." *Psicología Política* 18 (1999): 31–47.

Hill, Daniel. *Affect Regulation Theory: A Clinical Model*. New York: Norton, 2015.

Holt-Lunstad, Julianne, Timothy Smith, and J. Bradley Layton. "Social Relationships and Mortality Risk: A Meta-Analytic Review." *PLOS Medicine* 7 (2010), https://doi.org/10.1371/journal.pmed.1000316.

Holt-Lunstad, Julianne, Timothy Smith, and Mark Baker. "Loneliness and Social Isolation as Risk Factors for Mortality: A Meta-Analytic Review." *Perspectives on Psychological Science* 10 (2015): 227–37.

Hood, Ralph W., Jr., Peter C. Hill, and Bernard Spilka. *The Psychology of Religion: An Empirical Approach.* 4th ed. New York: Guilford, 2009.

Hopkins, Denise Dumbkowski. *Psalms Books 2–3.* Wisdom Commentary 21. Collegeville, MN: Liturgical Press, 2016.

Hossfeld, Frank-Lothar, and Erich Zenger. *Psalms 2: A Commentary on Psalms 51–100.* Hermeneia. Translated by Linda M. Maloney. Minneapolis, MN: Augsburg Fortress, 2005.

———. *Psalms 3: A Commentary on Psalms 101–150.* Hermeneia. Translated by Linda M. Maloney. Minneapolis, MN: Augsburg Fortress, 2011.

Huehnergard, John. *A Grammar of Akkadian.* HSS 45. 3rd ed. Winona Lake, IN: Eisenbrauns, 2011.

Jacobson, Rolf A., and Karl N. Jacobson. *Invitation to the Psalms: A Reader's Guide for Discovery and Engagement.* Grand Rapids, MI: Baker Academic, 2013.

Janowski, Bernd. *Rettungsgewissheit und Epiphanie des Heils: Das Motiv der Hilfe Gottes "am Morgen" im Alten Orient und im Alten Testament.* WMANT 59. Neikirchen-Vluyn: Neukirchener Verlag, 1989.

Jaques, Margaret. *Le vocabulaire des sentiments dans les textes sumériens: Recherche sur le lexique sumérien et akkadien.* AOAT 332. Münster: Ugarit-Verlag, 2006.

———. *Mon dieu qu'ai-je fait? Les diĝir-šà-dab(5)-ba et la piété privée en Mesopotamie.* OBO 273. Göttingen: Vandenhoeck & Ruprecht, 2015.

Johnson, Philip S., and David G. Firth, eds. *Interpreting the Psalms: Issues and Approaches.* Downers Grove, IL: IVP Academic, 2005.

Karen, Robert. *Becoming Attached: How First Relationships Shape Our Capacity to Love.* Oxford: Oxford University Press, 1998.

King, Leonard W. *Babylonian Magic and Sorcery, Being "The Prayers of the Lifting of the Hand."* London: Luzac, 1896.

Kirkpatrick, Lee A. *Attachment, Evolution, and the Psychology of Religion.* New York: Guilford, 2005.

Kitching, Chris. "An Old Testament Wonder! Dramatic Moment the River Zin is Reborn as Flash Flood Sweeps across Arid Landscape in Israel's Negev Desert." *Daily Mail,* 1/16/2016, http://www.dailymail.co.uk/news/article-2913486/Zin-River-reborn-flash-flood-sweeps-arid-landscape-Israel-s-Negev-Desert.html.

Klassen, Pamela E. "Ritual." Pages 143–61 in *The Oxford Handbook of Religion and Emotion.* Edited by John Corrigan. Oxford: Oxford University Press, 2008.

Klein, Jacob. "Man and His God: A Wisdom Poem or Cultic Lament?" Pages 123–43 in *Approaches to Sumerian Literature: Studies in Honor of Stip (H. L. J. Vanstiphout).* Edited by P. Michalowski and N. Veldhuis. CM 35. Leiden: Brill, 2006.

van der Kolk, Bessel A. *The Body Keeps the Score: Brain, Mind, and Body in the Healing of Trauma.* New York: Viking, 2014.

———. Foreword to *The Polyvagel Theory: Neurophysiological Foundations of Emotions, Attachment, Communication, Self-Regulation,* by Stephen W. Porges. New York: Norton, 2011.

Kong, Wong Fook. "Use of Overarching Metaphors in Psalms 91 and 42/43." *Sino-Christian Studies* 9 (2010): 7–27.

Kraus, Fritz Rudolph. "Brief eines Bittstellers an eine Gottheit." *JAOS* 103 (1983): 205–9.

———. "Ein altbabylonischer Privatbrief an eine Gottheit." *RA* 65 (1971): 27–36.

———. "Eine Neue Probe Akkadischer Literatur: Brief eines Bittstellers an eine Gottheit." *JAOS* 103 (1983): 205–9.

Kuckhoff, Antonius. *Psalm 6 und die Bitten im Psalter: Ein paradigmatisches Bitt- und Klagegebet im Horizont des Gesamtpsalters*. BBB 160. Göttingen: Bonn University Press, 2011.

Lambert, David A. *How Repentance Became Biblical: Judaism, Christianity, and the Interpretation of Scripture*. Oxford: Oxford University Press, 2016.

Lambert, W. G. *Babylonian Oracle Questions*. MC 13. Winona Lake, IN: Eisenbrauns, 2007.

———. *Babylonian Wisdom Literature*. Oxford: Oxford University Press, 1960. Repr., Winona Lake, IN: Eisenbrauns, 1996.

———. "A Further Attempt at a Man and His God." Pages 187–201 in *Language, Literature, and History: Philological and Historical Studies Presented to Erica Reiner*. AOS 67. New Haven, CT: American Oriental Society, 1987.

———. "Three Literary Prayers of the Babylonians." *AfO* 19 (1959): 47–66.

Lane, Carrie J. "Evolution of Gender Differences in Adult Crying." PhD diss., University of Texas at Arlington, 2006.

Lenzi, Alan. "Corpus of Akkadian Shuila Prayers Online." http://www1.pacific.edu/~alenzi/shuilas/catalog.html.

———. "Invoking the God: Interpreting Invocations in Mesopotamian Prayers and Biblical Laments of the Individual." *JBL* 129 (2010): 303–15.

———. *Reading Akkadian Prayers and Hymns*. ANEM 3. Atlanta, GA: Society of Biblical Literature, 2011.

Levine, Herbert. *Sing unto God a New Song: A Contemporary Reading of the Psalms*. Bloomington: Indiana University Press, 1995.

Lewis, Deane. "The Owl Pages." https://www.owlpages.com/owls/.

Lindström, Fredrik. *Suffering and Sin: Interpretation of Illness in the Individual Complaint Psalms*. ConBOT 37. Stockholm: Almqvist & Wiksell, 1994.

Lloyd, Peter, and Charles Fernyhough, eds. *Lev Vygotsky: Critical Assessments*. 4 vols. London: Routledge, 1999.

Loretz, Oswald. "Psalm 6: Klagelied enes Einzeln: Totenklage im Keret-Epos und Weinen in Ps 6,7b–8 und Ps 55,4." Pages 75–102 in *Psalmstudien: Kolometrie, Strophik und Theologie ausgewählter Psalmen*. Berlin: de Gruyter, 2002.

Lucas, Ernest C. *The Psalms and Wisdom Literature*, vol. 3 of *Exploring the Old Testament*. London: SPCK, 2003.

Lutz, Tom. *Crying: The Natural and Cultural History of Tears*. New York: Norton, 1999.

Maas, Joyce, Anja Laan, and Ad Vingerhoets. "Attachment, Emotion Regulation, and Adult Crying." Pages 181–95 in *Emotion Regulation and Well-Being*. Edited by Ivan Nyklíček, Ad Vingerhoets, and Marcel Zeelenberg. New York: Springer, 2011.

Mandolfo, Carleen. *Daughter Zion Talks Back to the Prophets: A Dialogic Theology of the Book of Lamentation*. SemeiaSt 58. Atlanta, GA: Society of Biblical Literature, 2007.

———. *God in the Dock: Dialogic Tension in the Psalms of Lament*. JSOTSup 357. Sheffield: Sheffield Academic Press and New York: Bloomsbury T&T Clark, 2002.

Maul, Stefan. *"Herzberuhigungsklagen": Die sumerisch-akkadischen Eršahunga-Gebete*. Weisbaden: Harrassowitz, 1988.

———. *Zukunftsbewältigung: Eine Untersuching altorientalischen Denkens abhand der babylonisch-assyrischen Löseritual (Namburbi)*. Mainz: von Zabern, 1994.

———. "Zwei neue 'Herzberuhigungsklagen.'" *RA* 85 (1991): 67–74.

Mayer, Werner. *Untersuchungen zur Formensprache der babylonische "Gebetsbeschwörigen"*. StPohl

5. Rome: Biblical Institute Press, 1976.

Mays, James L. "Psalm 13." *Int* 34 (1980): 279–83.

McKay, J. W. "Psalms of Vigil." *ZAW* 91 (1979): 231–47.

Miceli, Maria, and Cristiano Castelfranchi. "Crying: Discussing Its Basic Reasons and Uses." *New Ideas in Psychology* 21 (2003): 247–63.

Mikulincer, Mario, and Philip R. Shaver. *Attachment in Adulthood: Structure, Dynamics, and Change*. 2nd ed. New York: Guilford, 2016.

Mooney, Carol Gerhart. *Theories of Attachment: Introduction to Bowlbly, Ainsworth, Gerber, Brazelton, Kennell and Klaus*. Redleaf Professional Library. St. Paul, MN: Redleaf, 2010.

Mowinckel, Sigmund. *Psalm Studies*. 2 vols. History of Biblical Studies 2. Translated by Mark E. Biddle. Atlanta, GA: SBL Press, 2014.

Nelson, Judith Kay. "Crying in Psychotherapy: Its Meaning, Assessment, and Management Based on Attachment Theory." Pages 202–14 in *Emotion Regulation: Conceptual and Clinical Issues*. Edited by Ad Vingerhoets, Ivan Nyklíček, and Johan Denollet. New York: Springer, 2008.

———. *Seeing Through Tears: Crying and Attachment*. New York: Routledge, 2005.

Newsom, Carol. *The Book of Job: A Contest of Moral Imaginations*. Oxford: Oxford University Press, 2003.

Nougayrol, Jean. "Une version ancienne du 'juste souffant'." *RB* 59 (1952): 239–50.

Nussbaum, Martha. *Upheavals of Thought: The Intelligence of Emotions*. Cambridge: Cambridge University Press, 2001.

Olyan, Saul. *Biblical Mourning: Ritual and Social Dimensions*. Oxford: Oxford University Press, 2004.

Oshima, Takayoshi. *Babylonian Prayers to Marduk*. ORA 7. Tübingen: Mohr Siebeck, 2011.

Pennebaker, James W. *Opening Up: The Healing Power of Expressing Emotions*. Rev. ed. New York: Guilford, 1997.

Pennebaker, James W., and Amy L. Gonzales. "Making History: Social and Psychological Processes underlying Collective Memory." Pages 171–93 in *Memory in Mind and Culture*. Edited by Pascal Boyer and James B. Wertsch. Cambridge: Cambridge University Press, 2009.

Pierce, Gregory, and I. G. Sarason, eds. *Handbook of Social Support and the Family*. New York: Springer, 1996.

Porges, Stephen W. *The Pocket Guide to the Polyvagal Theory: The Transformative Power of Feeling Safe*. Norton Series on Interpersonal Neurobiology. New York: Norton, 2017.

———. *The Polyvagal Theory: Neurophysiological Foundations of Emotions, Attachment, Communication, Self-Regulation*. Norton Series on Interpersonal Neurobiology. New York: Norton, 2011.

Prinsloo, Willem S. "Psalm 116: Disconnected Text or Symmetrical Whole?" *Bib* 74 (1993): 71–84.

Provine, Robert R. "Emotional Tears and NGF: A Biographical Appreciation and Research Beginning." *Archives Italiennes de Biologie* 149 (2011): 169–74.

Ramage, Matthew. "Christian Discernment of Divine Revelation: Benedict XVI and the International Theological Commission on the Dark Passages of the Old Testament." *ScrTh* 47 (2015): 71–83.

Rimé, Bernard. "Emotion Elicits the Social Sharing of Emotion: Theory and Empirical Review." *Emotion Review* 1 (2009): 60–85.

———. *Le partage social des émotions*. Paris: Presses universitaires de France, 2005.

———. "Mental Rumination, Social Sharing, and the Recovery from Emotional Exposure." Pages 279–91 in *Emotion, Disclosure, and Health*. Edited by James Pennebaker. Washington, DC: American Psychological Association, 1995.

Rimé, Bernard, Dario Paez, Patrick Kanyangara, and Vincent Yzerbyt. "The Social Sharing of Emotions in Interpersonal and in Collective Situations: Common Psychosocial Consequences." Pages 147–63 in *Emotion Regulation and Well-Being*. Edited by Ivan Nyklíček, Ad Vingerhoets, and Marcel Zeelenberg. New York: Springer, 2011.

Rimé, Bernard, Susanna Corsini, Gwénola Herbette. "Emotion, Verbal Expression, and the Social Sharing of Emotion." Pages 185–208 in *The Verbal Communication of Emotions: Interdisciplinary Perspectives*. Edited by Susan Fussell. Mahwah, NJ: Earlbaum, 2002.

Rimé, Bernard, Gwénola Herbette, and Susanna Corsini. "The Social Sharing of Emotion: Illusory and Real Benefits of Talking about Emotional Experiences." Pages 27–41 in *Emotional Expression and Health: Advances in Theory, Assessment, and Clinical Applications*. Edited by Ivan Nyklíček, Lydia Temoshok, and Ad Vingerhoets. New York: Brunner-Routledge, 2004.

Ruiz, Eleuterio Ramón. "El silencio en el primero libro del Salterio (Salmos 1–41): Primera parte." *RevistB* 67 (2005): 31–83.

———. "El silencio en el primero libro del Salterio (Salmos 1–41): Segunda parte." *RevistB* 67 (2005): 163–78.

Rydé, K., M. Friedrichsen, and P. Strang. "Crying: A Force to Balance Emotions among Cancer Patients in Palliative Home Care." *Palliative and Support Care* 5 (2007): 51–59.

Sabourin, Leopold. *The Psalms: Their Origin and Meaning*. Staten Island, NY: Alba House, 1974.

Sapolsky, Robert. "The Trouble with Testosterone: Will Boys Just Be Boys?" Pages 149–59 in *The Trouble with Testosterone and Other Essays on the Biology of the Human Predicament*. New York: Simon & Schuster, 1998.

Savran, George. "'How Can We Sing a Song of the Lord?': The Strategy of Lament in Psalm 137." *ZAW* 112 (2000): 43–58.

Schmidt, Hans. *Die Psalmen*. HAT 15. Tübingen: J. C. B. Mohr, 1934.

Schore, Allan N. *Affect Dysregulation and Disorders of the Self*. Norton Series on Interpersonal Neurobiology. New York: Norton, 2003.

———. *Affect Regulation and the Origin of the Self: The Neurobiology of Emotional Development*. New York: Taylor and Francis, 1994.

———. *Affect Regulation and the Repair of the Self*. Norton Series on Interpersonal Neurobiology. New York: Norton, 2003.

———. *The Science of the Art of Psychotherapy*. Norton Series on Interpersonal Neurobiology. New York: Norton, 2012.

Schwemer, Daniel. "Hittite Prayers to the Sun-God for Appeasing an Angry Personal God: A Critical Edition of *CTH* 372–74." Pages 349–93 in *Mon dieu qu'ai-je fait? Les diĝir-šà-dab(5)-ba et la piété privée en Mesopotamie*. Edited by Margaret Jaques. OBO 273. Göttingen, Vandenhoeck & Ruprecht, 2015.

Scrimali, Tullio. *Neuroscience-Based Cognitive Therapy: New Methods for Assessment, Treatment and Self-Regulation*. Malden, MA: Wiley-Blackwell, 2012.

Seybold, Klaus. *Die Psalmen*, HAT 1/15. Tübingen: Mohr Siebeck, 1996.

———. *Das Gebet des Kranken im Alten Testament*. BWANT 99. Stuttgart: Kohlhammer, 1973.

Sharp, Shane. "How Does Prayer Help Manage Emotions?" *Social Psychology Quarterly* 73 (2010): 417–37.

Shaver, Philip R., and Mario Mikulincer. "Adult Attachment and Emotion Regulation." Pages 507–33 in *Handbook of Emotion Regulation*. Edited by James Gross. 2nd ed. New York: Guilford, 2014.

Shaver, Phillip R., and R. Chris Fraley, "Attachment, Loss, and Grief: Bowlby's Views and Contemporary Views." Pages 40–62 in *Handbook of Attachment: Theory, Research, and Clinical Applications*. Edited by Jude Cassidy and Phillip R. Shaver. 3rd ed. New York: Guilford, 2016.

Shiller, Virginia M. *The Attachment Bond: Affectional Ties across the Lifespan*. Lanham, MD: Lexington, 2017.

Singer, Itamar. *Hittite Prayers*. WAW. Atlanta, GA: Society of Biblical Literature, 2002.

von Soden, Wolfram. "Ist im Alten Testament schon vom Schwimmen die Rede?" *ZAH* 4 (1991): 165–70.

Soltis, Joseph. "The Signal Functions of Early Infant Crying." *Behavioral and Brain Sciences* 27 (2004): 443–90.

Soriano, Cristina. "Emotion and Conceptual Metaphor." Pages 206–14 in *Methods of Exploring Emotions*. Edited by Helena Flam and Jochen Kleres. London: Routledge, 2015.

Sõukand, Renata, Raivo Kalle, and Ingvar Svanberg. "Uninvited Guests: Traditional Insect Repellents in Estonia Used against the Clothes Moth *Tineola bisselliella*, Human Flea *Pulex irritans*, and Bedbug *Cimex lectularius*." *Journal of Insect Science* 10 (2010): 1–18.

Spilka, Bernard, and Kevin L. Ladd. *The Psychology of Prayer: A Scientific Approach*. New York: Guilford, 2013.

Starr, Ivan. *The Rituals of the Diviner*. BMes 12. Malibu, CA: Undena, 1983.

Steitler, Charles. "A Glossary of the Hittite Prayers to the Sun-God (CTH 372–74)." Pages 421–55 in *Mon dieu qu'ai-je fait? Les digîr-šà-dab(5)-ba et la piété privée en Mesopotamie*. Edited by Margaret Jaques. OBO 273. Göttingen: Vandenhoeck & Ruprecht, 2015.

Stern, Karen B. "Keeping the Dead in Their Place: Mortuary Practices and Jewish Cultural Identity in Roman North Africa." Pages 307–34 in *Cultural Identity on the Ancient Mediterranean*. Edited by Erich S. Gruen. Los Angeles, CA: Getty Research Institute, 2011.

Strawn, Brent. "Poetic Attachment: Psychology, Psycholinguistics, and the Psalms." Pages 404–23 in *The Oxford Handbook to the Psalms*. Edited by William Brown. Oxford: Oxford University Press, 2016.

———. "Trauma, Psalmic Disclosure, and Authentic Happiness." Pages 143–60 in *Bible through the Lens of Trauma*. Edited by Elizabeth Boase and Christopher Frechette. SemeiaSt 86. Atlanta, GA: SBL Press, 2016.

Strong, Anna Louise. *I Change Worlds: The Remaking of an American*. New York: Henry Holt, 1935.

———. *The Psychology of Prayer*. Chicago, IL: University of Chicago Press, 1909.

Stuart. D. "Moth." *ISBE* 3:426.

Sudak, Donna M. *Cognitive Behavioral Therapy for Clinicians*. Philadelphia, PA: Lippincott Williams and Wilkins, 2006.

Taylor, Shelley. "Social Support: A Review." Pages 192–217 in *The Oxford Handbook of Health Psychology*. Oxford: Oxford University Press, 2012.

Tolin, David F. *Doing CBT: A Comprehensive Guide to Working and Behaviors, Thoughts, and Emotions*. New York: Guilford, 2016.

van der Toorn, Karel. *Family Religion in Babylonia, Syria and Israel: Continuity and Change in the Forms of Religious Life*. SHCANE 7. Leiden: Brill, 1996.

———. *Sin and Sanction in Israel and Mesopotamia: A Comparative Study*. Assen: Van Gorcum, 1985.
de la Torre, Mónica Padilla, Elodie F. Briefer, Tom Reader, and Alan G. McElligot. "Acoustic Analysis of Cattle (Bous Taurus) Mother-Offspring Contact Calls from a Source-Filter Theory Perspective." *Applied Animal Behavior Science* 163 (2015): 58–68.
Trimble, Michael. *Why Humans Like to Cry: Tragedy, Evolution and the Brain*. Oxford: Oxford University Press, 2012.
Ullman, Sarah E., and Raymond A. Knight. "The Efficacy of Women's Resistance in Rape Situations." *Psychology of Women Quarterly* 17 (1993): 23–38.
Vesco, Jean-Luc. *Le psautier de David traduit et commenté*. LD 210–11. 2 vols. Paris: Cerf, 2006.
Villanueva, Federico G. *The "Uncertainty of a Hearing": A Study of the Sudden Change of Mood in the Psalms of Lament*. VTSup 121. Leiden: Brill, 2008.
Vingerhoets, Ad. "Crying: A Biosocial Phenomenon." Pages 87–96 in *Tears in the Greco-Roman World*. Edited by Thorsten Fögen. Berlin: de Gruyter, 2009.
———. *Why Only Humans Weep: Unraveling the Mystery of Tears*. Oxford: Oxford University Press, 2013.
Vingerhoets, Ad, and Jan Scheirs. "Sex Differences in Crying: Empirical Findings and Possible Explanations." Pages 143–65 in *Gender and Emotion: Social Psychological Perspectives*. Edited by Agneta Fischer. Cambridge: Cambridge University Press, 2000.
Vingerhoets, Ad, and Randolph Cornelius, eds. *Adult Crying: A Biopsychosocial Approach*. New York: Routledge, 2001.
Vygotsky, Lev. *Thought and Language*. Edited and translated by Eugenia Hanfmann, Gertrude Vakar, and Alex Kozulin. Cambridge, MA: MIT Press, 2012.
———. *The Vygotsky Reader*. Edited by René van der Veer and Jaan Valsinger. Oxford: Blackwell, 1994.
Wallace, Howard Neil. *Words to God, Word from God: The Psalms in the Prayer and Preaching of the Church*. Hampshire: Ashgate, 2005.
Walsh, Carey Ellen. *The Fruit of the Vine: Viticulture in Ancient Israel*. HSM 60. Winona Lake, IN: Eisenbrauns, 2000.
Walter, Chip. *Thumbs, Toes, and Tears and Other Traits that Make Us Human*. New York: Walker, 2006.
Wathey, John C. *The Illusion of God's Presence: The Biological Origins of Spiritual Longing*. Amherst, NY: Prometheus, 2015.
Watts, J. M., and J. M. Stookey. "Vocal Behavior in Cattle: The Animal's Commentary on Its Biological Processes and Welfare." *Applied Animal Behavior Science* 67 (2000): 15–33.
Weiser, Artur. *The Psalms*. Translated by H. Hartwell. OTL. London: SCM, 1962.
Westermann, Claus. *Praise and Lament in the Psalms*. Translated by Keith R. Krimm and Richard N. Soulen. Atlanta, GA: John Knox, 1981.
Wiley, Norbert. *Inner Speech and the Dialogical Self*. Philadelphia, PA: Temple University Press, 2016.
Wilson, Gerald H. "The Use of 'Untitled' Psalms in the Psalter." *ZAW* 97 (1985): 404–13.
Witt, Andrew. "Hearing Psalm 102 in the Context of the Psalter." *VT* 62 (2012): 582–606.
van Wolde, Ellen. "Sentiments as Culturally Constructed Emotions: Anger and Love in the Hebrew Bible." *BibInt* 16 (2008): 1–24.
Young, Sarah. *Jesus Calling Bible Storybook*. Nashville, TN: Tommy Nelson, 2012.
Zeno-Canto Foundation. "Xeno-Canto: Sharing Bird Sounds from Around the World." https://www.xeno-canto.org.

Zernecke, Anna Elise. *Gott und Mensch in Klagegebeten aus Israel und Mesopotamien. Die Handerhebungensgebete Ištar 10 und Ištar 2 und die Klagepsalment Ps 38 un Ps 22 im Vergleich.* AOAT 387. Münster: Ugarit-Verlag, 2011.

———. "How to Approach a Deity: The Growth of a Prayer Addressed to Ištar." Pages 124–43 in *Mediating Between Heaven and Earth: Communication with the Divine in the Ancient Near East.* Edited by C. L. Crouch, Jonathan Stökl, and Anna Elise Zernecke. LHBOTS 566. New York: Bloomsbury, 2014.

———. "A Shuilla: Ishtar 2: 'The Great Ishatar Prayer'." Pages 256–90 in *Reading Akkadian Prayers and Hymns.* Edited by Alan Lenzi. ANEM 3. Atlanta, GA: Society of Biblical Literature, 2011.

Zgoll, Annette. *Die Kunst des Betens: Form und Funktion. Theologie und Psychagogik in babylonisch-assyrischen Handerhebungensgebeten zu Ištar.* AOAT 308. Münster, Ugarit-Verlag, 2003.

Zhixiong, Niu. *"The King Lifted Up His Voice and Wept": David's Mourning in the Second Book of Samuel.* Rome: Editrice Pontificia Università Gregoriana, 2013.

Ziegler, Joseph. "Dir Hilfe Gottes 'am Morgen'." Pages 281–88 in *Alttestamenliche Studien: Friedrich Nötscher zum 60. Geburtstg Gewidmet.* Bonn: Hanstein, 1950.

Zimmern, Heinrich. *Beiträge zur Kenntnis der babylonischen Religion.* Leipzig: Hinrichs, 1901.

Zoucha-Jensen, Janice M., and Ann Coyne. "The Effect of Resistance Strategies on Rape." *American Journal of Public Health* 83 (1993): 1633–34.

Index

INDEX OF ANCIENT TEXTS

Old Testament

Genesis 23
21:16 121
21:17 7
42:24 31
43:29–30 32
43:30 31
44:18–34 35
45:1–3 32
45:18 35

Exodus 17
3:22 103
12:35 103
32:32 107

Leviticus 17

Numbers 17

Deuteronomy 17
1:45 27
20:5 123

Joshua
9:4 107
9:12–13 107

Judges
2:4 27
20:23–26 27
20:26 113, 121

1 Samuel
1:15 105–6
6 139
6:12 139
16:20 107

2 Samuel
12:16 113
19:1–2 121
19:1–8 23

1 Kings
8:34 117
8:63 123

2 Kings
20:3–6 7
20:5 100, 108, 132
22:11–13 26
22:17 27
22:19 138
22:19–20 27

Ezra
6:16–17 123

Nehemiah
1:4 27
1:7 27

1 Maccabees
4:52–59 123

Job
2:12–13 121
4:19 103
7:19 104
7:20–21 109
13:28 103
14:6 104
16:20 132
19:23 107
27:15 129
30:6 105
30:16 131

Psalms
1 130
3 94
4 94–95
4:4–6 95
5:4 99
6 14, 96–101, 106, 110, 113, 115, 124, 133–34
6:2 97, 103, 124
6:3 97, 124
6:4 97
6:5 97
6:6 124
6:7 124, 132
6:7–8 98
6:7–10 7
6:8 97
6:8–9 137
6:9 104, 113, 132
6:9–10 100
6:9–11 99
6:11 97
9 134
10 134
13 113, 134
16:7 99
17:3 99
18 128
18:5 100
19 130
22 134
22:26 123
22:32 123
23 116
29 122
30 113, 122–24, 126, 134
30:2 123
30:3 124
30:4 123–24
30:5 124
30:5–6 123, 137
30:6 99, 124, 132
30:6–7 124
30:7 124, 127, 137
30:7–12 123
30:8 124
30:9 124
30:10 124
30:10–11 137
30:11 124
30:12 124
30:13 123
31 107
32 113
34:4 123
35 113, 134
35:13–14 110
37 130
38 113
39 101–4, 110, 113, 115, 134
39:2 137
39:2–3 104
39:2–4 101
39:3–4 101
39:5–6 101
39:5–7 101
39:6 101
39:7 101, 137
39:8–12 101
39:10 104
39:11 103

39:11–14	102–3
39:12	102–3, 137
39:13	104, 108, 132
39:13–14	101
39:14	7, 104
40:4	114, 116, 132, 139
41	113
42	100, 105–6, 108, 110, 115, 132–34
42:2	105
42:2–3	7, 137
42:2–4	105
42:4	99, 113, 117, 132
42:5	106, 137
42:5–6	106
42:6	105
42:6–7	137
42:8	100, 105
42:9	99
42:10	105, 137
42:11	106
42:12	105, 137
43	105–6, 110, 115, 133–34
43:5	105, 137
44	134
46	120
46:6	99
48	120
49	130
51	113
56	107–8, 110, 115, 134, 139
56:2–10	107
56:2–3	107
56:4–5	107
56:5	107
56:6–8	107
56:7	107
56:9	107, 132
56:9–12	107
56:10–14	107
56:11	107
56:13–14	107
56:14	107
59	107
60	134
69	108–11, 113, 115, 130–31, 134, 138
69:2	108
69:2–3	100
69:2–5	108
69:3	108
69:4	110
69:5	108
69:6	108–9
69:6–13	108–9
69:7	109
69:7–8	109
69:8	109
69:10–13	109–10
69:11	110, 113, 132
69:13	110
69:14	108
69:14–19	108
69:15	108
69:16	108
69:19	108
69:19–29	111
69:20	108–9
69:20–29	108
69:21	109
69:30	108
69:30–37	108
69:32	109
69:36	108
71	107, 113
73	113, 130
74	134
76	120
77	134
77:7–10	99
78	128–30
78:1	128–29

78:1–8	128
78:5	128
78:7–8	128
78:8	129
78:9–19	128
78:10	129
78:21	129
78:31	129
78:38	129
78:40–72	128
78:49	129
78:50	129
78:58	129
78:59	129
78:62	129
78:62–64	128–29
78:64	132
78:65–72	129
79	134
80	115–18, 122, 133–34, 140
80:1	115
80:2	117
80:4	116
80:5	116
80:5–8	116
80:6	113–14, 116–17, 132, 139
80:8	116
80:15	116–17
80:18–19	116
80:20	116
84	120
85	134
88	113, 134
88:1–2	99
88:8	100
88:12–13	98
88:14	99
90	134
90:14	99
91	113
92:3	99
102	100, 106, 110–15, 132–34, 139
102:2	111, 113
102:2–12	111–12
102:3	113
102:4–10	113
102:4–12	112
102:5	114
102:6	113
102:9	116
102:10	106, 110, 113, 117, 132, 139
102:11	113–14
102:12	114
102:13–23	111
102:18	111
102:19	114
102:21	114
102:23	114
102:24–29	111
102:25	114
102:29	114
103	113
103:2	105
108	134
116	125–27, 134
116:1–2	125
116:3	125
116:3–4	126
116:4	125, 137
116:5	137
116:5–6	126
116:5–9	125–26
116:7	127, 137
116:8	126, 132
116:9	125
116:10	125
116:10–11	137
116:10–19	125
116:12	127
116:13	125
116:13–14	127

116:16–17 127
116:17 125
116:18–19 127
116:19 125
119 128, 130–32, 134
119:28 131–32
119:55 99
119:62 99
119:126 132
119:129–136 131
119:136 131–32
119:139 131
122 120
126 96, 118–19, 122
126:2–3 118
126:4–6 118–19
126:5 132
126:6 132
127 130
128 130
130 122, 133
134:1 99
137 120–22, 134
137:1 121, 132
137:1–3 120
137:1–4 120
137:2 121
137:4 121
137:5–6 120
137:7 121
137:7–9 120
137:8 121

Ecclesiastes
2:18–23 102
4:1 132

Sirach
12:16 132
24 130

Isaiah
5:1–7 117
15:9 132
38:5 100, 139
38:14 113, 139
50:9 103
51:8 103
58:3 113
59:11 113

Jeremiah
2:21 117
7:34 129
9:16–17 33–34
9:16–21 34
9:17 132
11:1 22
12:10 117
13:17 132
14:12 113
14:17 132
15:1 22
16:9 129
27:22 117
38 108

Lamentations
1 137
1:1–2 121
1:1–11 14
1:2 99
1:12–22 14
1:14 109
1:16 132
1:22 109
2:12 105
2:18 99
3:24 132
3:48 132

Ezekiel
7:16 113

24:15–24 129
24:16 132

Hosea
5:12 103
10:1 117

Malachi
3:16 107

NEW TESTAMENT

Matthew
6:19–20 103

Luke
12:23 103

James
5:2 103

AKKADIAN

AbB
6:135 79
6:135 4′–8′ 79

Dialogue between a Man and His God 61, 138–39
1–11 14, 67–68
12–16 14
13 69
5 138
5 68
55 69
58 69
59 69
66–67 69

Dingiršadabba
1 69–70
2 69–70
3 69–70
4 69–70
5 69
6 69
7 69
8 69
9 69, 85, 70–75
9 13′–18′ 70
9 16′ 72
9 17–18 72
9 19–23 72
9 20 73
9 25′–35′ 71–72
9 26′ 73
9 28 73
9 29–34 73
9 35 73
9 28 70
9 25′–26′ 64
10 69
11.1 69, 85–86, 73–74, 139
11.1 10 74
11.1 11 74
11.1 12–14 46, 61
11.1 2 74
11.1 8–14 73
11.10 69
11.2 69
11.3 69
11.3 41 70
11.4 69
11.4 55 70
11.5 69, 74–75, 85
11.5 98–104 74
11.5 101–102 64
11.5 108 75
11.6 69
11.7 69
11.8 69
11.9 69

Enūma Eliš
I.107–8 46

Eršaḫunga
1.1 53
1.1 11–17 53
1.1 38–39 53
1.14 56, 58–59, 85–86
1.14 18–21 58
1.14 21 57
1.14 22 59
1.14 23 59
1.15 85
1.15 2′ 57
1.15 4′–5′ 46
1.15b 59–62, 66, 85–86, 137–39
1.15b 1 61
1.15b 1′–9′ 60
1.15b 3′–4′ 60
1.15b 4′–5′ 61
1.15b 16′–17′ 72
1.15b 21′ 59
1.15b 22′–23′ 61
1.16 62–64, 66, 85, 138
1.16 2 62–63
1.16 4 62
1.16 6 62–63
1.16 8 63
1.16 33 62
1.16 35 62
1.16 43 62
1.16 52 63
1.16 53 62
1.16 55 62
1.16 57 62
1.16 59 63
1.16 61 63
1.16 rev. 2 63
1.16 rev. 4 63
1.16 rev. 6 63
1.16 rev. 8 63
1.2f 54–55, 66, 85–86
1.2f 10 54
1.2f 12–19 54
1.2f 16 54
1.2f 20–21 54
1.2f 26 55
1.2g 86
1.6b 56
1.6d 55–56, 66, 85
1.6d 2 56
1.6d 6′–14′ 55–56
1.6d 7 56
1.6d 8 56
1.7d 57–58, 66, 85
1.7d 8 58–59
1.7d 8′–14′ 57
1.7d 14′ 57
1.7d 16′ 57
1.7d 18′ 57
2.1a 69
2.1d 64–65, 85, 139
2.1d 2 64
2.1d 4 64
2.1d 10′–12′ 64
2.1d 16′ 64
2.1d 18′ 64
2.1d 19′–22′ 72
2.1d 20′ 64
2.1d 22′ 64
2.1d 24′ 64
2.1d 26′ 64
2.3 65–66, 86
2.3 13–18 65
2.3 24 65
2.3 25–27 66

Gilgameš
XII 100 50
XII 104 50

Ishtar
2 43–48, 51, 67, 81, 85–86, 137, 139
2.1–41 43
2.26 44

2.27–30 43–44
2.41 45
2.42–55 43–44
2.45 44
2.45–50 44
2.47 44–45
2.49 47
2.50 44–45, 47, 56
2.51 44
2.51–52 45
2.52 44
2.56–78 43–44, 46
2.62–68 46
2.64–65 61
2.67 69
2.67–68 47
2.77 47
2.79–102 43
2.85–86 47
2.103–105 43
10 48–51, 86, 139
10.1–6 48
10.8–18 48
10.11 48
10.12 48
10.12–27 48
10.13 51
10.19 48
10.19–38 48
10.20 50
10.22 50
10.25 50
10.32–38 51
10.39–42 48

Literary Prayer
to Ishtar 81–82, 85–86, 139
67–70 81
73–80 81
94 81
144–150 81–82
166 82

Literary Prayer
to Marduk 82–85, 138
1–4 82–83
57–59 83
66–70 83
104–10 83
129–134 83
131 83
137–40 84

Ludlul Bēl Nēmeqi 80, 82
I 107–10 61
II 60 82
II 92 71

Nusku
13 42–43
13.104–106 42

UGARITIC

KTU 1.14 i.28–30 99

HITTITE

Prayer of a King 76
Prayer of a Mortal 76
Prayer of Kantuzili 76

CLASSICAL

Iliad 32
9.433 27
9.436 27
9.612 27
10.372–464 27
10.377 27
11.136 27
19.287 33
19.300 33
19.301–2 33
19.310–11 33
19.338–39 33

Odyssey 23
22.447 27

AUTHORS

Abusch, Tzvi 87
Aguiar, Patrícia 13
Ainsworth, Mary Salter 4
Allen, Leslie C. 110
Alonzo Schökel, Luis 105, 108, 114, 117, 126–27
Anderson-Stojanovic, Virginia R. 108
Archer, Margaret S. 16
Auffret, Pierre 97, 101, 120
Augustine 98
Aun, John 121
Austen, Jane 28–31, 135
Avalos, Hector 86
Báez, Silvio José 101
Baker, Mark x
Bakermans-Kraneburg, Marian J. 9
Bakhtin, Mikhail 16, 18, 94
Baloian, Bruce Edward 134
Barré, Michael L. 126
Basabe, N. 13
Bauer, Christian 52
Baylin, Jonathan 8
Beebe, Beatrice 16
Begrich, Joachim 19, 93
Bellelli, G. 13
Bellinger, William H. 92, 94–95, 121, 130
Beristain, Carlos Martín 13
Berlin, Adele 106
Berlin, Andrea M. 108
Blechman, Andrew D. 47
Boer, Roland 18
Bollingmo, Guri C. 22
Borowski, Oded 113
Bosworth, David A. 1, 5, 20, 22–23, 28, 34, 40, 50, 69, 72, 90
Bottéro, Jean 56
Bowlby, John 4
Broyles, Craig C. 89, 92, 95, 109, 117, 123, 133–34, 136
Brueggemann, Walter 19–20, 89–91, 94
Burton, Tara Isabella 31
Byrne, Paula 31
Calhoun, Lawrence G. 22
Carniti, Cecilia 126
Cassidy, Jude 4, 20
Castelfranchi, Cristiano 1
Charney, Davida H. 96
Clark, Margaret S. 11, 12
Clifford, Richard J. 97, 101, 108–9, 116, 118, 120, 125, 130
Cornelius, Randolph 1
Cornell Lab of Ornithology 47
Correia, Isabel 13
Cotrill, Amy 111
Coyne, Ann 28
Curci, Antonietta 11, 13
Day, Andrew 23
Day, John 92, 95, 130
de la Torre, Mónica Padilla 61
Duprez, Christelle 11
Ebeling, Erich 41
Ebersole, Gary L. 32
Eder, Sigrid 124
Edlund, John E. 13
Eksner, H. Julia 98, 116
Erbele-Küster, Dorothea 93
Farber, Walter 40, 72
Fernyhough, Charles 15–16, 18
Finkel, Eli J. 11, 12
Firth, David G. 92
Fischer, Agneta H. 25
Flesher, LeAnn Snow 95–96
Fløysvik, Ingvar 133–34

Fonagy, Peter 8
Forti, Tova L. 113–14
Foster, Benjamin R. xi, 39, 59, 68, 80–81
Fraley, R. Chris 4, 7, 20
Frechette, Christopher 14, 41, 42
Friedrichsen, M. 24
Furnham, Adrian 13
Geller, Markham J. 50, 52, 86–87
Gerstenberger, Erhard S. 110–11
Gillath, Omri 4, 7
Gillingham, Susan E. 92, 95, 130
Goldingay, John 99, 107, 109, 123, 130
Gonzales, Amy L. 13
González, José Luis 13
Grant, Deena 97–98, 114, 134
Green, Barbara 18
Grossmann, Karin 1
Guillaume, Alfred 121
Gunkel, Hermann 19, 89, 91–92, 94–95, 122, 125, 130
Hackett, Louisa 23
Hart, Susan 4
Hasson, Oren 21
Hays, Christopher B. 121
Heeßel, Nils P. 87
Heiler, Friedrich 93
Hendricks, Michelle C. 1, 24–25
Hermann, Judith 14
Herranz, J. K. 13
Hill, Daniel 10
Hill, Peter C. 9
Holt-Lunstad, Julianne x
Hood, Ralph W. 9
Hopkins, Denise Dumbkowski 110, 117
Hossfeld, Frank-Lothar 111, 113, 118, 129
Huehnergard, John 68
Hughes, Daniel 8
van Ijzendoorn, Marinus H. 9
Jacobson, Karl N. 94, 123
Jacobson, Rolf A. 94, 123
Janowski, Bernd 99
Jaques, Margaret 67–74, 76
Johnson, Brian S. 13
Johnson, Philip S. 92
Kalle, Raivo 103
Karantzas, Gery C. 4, 7
Karen, Robert 4
King, Leonard W. 41
Kirkpatrick, Lee A. 5, 9–10
Kitching, Chris 119
Klassen, Pamela E. 34–35
Klein, Jacob 68
Knight, Raymond A. 28
van der Kolk, Bessel A. 8
Kong, Wong Fook 106
Kraus, Fritz Rudolph 79
Kuckhoff, Antonius 98–100
Laan, Anja 6
Lachmann, Frank M. 16
Ladd, Kevin L. 3
Lambert, David A. 22
Lambert, W. G. 50, 68, 77–78, 80–83
Lane, Carrie J. 26
Layton, J. Bradley x
Lenzi, Alan xi, 39–41, 43, 51, 62, 70, 78–80
Leoni, G. 13
Levine, Herbert 96
Lewis, Deane 113
Lindström, Fredrik 97, 109
Lloyd, Peter 16
Loretz, Oswald 99
Lucas, Ernest C. 92
Lutz, Tom 1
Maas, Joyce 6
Mandolfo, Carleen 18, 93–95, 102, 126
Manstead, Antont S. R. 25

Maul, Stefan 42–43, 52–59, 62, 64–65, 69, 72, 76
Mayer, Werner 41, 43, 67, 70
Mays, James L. 96
McKay, J. W. 99
Mead, George Herbert 16
Miceli, Maria 1
Mikulincer, Mario 4, 8
Mohr, Philip 23
Mooney, Carl Gerhart 4
Mowinckel, Sigmund 122
Nelson, Judith Kay 1, 4, 24, 28
Newsom, Carol 18
Nougayrol, Jean 68
Nussbaum, Martha 12
Olyan, Saul 35, 111
Oshima, Takayoshi 82–84
Páez, Darío 13
Pierce, Charles Sanders 16
Pierce, Gregory 12
Porges, Stephen W. 8
Prinsloo, Willem S. 125
Provine, Robert R. 21
Ramage, Matthew 121
Rimé, Bernard 11–12, 15
Ruiz, Eleuterio Ramón 101
Rydé, K. 24
Sabourin, Leopold 92, 94
Sagarin, Brad J. 13
Sapolsky, Robert 26
Sarason, I. G. 12
Savran, George 121
Scheirs, Jan 25
Schmidt, Hans 97
Schore, Allan N. 8
Schwemer, Daniel 76
Scrimali, Tullio 17
Seybold, Klaus 92, 113
Sharp, Shane 3
Shaver, Philip R. 4, 8, 20
Shiller, Virginia M. 4, 6, 8
Singer, Itamar 76
Smith, Timothy x
von Soden, Wolfram 99
Soltis, Joseph 21
Soriano, Cristina 98, 116
Sõukand, Renata 103
Spilka, Bernard 3, 9
Starr, Ivan 77
Steitler, Charles 76
Stern, Karen B. 108
Stookey, J. M. 61
Strang, P. 24
Strawn, Brent 14
Strong, Anna Louise ix–x
Stuart, D. 103
Sudak, Donna M. 17
Svanberg, Ingvar 103
Taylor, Shelley 12
Tolin, David F. 17
van der Toorn, Karel 59, 67, 69, 79, 86–87
Trimble, Michael 1
Ullman, Sarah E. 28
Vala, Jorge 13
Vesco, Jean-Luc 95, 122
Villanueva, Federico G. 20, 94, 97, 107
Vingerhoets, Ad 1, 6, 11–12, 14, 20–21, 23–26, 28, 32–33, 35
Vygotsky, Lev 15–16
Wallace, Howard Neil 94
Walsh, Carey Ellen 107
Walter, Chip 1, 15
Wathey, John C. 1–2
Watts, J. M. 61
Weiser, Artur 93, 97
Westermann, Claus 89, 91, 96, 122
Wiley, Norbert 16, 18
Wilson, Gerald H. 105
Witt, Andrew 111
van Wolde, Ellen 98, 116, 134
Young, Sarah 17
Zenger, Erich 111, 113, 118, 129
Zernecke, Anna Elise 43–45, 47–48

www.ingramcontent.com/pod-product-compliance
Lightning Source LLC
Chambersburg PA
CBHW021858230426
43671CB00006B/442
* 9 7 8 1 6 2 8 3 7 2 3 5 9 *